Always Another Mountain

A woman hiking the Appalachian Trail from Springer Mountain to Mount Katahdin

Danie Martin

"Always Another Mountain," by Danie Martin. ISBN 1-58939-693-6.

Published 2005 by Virtualbookworm.com Publishing Inc., P.O. Box 9949, College Station, TX 77842, US. ©2005, Danie Martin. All rights reserved. No part of this publication may be reproduced, stored in a retrieval system, or transmitted in any form or by any means, electronic, mechanical, recording or otherwise, without the prior written permission of Danie Martin.

Manufactured in the United States of America.

To Keith B. Shaw Sr., 1929-2004

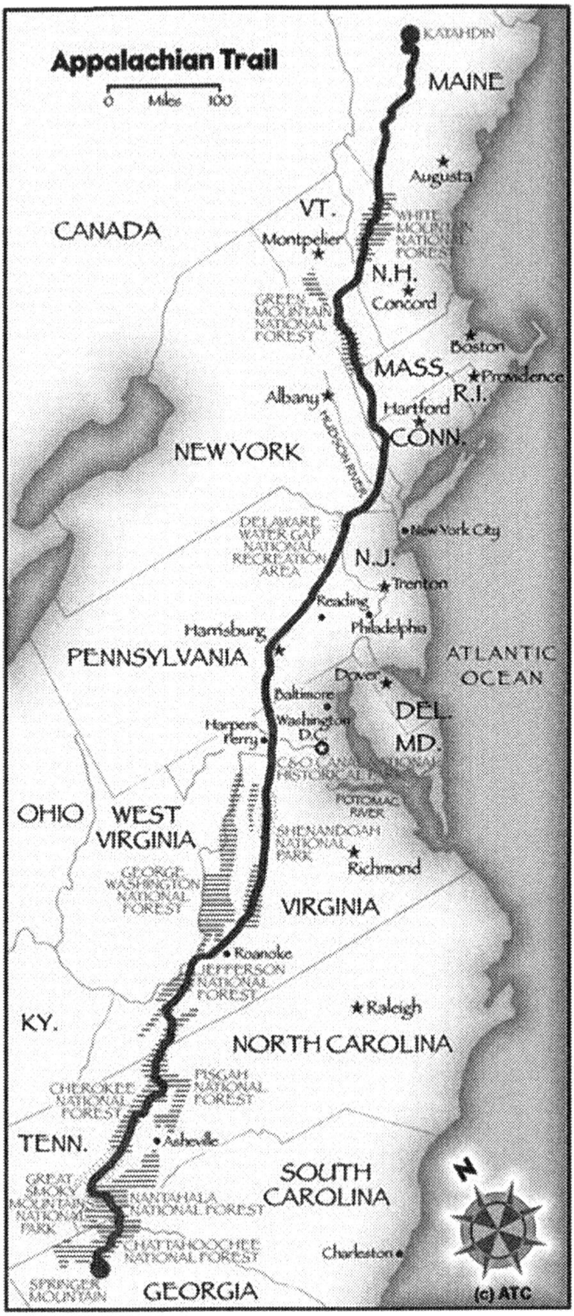

Appalachian Trail
0 Miles 100
KATAHDIN
MAINE
Augusta
VT.
CANADA
Montpelier
WHITE MOUNTAIN NATIONAL FOREST
N.H.
Concord
GREEN MOUNTAIN NATIONAL FOREST
Boston
MASS.
Providence
R.I.
Albany
Hartford
CONN.
NEW YORK
HUDSON RIVER
DELAWARE WATER GAP NATIONAL RECREATION AREA
New York City
N.J.
Trenton
Reading
Philadelphia
Harrisburg
PENNSYLVANIA
ATLANTIC OCEAN
Dover
Baltimore
DEL.
Harpers Ferry
Washington D.C.
MD.
C&O CANAL NATIONAL HISTORICAL PARK
POTOMAC RIVER
OHIO
WEST VIRGINIA
SHENANDOAH NATIONAL PARK
Richmond
GEORGE WASHINGTON NATIONAL FOREST
VIRGINIA
Roanoke
JEFFERSON NATIONAL FOREST
Raleigh
KY.
NORTH CAROLINA
CHEROKEE NATIONAL FOREST
PISGAH NATIONAL FOREST
TENN.
Asheville
SOUTH CAROLINA
GREAT SMOKY MOUNTAIN NATIONAL PARK
NANTAHALA NATIONAL FOREST
CHATTAHOOCHEE NATIONAL FOREST
Charleston
SPRINGER MOUNTAIN
GEORGIA
N
(c) ATC

ACKNOWLEDGEMENTS

I want to thank all the countless people who make thruhiking the Appalachian Trail possible: Trail Maintainers and Ridgerunners, Caretakers, fellow hikers, the Trail Angels who make our lives easier with their generosity, Hostel keepers, Postal Workers, the loved ones left at home, and all the ordinary people who help us along. My particular thanks go to my faithful journal transcriber Kerry.

INTRODUCTION

WHILE GATHERING INFORMATION IN PREPARATION for my 2004 Appalachian Trail thruhike I was frustrated that there were no memoirs published by women my age who completed the Trail and by the fact that the accounts by women I could find were nearly ten years old. This book was published to fill that lack. It started out as an online journal I kept while thruhiking. I decided to publish it in its entirety rather than focusing on just the most interesting parts. That means it has slow, less interesting sections left in, but after all, so does a thruhike! Leaving it whole seemed a more authentic record of what it is like to thruhike the Appalachian Trail. The original journal has been edited for clarity and spelling and some added comments inserted in brackets. The distances were corrected to those in the 2004 edition of the Appalachian Trail Data Book published by the Appalachian Trail Conference.

The Appalachian Trail was first conceived by Benton MacKaye in 1921 and was completed in 1937. It now stretches 2174 miles along the spine of the Appalachians from Springer Mountain Georgia to Mount Katahdin Maine. In 1948 Earl Shaffer became the first person to hike it from end to end in one continuous hike; the first thruhiker. Every year over 1500 hikers set out to thruhike the Trail, swarming north like a herd of migrating lemmings. Only 10-15% succeed. Thousands more hike just a section of the trail or come as dayhikers

I first heard the term Appalachian Trail while growing up in Ohio in the 1960s. In the early 1990s I was visiting in-laws at Falls Village CT and the trail was nearly in their back yard. We stood upon the footpath and there was something compelling about it, thinking of all those hikers who hiked past from distant places.

I first really went backpacking two summers ago when living in California. Two women friends invited me to hike the ten mile trail to Sykes Springs at Big Sur. Before I knew it I was hooked, buying gear and heading out on trips alone in Big Sur and the Sierras. When we decided a year earlier to relocate to Philadelphia in 2004, all I could think of was the nearby Appalachian Trail. My awareness of the Trail had become a dream. I started reading backpacking and Trail books and studying trail journals for every bit of wisdom I could squeeze out of them. I ordered a lightweight Wanderlust Nomad tent and started accumulating gear.

As a 44 year old woman, I was a bit atypical for a thruhiker. Most thruhikers I met on my hike were either in their twenties or are fifty or older, either just out of college or retired. But like many others I had some personal reasons for hiking.

Although in good physical condition, I did have some problems I had to take into account. My body showed the effects of an active life that included military service and nearly thirty marathons and ultra marathons. I had a loose cartilage in my right knee. In 2002 I was hit by a car while training for a marathon and slightly injured. A torn hamstring in my right hip was still causing trouble just two months before my hike. Years ago I developed epilepsy from a head injury and I have to take medication daily to prevent seizures. On top of that, I was on hormone replacement therapy and I had recently been diagnosed with osteopenia, moderately low bone density. The move to Philadelphia meant a break between jobs and so an opportunity to hike the Trail. With my bone density problems, who knew if I would still be fit enough to hike when I was old enough to retire? So I decided to seize the opportunity while it was there, and hike the Trail.

Planning my hike meant making a lot of decisions. The Appalachian Trail is like the ordinary person's equivalent of going on a polar expedition: it takes about the same time commitment and requires nearly the same scale of logistics.

I decided early on to use trekking poles. They would ease the strain on my knee and hamstring and would also double as the poles for my Nomad Tent. I also decided to keep my pack weight as low as I could without compromising safety. There is an Ultra Light school of backpacking but to me that meant compromising too much on safety. So I decided to aim towards lightweight but not Ultra Light. I also decided on a synthetic sleeping bag. It is heavier than down, but keeps its insulation value better when wet. I already owned an MSR Pocket Rocket stove and when I learned fuel canisters seemed available I decided to start with it because it is quick heating. I thought I might switch to an alcohol stove after things warm up. I planned to switch sleeping bags in Southern Virginia to a lighter one for summer use and back again in New Hampshire to my winter weight bag. I chose the Mountainsmith Chimera backpack, which only weighed about 3 and a half pounds and had the full padding and suspension system found in heavier packs. For a knife, I brought a tiny Swiss Army Knife and hooked it to the key ring of an even tinier Photon LED flashlight the size of a quarter. I even cut the pages out of my guidebook and Trail Data Book and trimmed off the margins. I would only carry a week or so of pages and maps with me, mailing the rest ahead in a "bounce box." It is called a bounce box because you mail it to yourself at a post office a week or two up the trail, take what you need from it when you arrive, then mail it ahead again, so it "bounces" up the Trail. I would also use the bounce box to carry spare water filter elements, bulk jars of vitamins, soap and hand sanitizer so I could buy in bulk but carry a small supply, along with anything else I might need later but did not want to carry.

I decided to buy food at towns along the trail rather than buying it in advance and having to have someone mail it. That would make me more independent and allow changing my diet as I went. The downside would be that sometimes I might have to make do with a limited selection of available food.

Rather than trust the mail system, I decided to carry a three month supply of hormones and seizure medication with me, accepting the extra weight for the peace of mind knowing I would not run out. The seizure medication is sensitive to moisture, so I had to be sure to keep it dry. I got a 2 oz. Nalgene bottle for each medication to hold the main supply to keep it safe and dry. I used a smaller bottle to hold the day-to-day supply of seizure medication and a waterproof ziplock bag for the hormones and dietary supplements. I used Centrum Performance vitamins since they combine a multivitamin and a B-complex in one tablet. I also took calcium supplement tablets to help maintain my bone density. I only carried enough of those to get to the next mail stop, sending the main supply ahead in my bounce box.

Being a woman hiking alone meant other considerations. Many friends urged me to bring a cell-phone and a few even said to bring a gun! A gun was out of the question being heavy, of dubious value, and potentially dangerous. Besides, guns are illegal on sections of the trail. I thought more about a cell-phone but rejected that as well. The charger would be heavy and I could not count on getting reception or of finding an outlet to recharge the batteries. Instead I decided simply to keep my housemate informed on where I was and when I expected to contact her next. I also resolved to minimize the hazards of hitching rides to towns for supplies by picking towns on or near the Trail whenever possible to minimize the hitches I would have to make.

To stay in contact with the outside world I brought a phone card and a Pocketmail. That is a device with a built in modem that let me type and store emails then send and receive them from ordinary pay phones. I also used it to keep my journal. I typed each day's entry and when I got to a phone I emailed them to my friend Kerry back home. She then posted the entries to an online journal at a website called TrailJournals.com.

One last detail was my Trailname. Rather than their real name, it is traditional for thruhikers to be known by a trailname given to them by other hikers or that they choose. I chose the name Mouse because I am rather like a mouse; quiet, soft spoken, and a bit retiring but apt to turn unexpectedly sociable (like shelter mice do when they come out at night).

Friday, March 19, 2004
Atlanta, GA

    My housemate and I went by train to Atlanta Georgia for a last few days together before I start the trail. We had reserved for an economy rental car, so were amused when the rental agency gave us a bright yellow Mustang convertible! The weather was warm and nice so we had fun going off to see Stone Mountain, driving with the top down and our hair blowing in the wind. It was like Thelma and Louise! We also explored downtown Atlanta. Then I found the local REI where I bought a fuel canister for my stove and finally found the perfect long pants. Convertible pants that double as long pants and shorts are popular on the Trail but I rejected them for their weight. I found lightweight nylon shell pants with a built-in drawstring that would adjust as my weight dropped. I also got three days of food. I went carefully through my gear one last time, setting aside every possible item I could do without to be sent back home. I inspected everything that was left equally carefully to be sure I had not left anything I might need and loaded my pack. I feel a bit nostalgic and a bit apprehensive about what lies ahead. Tomorrow I get picked up at 8AM to get dropped off at Springer Mountain!

    -Mouse

Saturday, March 20, 2004
Destination: Hawk Mountain Shelter
From: Atlanta
Today's Miles: 7.6
Trip Miles: 7.6

    One last hotel breakfast in bed, then I went down to the lobby to meet Bill Porter, who would be driving me to Springer Mountain. His wife Judith came along for the ride and we had a nice conversation on the drive. Much to my delight, Bill offered to take me first to Amicalola Park Headquarters. That allowed me to sign in as a thruhiker at the trail register there and go through the traditional pack-weighing ceremony at the hanging scale outside the Lodge. Next a quick stop to admire the falls, then on to where US Forest Service Road 42 intersects the Trail .9 miles north of the start of the Trail. There they both gave me a hug for luck and I backtracked south towards the Summit.

I got there at about 11am and found a small crowd of dayhikers. I signed the register and had someone snap my picture in the traditional pose by the plaque that marked the start of the trail.

The weather started cloudy and a bit chilly but cleared and got up above 70 degrees as the day wore on. I got to Hawk Mountain Shelter just after 4pm. I was a bit sore but no major damage.

It was a bit bigger than most shelters, with a loft as well as the usual sleeping platform. There were already about 18 hikers but they had reserved the loft for the women so I had a space inside. I laid out my pad and sleeping bag, and then fixed ramen noodles with tuna for supper. After cleaning up I sat and wrote and listened to the conversation until time for bed. Besides the two women sharing the loft with me, there were three other women sleeping in tents.

The two in the loft were friends who had met in college and were hiking together the year after their graduation. As we went to bed one of them remarked that she had seen lightning in the distance. Sure enough, a storm blew up with lots of lightning REALLY close to the shelter. Again and again the interior of the shelter was brightly lit by a nearby bolt. It made me glad I was inside and not out in my tent! It was a stunning display of the sort of violent weather we might encounter in the mountains. I hoped no one outside would get hit and fortunately none were.

Next morning was chilly and windy. I piled on both my Polartec top and Gore-Tex top before going out to cook breakfast. Some hot oatmeal and hot chocolate revived me though, and got me in the mood to hike. I was moving out at 8am while my loft-mates were still packing up.

-Mouse

Sunday, March 21, 2004
Destination: Gooch Gap
From: Hawk Mountain
Today's Miles: 8.3
Trip Miles: 16.4

Today I hiked at a fairly slow pace and aimed for Gooch Mountain Shelter only about 7 miles away. My weight when I started was about 10-15 pounds heavier than back when I ran the New York Marathon in 2002 and I had hurt my right hamstring while training for that. So I am not in the best shape and want to give my body a chance to ease into longer distances.

The day was very windy and in the 40's and 50's. I wore my Polartec top until about noon when I turned into a sheltered valley out of the wind. At points one can see down into a lowland to the east. Then I could begin to grasp the Trail's location high up on the Blue Ridge.

All through the day I was passed by other hikers only to pass them when they stopped for breaks, then get passed again and so on. Our different break schedules made it hard to tell who actually was covering the most ground. Since I did not plan to hike as far as yesterday I took infrequent short breaks knowing I could rest at Gooch.

I did not expect to reach the shelter until about 2pm so was a bit astonished to see a roof through the trees to my left. Sure enough, it was Gooch Mountain Shelter. There were already a few men I'd seen at Hawk Mountain and I took my air mattress and climbed to the loft to claim a spot. No sooner did I have it inflated then the men started packing up. They were headed for the site of the old shelter at Gooch Gap to get a couple miles head start. That made sense, since the Woods Hole Shelter was over 12 miles away. Also a dayhiker had told me a cold front was moving in so it was expected to drop into the 30's tonight and this shelter site was quite windy. So I ended up packing up and leaving the nice new shelter to follow them. First I left a note in the shelter register. That way the two women I'd shared the loft with at Hawk Mountain would know what happened to me. Given choice of sharing their company again I chose instead to trim a couple miles off the next day's hike.

[In every shelter is a register where hikers can sign in. It is usually just a plain spiral-bound notebook with a pen or pencil. Hikers are encouraged to sign everywhere they stop in, both to keep track of usage and to help locate a hiker in an emergency. Hikers also use registers to communicate to each other, to alert others to problems and even as a form of self-expression.]

The new shelter was not on the map so I was not quite sure where I was starting from. So I worried about missing the Gooch Gap campsite and having to stealth camp somewhere. But crossing the road at Gooch Gap I found it, with 3 of the men already there setting up tents.

I quickly got my tent up then fetched water from the stream. I had brought a six liter Platypus bag to allow me to get a full night's water in one trip. Then I entertained myself untangling my new nylon cord and getting it looped over a high branch to hang my food after supper in case of bears. Then I started writing my journal. By 4 it was getting chilly and I began thinking about supper.

-Mouse

Monday, March 22, 2004
Destination: Woods Hole Shelter
From: Gooch Gap
Today's Miles: 10.2
Trip Miles: 26.6

I was cold last night despite wearing most of my clothing inside my sleeping bag. When I woke up I checked the thermometer on my pack. It said it was 40 degrees, which seemed pretty warm for how it felt. Just as I was thinking my sleeping bag must be really under-rated I noticed the frost on the netting of my tent. Someone else said it was about 24 degrees. I had to break the ice in my water bag to cook breakfast and when I washed up the rinse water froze to my pot before I could dry it off. Brrrrrr! I guess I must have been lying on the thermometer and warming it up so it gave a false reading.

I found myself hiking more strongly. I was the last one to leave the campsite and was passed by two men and then by a man in sandals carrying a guitar and accompanied by two small dogs. By early afternoon I re-passed all of them. Knowing that space in the next shelter was limited and that if I slowed they would all pass me and gobble up the shelter, I hiked as fast as I could without stopping for an instant. The two dogs ran along by my feet all the way to the turnoff to Woods Hole Shelter.

Much to my surprise, I was the first one there. The floor was wood slats with gaps between, so to try and keep the cold draft out I laid out my tent on the floor, added a space blanket over that then put my air mattress on top. I also could not find my balaclava hat so to keep my head warm I had to settle for wearing a pack towel on my head under my regular brimmed hat. It looked strange, but kept me warm.

I am hoping to get away in time to get a bed space in the hostel at Neels Gap tomorrow. I can also replace my balaclava and maybe get a pair of fleece pants.

Now it is 5pm and the shelter is more than full. Three more men have shown up, then a woman from Germany and a male-female couple who decided to move on. Four men are in the shelter leaving a respectful (and probably chilly) gap between them and me. The other man is tenting and the German is in a bivy-sack on the ground outside along the side of the hut. I am probably going to bed soon, adding my Gortex pants to last night's ensemble in hopes of sleeping warmer. I could add the silkweight Capilene bottoms and midweight top, but this way means less undressing in the morning. I sure hope five bodies generate more heat than mine did last night. Oh well, there is always the climb over Blood Mountain in the morning to warm me up!

No sooner did we go to bed than another half-dozen or so arrived! Everyone in the shelter lay with their heads out of their sleeping bags watching the new arrivals set up camp. I couldn't help giggling; we looked just like we were watching TV! I guess it does not take much to be entertained out here.

During the night I felt a BIT warmer perhaps. Still, I missed my nice comfy balaclava. Then next morning while trying to clear away my muddle of cap and pack towel, I found something in the way. It was my BALACLAVA! It had hung unnoticed and forgotten around my neck ever since I pulled it back off my head on the first warm moment of the previous day.

Was I happy to see it again! Like much of my equipment, it has a story behind it. I wanted a fleece balaclava but everywhere I looked they were too big, heavy, loose and bulky. I looked all over the San Francisco area: REI, Any Mountain, Patagonia, Marmot Mountain House's beautiful Chalet-looking former church in Berkeley. Finally high up in the sky in the ski shop at the top of the big gondola lift at Squaw Valley Ski Area I found just what I needed. It is a warm stocking-cap with a built-in neckpiece that converts it to a nice snug-fitting balaclava. In just two days I have fallen in love with it and am very glad to have it back.

Anxious to beat the rush for the twelve bunks in the hostel at Neels Gap, I packed hurriedly, jammed my gorp bag and a couple Snickers bars into the top pocket of my pack for later, then hit the Trail.

-Mouse

Tuesday, March 23, 2004
Destination: Neels Gap
From: Woods Hole Shelter
Today's Miles: 4.1
Trip Miles: 30.7

    The Trail led steeply up Blood Mountain, breaking again and again into flights of rugged stone stairs. Even the soil was frozen as hard as concrete. It was colder still in the shadow of the mountain. I seem to be getting a bit more in shape; I could keep a slow but steady climb with no pauses for breath. Finally only Danny, the young hiker I'd been passing and being passed by for two days, was still with me. We hiked together over the crest and partway down before he pulled ahead of me again, this time for good.

    The descent was even more rugged, passing through wide slabs of exposed bedrock with the white blazes painted on the stone instead of trees to mark the way on and off the slabs. There began long gentle switchbacks that made for fast hiking mixed with more rugged stone steps and scrambles through boulders. Several times I had to take both poles in one hand to free the other to help me slide down steps too high for my knees to step down safely.

    For some time I heard the unfamiliar sound of passing cars and trucks. When I finally saw the roadway I let out a whoop. I was nearly there! Moments later I was at the hostel signing up for a bunk. The Walasi-Yi Center is the only place along the AT where the trail goes THROUGH a building. It is a stone structure originally built as a trailside inn. Now one side has an outfitter or hiking equipment store as well as a laundry room and showers. The other side has a hostel in the basement with a bunkroom and a sitting room with TV and VCR. The Trail passes through an archway between the two sides. The bunkroom is chilly and the bunks have no bedding, so you sleep in your sleeping bag just like in the shelters.

    I spent the morning buying food in the store, showering and doing laundry. I ran into Danny and we agreed to put our laundry together to save money since neither of us had a full load. We keep running into each other anyway. Good thing I already have a Trail Name; having both a Danny and a Danie hiking at once would be pretty confusing!

    Things have gone well so far, even if a bit cold. In the store they said a hiker's thermometer up on Blood Mountain the previous morning read 9 degrees! So it must have been in the teens where I was. Still, there are higher mountains and it could get colder still, as well as wet. So I reluctantly splurged $80 on a Marmot sleeping bag cover and accepted the extra one and a quarter pounds in weight in order to improve the warmth of my bag by 10 degrees. Freezing to death is not a happy thought, and a warm sleeping bag is the last refuge in an emergency so the cover could save my life if the weather gets much colder. Still, the extra weight rankles a bit. Most of the rest of my equipment performed pretty well. I did have trouble with my Smartwool socks gathering between my toes and the balls of my feet. Too much of that is sure to cause blisters, so I bought a pair of the next smaller size to see if that helps.

I have not had a single blister or any serious aches or pains. My Ibuprofen stays unused in my pack. But I have probably been pushing much harder than is wise. It got me a bunk today, but I doubt that I should make a habit of it any time soon. Too much too soon and I risk an injury. It was only last month that I was doing physical therapy for my stretched hamstring and on the train ride from Philadelphia I had such shooting pains, I limped to the porter's station for ice to sooth it. So I really ought not to push my luck. I also should stop skimping on food, one can't keep that up too long on the Trail either. Well, with my new "security blanket" I can worry less about cold nights.

The outfitter here reminds me of "Clean Sweep," the show where professional organizers ruthlessly force people to abandon their clutter. If one asks for help reducing pack weight, they are just as thorough here. Cotton clothes? Replace them! Heavy stove? Replace it with a featherweight alcohol one. They will let you keep ONE luxury item, the rest goes home. One hiker in our group dropped 18 pounds from his pack! Other hikers need less help but are glad to send home boxes of excess gear. Every year they ship home vast numbers of boxes.

I solved another mystery that afternoon. When I arrived at Neels Gap I noticed my glasses were rubbing my ear painfully. On examination I found a rough spot just as if they had been scrapped against a rock. This was odd since they had never left my head except to lay in my tent or safe inside a boot at night. Then I remembered the mouse I'd heard poking around my boots the previous night. That mouse must have chewed my glasses! I'd heard of them holing fabric and shredding toilet paper for nests, but never eating glasses!

That evening anyone who wanted was shuttled by van to an All You Can Eat buffet (AYCE) in a nearby town. There I filled up on veggies and cottage cheese. Vitamins and calcium are hard to find in Trail food, which is heavy on fat protein and carbohydrates.

By the time we'd all spent the day cleaning and laundering, having a meal together, watching a video of a movie and were going to bed the bunkroomful of hikers no longer felt like strangers. We have acculturated into the thruhiker community, a literal extended family that stretches out each year along the length of the Appalachian Trail.

-Mouse

Wednesday, March 24, 2004
Destination: Low Gap Shelter
From: Neels Gap
Today's Miles: 10.6
Trip Miles: 41.30

My pack felt overloaded for a 3 day trip to Dick's Gap when I left the next morning. That made it hard on my feet and by the time I reached Low Gap tender spots were starting to form. To make it worse, the second half has no water sources and I missed the last spring. So I only had a pint and a half of water for that leg and the weather was in the 60s so hiking in winter clothing was thirsty work. Except for those things it was a pleasant day's hike, with some high climbs and descents but much of it on a high ridge line with excellent views. I even saw my first flower!

The shelter has lots of flies so I am tenting up the hill.

I'm not sure that I can do another day like this tomorrow. Also there seems to be a forest fire up ahead that might stop us until it is out. I checked my food and should be able to stretch it out for 4 nights. That would let me do four 7-8 mile days instead of a 13 mile day and two 10 mile days. Another option would be to go to the town of Helen tomorrow but that wastes a day very soon after my last resupply.

Tomorrow I will see how it goes and plan from there.

-Mouse

Thursday, March 25, 2004
Destination: Cheese Factory Site
From: Low Gap Shelter
Today's Miles: 13.0
Trip Miles: 54.3

    I made it!!! All 13 miles to the Cheese Factory. I guess with a trailname of Mouse it was preordained. The first 5 miles were quite nice, fairly flat and smooth making for fast hiking. Early on I ran into the German woman, Sylke, with another hiker. They were trying to fix his trekking pole, one section of which had come off and would not go back in and lock properly. I joined them and we fiddled a bit with a screwdriver unsuccessfully. Then the plastic expansion piece came off exposing the little butterfly nut. That reminded me of when I had the same problem at home when I first bought my trekking poles. If you turn the shaft to unlock it and turn too far, the butterfly nut jams against the pole. The screw was not the problem, the nut just needed loosened. By now several more hikers had gathered and we asked if anyone had a microtool. No one did, so I finally used my teeth to free the nut, then reassembled the pole. The trick is to unscrew it only far enough to let the section slide freely. Any further and the nut jams.

    Later Sylke caught up with me yet again and then we met Danny. The three of us hiked the rest of the day together. It was only noon when we reached Blue Mountain Shelter where I had considered stopping for the day. That meant plenty of time to reach the Cheese factory. But first we had to climb Blue Mountain, descend 1000 feet into Unicoi Gap, climb another 1000 feet up Rocky Mountain (I guess to appreciate the slight difference in view between the two?), down ANOTHER 1000 feet into Indian Grave Gap and up 400 to get to the Cheese Factory. It was a nice pleasant sunny day and nice hiking despite all the climbing, warm enough that I hiked most of it in T-shirt. Still, the ups downs and mileage took their toll. I used up most of a sheet of moleskin warding off blisters, dipped into my supply of Ibuprofen for the first time, and had to use my water bottle full of cold water like an ice pack in the evening to soothe my Achilles tendons, holding it upright between my ankles in the foot of my sleeping bag.

    The Cheese Factory is a campsite on a ridge just before Blue Mountain at the site of a mid-1800s cheese factory. We pitched our tents just off the Trail. We were joined by four more hikers, had a campfire and a nice evening talking and getting acquainted.

    -Mouse

Friday, March 26, 2004
Destination: Hiawassee
From: Cheese Factory
Today's Miles: 12.5
Trip Miles: 66.8

This morning coming up Tray Mountain I let a trim 50 something woman pass and she disappeared up the slope like I was standing still. At the top I introduced myself and learned her trailname was "The Walking Stomach." She had earned it as a trail maintainer in Connecticut by outeating her coworkers on a snack break. We ran into each other several times during the day, greeting each other with a jaunty "Hello Stomach!"; "Hello Mouse!."

Let's see, back at Neels Gap I resolved to slow down. Ten miles later at Low Gap I was SURE I needed to. Then I went 13 miles yesterday and now I've gone and done it again! I got to Deep Gap just after two and talking to Danny and The Walking Stomach I decided I could go ahead to Dicks Creek Gap in time to get a ride into Hiawassee and sleep in a nice comfy bed. I seem to have misplaced my brain; I was sure it was here someplace, but it seems to be missing. My plan worked, but when I got my boots off, ouch ouch ouch! No muscle or tendon problems, but my feet! They felt VERY overused and one heel had a raw spot for good measure despite having been covered with moleskin and duct tape.

Still, I'm unrepentant. First it let me play Trail Angel. Two days ago I found a gray stocking cap lying on the Trail, but have been unable to catch up with the owner. Whoever it was almost surely got off here to resupply, so I hung the cap on the Trail sign on the north side of the gap where they would see it getting back on the Trail. And it gave me a shower and a nice comfy bed tonight and a full day of rest tomorrow.

Hitchhiking was a new experience for me, and one that as a woman hiking alone I was worried about. So I approached the highway and the task of getting 11 miles to Hiawassee with apprehension. But it turned out to be effortless. A very nice man was waiting with his van to offer a ride to any hikers who showed up. He took me to the Hiawassee Inn, waited until we were sure there was a room for me and offered a ride back to the Trail if I needed it. The innkeepers gushed hospitality and called me "Sugar" and "Hon" and offered everything a tired hiker could dream of. After they shuttled us to another of those wonderful under $7 all you can eat southern buffets another hiker named Pirate paid for my dinner as well as his, no matter how much I said I could pay for myself. So much hospitality and niceness! I seem to be getting more than my share of trail magic.

-Mouse

**Saturday, March 27, 2004
Destination: Hiawassee
From: Hiawassee
Today's Miles: 0.0
Trip Miles: 66.8**

Today I walked to the public library to try to post my first journal entries to be sure my online journal works properly. Rather oddly, I needed my drivers license to sign up to use the computer. Good thing I brought it! I spent the rest of the day resting my sore feet. Tomorrow, back to the Trail, probably bound for the campsite at Bly Gap on the GA/NC border.

-Mouse

**Sunday, March 28, 2004
Destination: Muskrat Creek Shelter
From: Hiawassee
Today's Miles: 11.6
Trip Miles: 78.4**

Well, I went and did it again! I meant to stop at Bly Gap and when I got there it was only 1:30 and so now I am at Muskrat Shelter, 3 miles up the Trail with sore feet and Achilles tendons. I wonder, will I ever learn?
The Trail was crowded with more than one youth group out hiking. The first thing into North Carolina were 2 ferocious hills. More and more greenery is ap-

pearing in the underbrush including some ferns and scattered wildflowers, and the buds in the trees are showing signs of coming out.

Sylke is here as well as many others I've been keeping pace with. Some stayed one night in Hiawassee or the Blueberry Patch hostel and some like Sylke just hiked right through Dicks Creek Gap. I got a space in the shelter, which is just as well as a cold front is coming through and there could be rain tonight.

-Mouse

Monday, March 29, 2004
Destination: Carter Gap Shelter
From: Muskrat Creek Shelter
Today's Miles: 12.5
Trip Miles: 90.9

A little rain off and on at night but cleared away by morning. Sylke said farewell; she is taking a non-AT shortcut to Standing Indian Campground to call her mother. That puts her so far ahead I probably won't see her again before she gets off north of Franklin.

Another long day. (Sorry, feet) Went past Standing Indian Mountain Shelter at 10:30 a.m., and on to the next one. The mountain is the highest so far, about 5,500 feet. The Trail went up 1,500 feet nearly to the top, down again, around the Nantahala River headwaters, then up and over a ridge to the shelter. Once there I found Danny had gone on 4 miles to get a head start on hiking to Rainbow Campground at Wallace Gap. I doubt if I can get there tomorrow. My feet are sore and the Trail leads up what appears to be a very steep ascent at Albert Mountain. So Danny may have outrun me as well.

Again I got a spot inside the shelter, meaning less privacy but a faster start in the morning. I ate two days worth of dinners in hopes of reducing the load I have to lug up Albert Mountain.

At Deep Gap just before the Mountain a sign warned, "There are reports of a bear ranging between Deep Gap and Wayah Gap taking packs from hikers. It does not exhibit fear of humans. Use extreme caution." Perfect! An ursine Robin Hood stalking the next 30 miles or so of trail. Lovely! I could just imagine it ambushing me and grabbing my pack.

It is 6 p.m. and The Walking Stomach just showed up along . So I am not totally with strangers.

-Mouse

[By now I was settling into a routine. Get up and have oatmeal or Poptarts for breakfast, visit the privy or go into the woods and dig a cathole, pack up and hike. Snack every hour or so and a bigger snack of Gorp or whatever midday for lunch. Then on to a shelter or campsite. I carried my tent on the outside of my pack in case I needed to put it up in a hurry. I also carried my air mattress on the outside. When you get to a shelter the first thing you do is reserve a sleeping space by laying out your mattress on the floor, so I wanted my mattress easy to get to. Next I threw on an extra layer or so of clothing; as soon as you stop the body chills quickly without extra insulation. Then down to the stream or spring to get water and then cook supper. I usually used unfiltered water for cooking since I will boil it anyway. I topped off my water filter bottle before bed so the filter element was surrounded by water to protect it from freezing, or if it was really cold I took it into my sleeping bag to keep it warm. The evenings were cold enough I usually ate lying in my sleeping bag for warmth and settled down to sleep soon after.]

Tuesday, March 30, 2004
Destination: Wallace Gap
From: Carter Gap Shelter
Today's Miles: 12.8
Trip Miles: 103.7

After hours of rising wind the rain starts at 4:00 a.m., noisily hammering on the tin roof of the shelter. It is still coming down when I glance at my watch at 6:15 a.m. It looks like a late morning to let the rain stop. Then I peek outside my sleeping bag and am surprised see Stomach industriously packing away her sleeping bag. In a moment her friend gets up too and I know I HAVE to get up as well. If all the other women in the shelter are hiking despite the rain, how can I stay behind? I pack up, put on my rainsuit, put the rain cover on my pack, and by 7:00 I am on the Trail leaving all the men behind.

The Walking Stomach and I keep passing each other as we head for Albert Mountain. At 10:00 the rain stops. In a covered spot in the rocks I pack away my raingear and change to my long nylon pants, which should hold up to rocks better than the tights I'd worn under my Gore-Tex. As I start off again, Stomach's friend appears and we start up the mountain.

The Trail gets steep, breaks into long stairs, then hits sections of rock not really vertical, but too steep for poles. I let them dangle by their wrist straps and climb on all fours, grabbing rocks and trees to pull myself up.

Finally I get to the top where I find The Walking Stomach and a young couple from New Paltz NY. There is a fire tower and the clouds have broken enough for a wonderful view of the landscape from the top. I come down just as Stomach's friend arrives and we take some pictures. Her name is Little Tree. By 11:00 a.m. I am back on the Trail. At 11:30 I am at the Big Spring Shelter still going strong, so I make for Wallace Gap.

The Walking Stomach passes me. She is going to spend the night at Rock Gap Shelter, a mile short of Wallace Gap. I wave as I pass the shelter, then push on to Wallace Gap and turn west on the road. It is only one mile to Rainbow Springs campground but hiking on the hard pavement makes it seem to take forever.

At the campground the first person I see is Danny. He has just bought his FOURTH water treatment system in 100 miles. He sent his filter home at Neels Gap to switch to chemicals to save weight. He didn't like the taste so switched to a filter bottle at Hiawassee. But he did not like how hard it was to squeeze water through it. So here he went and bought a filter just like the one he had mailed home at Neels Gap! He is having trouble being satisfied with the different pros and cons of the alternative ways to treat water.

The new bunkhouse is interesting. It is a large yurt, a type of circular tent traditional in Mongolia. It has the traditional expanding wood frame but a plastic sheet covering instead of felt rugs and a plastic dome over the center of the roof where the opening for smoke would be in an actual yurt. It is crowded with double deck bunks. There are so many hikers already here I have to settle for an upper bunk.

The Weather channel says heavy thunderstorms just west of here this evening, so tomorrow could be rainy. If so, I might stay and give my feet the rest I have been promising them.

-Mouse

Wednesday, March 31, 2004
Destination: Winding Stair Gap
From: Wallace Gap
Today's Miles: 3.1
Trip Miles: 106.8

Talk about short days! I had toyed with staying at the campground another day to rest my feet. This morning there were scattered patches of blue sky and EVERYONE was packing to leave, so I decided to head out too. The forecast said rain with possible snow at 3,000 feet and rain Thursday and Friday. However the woman who worked in the camp store related that a year ago at 7:30am it had looked sunny and promising like now but by 9am it had been snowing hard.

Sleet started just before Winding Stair Gap and as I crossed the highway a few flakes had appeared. Before I had gone half a mile, it was snowing lustily. I began to have doubts about making another four miles to the shelter, camping at 5,000 feet, then going on through two more days of rain. Just before rounding a ridge that would have blocked the final view of the road far away, visibility was dropping fast and going on looked like a very dubious proposition. I decided to head down and hole up in Franklin. By the time I got back to the road the ground was covered and I was starting to look like a snowwoman. Along the way I passed Danny and asked him to let everyone know I had gone to Franklin and was not lying frozen somewhere. Then I sternly admonished HIM not to end up lying frozen somewhere! I met three hikers at the road, two going on and one looking for a ride down. In a few moments a car pulled up and an older couple offered us a ride to the town of Franklin, NC ten miles away.

The other hiker's name was Welsh Walker. She had the guidebook page for Franklin and got us to a motel that offered a shuttle back to the Trail in the morning. I think tomorrow I can go on. Two days of decreasingly rotten trail weather sounds better than three and with a warming trend slippery looking trail should be less of a danger.

For some days now my left foot in particular has had a painful bones-popping-out-the-ball-of-the-foot feeling that I get after running ten miles in worn out running shoes. So when the motel offered a shuttle to the local outfitters I went along and bought a set of Spenco insoles. My old insoles had been rather thin to begin with and now are mashed flat, so the new ones made a noticeable difference. Now I'm keeping my foot in a bucket of ice trying to soothe away the damage already done. Hopefully that and a little less mileage will make my foot happy again.

The rest of me is holding up well. My legs are going stronger, and the raw spots on my feet have healed so I went today without moleskin. If I can just fix the foot problem I will be a happy hiker.

-Mouse

[Each of the three published thruhiker memoirs I had read had described first hand near-death encounters with hypothermia. That gave me a healthy respect for possible hazards of winter hiking. So I tended to be rather conservative, choosing to try to avoid dangerous situations. Others hiked cheerfully into the worst weather with little regard for what could happen. It is hard to say in retrospect who was right, except to note that avoiding trouble means not having to deal with it.

By now I had learned there was a pattern to the weather. A cold front would bring several days of wet or snowy weather when the front passed through, followed by one or two very cold clear days as a high pressure zone took over, then several good hiking days. Whenever I was near a TV set I would check the Weather Channel to check the forecast and try to time things so that I went over the highest peaks during the good days. This cycle and the concern with avoiding or being ready for bad weather set the tone for my hike until Hot Springs NC. The ground was usually frozen and every morning crystals of frost thrust out of the ground in fascinating shapes. The high Smoky Mountains loomed off to the north under a white blanket of snow. But there were also increasing signs of spring: wildflowers starting to peep out and buds beginning to grow into leaves.]

Thursday, April 01, 2004
Destination: Silar Bald Shelter
From: Winding Stair Gap
Today's Miles: 3.7
Trip Miles: 110.5

The shuttle from the motel dropped me off at Winding Stair Gap at 9:30 am. It is about 40 degrees, cloudy, with snow and sleet. By the time I get to the shelter even the Trail is covered with snow, with just the tracks of the last footprints showing.

A couple are there and soon another woman named Katie arrives. We consult and the couple decides to move on to a campsite 4.5 miles away. It is only noon, but the site is 600 feet higher and this will probably be the coldest night, so Katie and I decide to stay here. It was my original destination before the snow hit so I have food.

So I am typing this with cold fingers while lying in my sleeping bag trying to stay warm. I feel the heat draining from beneath me. Finally the cold is too much and I try laying out my groundsheet, folded tent and emergency blanket for insulation then put the pad and sleeping bag on top. MUCH better!

A number of people show up, but most go on. We end up with six for the night, all men except for Katie and I. Then after supper one more appeared. He was SOUTHBOUND! He'd walked all the way from Roan Mountain, Virginia in this weather. He'd started last fall from his home near the Trail at Rockfish Gap then stopped for the winter. When he gets to Springer he will go to Maine and hike south to his home. Hikers call that a "flip-flop."

I had a good scare during the night. I woke up to find I could not feel or move my left hand and it was sticking out the opening of my sleeping bag. It was just like a lifeless piece of dead weight, a really unnerving phenomenon. A burst of fear swept through me and settled into a knot in my stomach as cold as the frozen landscape. "Oh great!" I thought, "I've kept my hand outside and it has frozen into an ice block." I frantically pulled my hand in and touched the fingers to my lips. The fingers were warm. Thank goodness! It was not frostbitten, it just had positional numbness, the nerves deadened from pressure applied to them by the position I had slept in. I straightened my arm and the feeling returned in seconds. What a relief.

-Mouse

Friday, April 02, 2004
Destination: Cold Spring Shelter
From: Silar Bald Shelter
Today's Miles: 12.2
Trip Miles: 122.6

I got going at 7:30 am. The ground was only crunchy instead of being concrete-hard so my decision to sleep low was a good one. At first the mud under the surface ice was still soft and the trail was free of snow. But it was overcast and foreboding and as I climbed towards Wayah Bald powdery snow appeared, then snowy footprints, then the trail became just a track in the snow. It became colder in proportion to the snowiness of the trail and the icy wind poured with the roar of a river through the gaps between the peaks. I have one last view of the town of Franklin nestled far below, the sun shining warmly on it as if to mock me and the icy world I had climbed into.

Soon the only way to keep warm was to keep moving. On the level spots I strode quickly, on steeper spots I shuffled up as fast as I could. As I got closer to the summit the wind became constant. The air got foggy and I realized I was way up inside the body of a cloud, like one of the ones that had been drifting high above the town of Franklin.

Hiking alone in a remote and snowy setting reminded me of the Jack London story "To Build a Fire" or Robert Scott's diary of his fatal trip to the South Pole. It was cold enough to die up here if one made the wrong mistake. I thought about the hiker who blithely set out at 2pm yesterday for the next shelter 12 miles away without even a flashlight and wondered if he was all right. In the last leg a hiker missed a turn and got lost for days on a side-trail. Someone said there were over 200 search and rescue workers out looking for him before he got found. That was during warm weather, now that kind of mistake could be fatal. That leaves me a bit keyed on edge and I watch the tracks carefully. When an orange-blazed side trail joins the Appalachian Trail I watch nervously for the blazes to be sure there are still white blazes and I have not strayed onto the side trail after it split off. My feet start to get cold and I discover I must keep brushing the snow off the tops of my boots or it melts and the water soaks through the uppers and wets my socks and chills my feet.

Suddenly I find myself at a parking spot with restrooms and trashcans. There must be a road to the top of Wayah Bald. The trails follow a paved blacktop sidewalk to a big display sign and then an old stone fire tower converted to an observation platform. Nearby is a rail with a sign. It is titled "The Ever-Changing View" and has all the landmarks labeled. All I can actually see is the inside of the cloud; the irony of all those labels and no view is irresistible so I stop and get out my camera to take a picture.

As I start descending the mountain the snow on the trail slowly fades to mud and the temperature eases somewhat. With relief I pass where the orange-blazed trail branches off.

The reprieve lasts for a few miles, then I start climbing again. It is high enough that it SHOULD be the last mile to the shelter. But it seems to go on forever, the temperature is dropping and visibility is dropping fast. More than once I see what looks like the roof-line of the shelter through the murk, only to find it is just a leaning tree. I am starting to worry when suddenly the shelter emerges from the gloom. Thank goodness!

It is 2pm and to my surprise I am the first here. I claim the most sheltered spot by the windward wall and set up my bed. Half an hour later Crash-Bang from last night arrives followed by Katie and Andrew from last night.

A bit later an older man, Stretch, arrives making five for the night. We spend the evening telling about ourselves and kidding each other. I think we are all a bit on edge from the long cold walk and relieved to have gotten safely to a shelter. It looks to be another cold night and I put on nearly everything I have. We figure it is so cold that the bears have gone back to bed so rather than bear bagging our food from trees most of us hang our food from the mouse protectors on the ceiling of the shelter. Most shelters have these, consisting of a cord with a stick tied at the end as a crosspiece for hanging and a tuna can in the middle attached through a hole punched in the center of the can. In theory if a mouse tries to climb down the cord, it slips on the tuna can and falls to the floor.

Because of the cold, someone half-jokingly says "Let's make a pact that none of us will die in the night. If anyone thinks they are about to freeze, they should say a code-word."

"Cheeseburgers" someone else suggested. We all laugh, because we have been talking constantly about the cheeseburgers at the Nantahala Outdoor Center so hardly five minutes pass without someone saying "cheeseburgers." We should be there tomorrow.

To my surprise it actually starts to warm up. During the night I unzip my sleeping bag a couple feet to spill the excess heat. Then Andrew complains about mice from across the shelter and I hear a scratching sound nearby so I hastily zip my bag shut before I have company. I am a bit squeamish about mice since a close encounter years ago and I really don't want one running across my face! It sounds like there could be a mouse between my bag and its cover but there is nothing I can do about it in the dark so after some effort I manage to ignore it enough to go back to sleep.

-Mouse

Saturday, April 03, 2004
Destination: Nantahala Outdoor Center
From: Cold Spring Shelter
Today's Miles: 11.5
Trip Miles: 134.1

I am the first to leave the shelter at 7:30 am. Remembering our pact, I bid farewell by saying "Cheeseburgers Cheeseburgers, help, Cheeseburgers!" Everyone laughs, since it is quite warm, well above freezing, and bid me farewell.

The ground is soft and the blanket of snow looks like Swiss cheese from holes made by wet clumps of thawing snow falling from the trees. As I enter rhododendron thickets instead of a long green tunnel it has become a low white one, the branches weighed down by heavy wet snow. From time to time more clumps fall from the branches and cascade onto me, as if the trees are children throwing snowballs at me.. I'm glad it is still early, it will get worse as the day warms up.

The snowy landscape finally relents as I descend to Tellico Gap. The clouds break and I can finally see the distant landscape for the first time in three days. It is windy and chilly as I climb back up Wesser Bald but only scattered bits of snow remain. I climb the observation tower for some pictures. I can still see the white through the trees on the mountains I have just crossed and to the north the Smokys are even more white. Then I start the long 3500 foot descent to the Nantahala River.

As I go down it is like another part of the world! More and more wildflowers appear and I see a tiny lizard and then three different kinds of butterflies flitting about happily as if the snow had never existed. Off in the distance I can hear the unfamiliar sound of a locomotive horn and later the rumble of railroad cars.

By the time I near the end of the steep 6.5 mile descent my feet are aching. I keep looking down, hoping to see the river and listening, hoping the roar I hear is the rapids instead of the wind in the trees. At last I see a parking lot by a road. I can hear someone announcing kayak races over a PA system. A few more switchbacks and I stumble into the NOC complex just after 2pm.

I check in at the office and get one of the last few bunks available. Then I go to the snack bar to get a barbeque sandwich and lemonade and sit down to eat and watch the races. Today is NOC's Spring Splash, with kayak racing and other events. As it is mainly a whitewater sport center we hikers are just a tiny presence.

Everywhere are t-shirt and shorts clad people, a surreal change from the frigid world I had just hiked out from.

Next I look for my room. In all the dozens of journals I have read, I don't remember any saying that a railroad track goes right through the NOC. Or that the bunkhouses are high up a steep hill! Just to get to the bathroom from my room takes 70 stair steps! Yikes! My feet and legs are sore from the long descent and the last thing I wanted to see were more stairs. Still, a shower feels good. There are no towels and I forgot to bring my pack towel from the room so I dry off with my almost clean midweight Capilene top then put on my only remaining clean clothes, a pair of shorts and spare t-shirt.

Feeling rejuvenated I head down the long hill to the outfitters to buy food for the next leg. Coming out of the store I discover Crash-Bang, Andrew, and Katie. They have arrived just too late to get bunks. They try calling other places to stay without luck, then we decide to have dinner together in the Rivers End Restaurant. Mmmmm, cheeseburgers.

They prepare to return to the shelter half a mile back up the Trail and I go to my room. Someone else has arrived, because there is a large dog sleeping happily on top of my clothes and sleeping bag! When I tell her to go to the floor she wakes up and looks at me irritatedly, like that is all hers and I should find somewhere else to sleep. Finally she reluctantly gets up and settles down under the other bunk bed to go back to sleep. A moment later there is a knock on the door; it is a manager with a note for the owner to get the dog out of the room or leave. Pets are not permitted at the NOC. Not long after the owner shows up. He seems unimpressed by the note but does go out taking the dog with him.

Just before 8pm comes another knock on the door. I'd heard sirens and it seems someone fell and needed taken away by ambulance. There was a dog with him and a staff person is trying to find out if it was my cabin-mate. I give what description I can and promise to let them know if he shows up tonight. If not, it is probably him who was hurt.

Later still, two security workers come to collect his belongings. It turns out it was him who had been hurt. They went through everything trying to find some form of ID. Just as they were about to give up, I spotted his name and address written on the outside of his pack. We had missed the obvious!

-Mouse

Sunday, April 04, 2004
Destination: Sassafras Shelter
From: Nantahala Outdoor Center
Today's Miles: 6.9
Trip Miles: 141.0

First I gathered the last forgotten belongings of the injured hiker to drop off at the office. They include the dog's backpack left on a shelf and her food-dish sitting outside the door. This was the first really serious injury I had encountered on my thruhike and it had a sobering effect on me. Then I went to the restaurant and had the first real breakfast since Atlanta: eggs, sausage, potatoes and two cups of hot chocolate. Stuffed to the gills, I waddled satiatedly back up the hill to pack and got on the Trail by 9:30 am.

It was a long climb up out of the Nantahala Gorge. At least it varied, sometimes steep, leaning into the poles and staggering upward, sometimes picking my way through jumbles of rocks, striding quickly when the slope is shallow enough and once in a while going downward. Along the way I realized the key to my room was still in my pocket. What with all the distractions, I'd forgotten to put it into the drop box when I left.

I came to another path leading to a ledge with a splendid view of the Nantahala Gorge, the cars drifting like tiny little ants 3000 feet below. I heard another locomotive horn and sat to see the train go by but it seemed to be heading in the wrong direction so after soaking in the vista a bit more I started uphill again.

Right after that I met two section hikers coming the other way who were willing to take the key back. Assuming they are less forgetful than me, the key will be back in a few hours instead of more than a week.

It got really steep and seemed to go on forever. False crest after false crest came and went only to reveal more climbing. I had seen a peak I thought was Cheoah Bald off in the distance ahead, part of tomorrow's hike, only to find myself standing on that same peak with even MORE climbing and Cheoah Bald still unimaginably far.

Finally I got to the top of Swimm Bald, 4500 feet high and the last crest before I dropped down to Sassafras Shelter. Balds are supposed to be mysterious southern mountains on whose crests trees don't grow, only grass. But every bald I have gone over so far have had trees. Swimm Bald seemed as wooded as the rest. But under clumps of rhododendrons I found small patches of snow, reminders of the recent storm.

The shelter was large, with two sleeping levels. It began to fill up. Katie and Crash-Bang appeared, but Andrew had decided to take a zero day at NOC. Checking the register I found Danny had sped ahead, trying to reach Fontana in time to watch the NBA basketball playoffs.

-Mouse

Monday, April 05, 2004
Destination: Cody Gap Campsite
From: Sassafras Shelter
Today's Miles: 11.9
Trip Miles: 152.9

As the price for the clear sky showing off a brilliant full moon last night, it was 24 degrees this morning. Brrrrrrr!

Thanks to daylight savings time I only got going at 8:00 am. Funny thing, it was not a bit brighter outside than 7:00 am was a few days ago! The first order of business was getting over 5,000 foot high Cheoah Bald. It seemed to take forever but in compensation it actually had a large-ish grassy patch on one side of the top. Finally a bald that was bald. It was even colder up there with lots of patches of snow and for a stretch on the shaded north side even the Trail was still covered in snow. Add in a chilly wind and I felt envious of the little village I saw far below surrounded by nice warm green fields.

My envy turned to dejection a few hours later when I realized the Trail was heading nearly all the way down to that village at Stecoah Gap and that I would have to climb all the way back up to the ridge top on the other side. Bleah! Still, it brought a reward. A section hiker who had shared the shelter mentioned this morning that he had left some oranges on a picnic table for us. Sure enough, there were three left. Trail Magic! In true thruhiker spirit I chose the one that had rolled onto the ground. Tradition says that a real Thru-hiker will pick up anything edible off the ground without a second thought and eat it. I did not have enough thruhiker appetite to eat the shreds of Hostess cupcake scattered near the table, but I courteously refrained from stepping on them in case someone after me was that ravenous.

Another hour and a half saw me back up on the ridgeline and after passing another peak I could finally see stretches of Fontana Lake, at the head of which I planned to find a warm dry bed, shower, rest and lots of real food. In sight beyond were the high snow-covered peaks of the Smoky Mountains, my next challenge.

I got to Brown Fork Shelter at 2:00 pm. I was not tired and it was the most uncomfortable looking shelter I had seen yet. An old log shelter, it's sleeping platform was waist high. About two feet in front of it was a gigantic log. One could not get in or out of bed without clambering over the log. Lovely!

Without regret I headed about 3 miles further up the Trail to Cody Gap. Here there was water and probably a campsite. Sure enough, when I got there at 4:20 pm I found both. Granted, the tentsite had a fair wind blowing through it and the water was far below in a meadow choked with poison ivy, but you can't have everything.

About an hour later Katie arrived along with an Australian trailnamed Ozzie. He decided to go on but Katie stayed, giving us a little two-woman village. About 6:00 a man named Rambler arrived all the way from NOC nineteen miles away and kept going. According to him everyone else from our shelter was behind us, some having started as late as 11:00 am. Maybe this will be where they all stop for the night.

It is 7:10 pm. Stretch has decided to tent here, Two Cents from Israel decided to go on after giving us all his candy bars so he would not have them during Passover. I have decided to name our little hamlet Mouseville and as the Mayor I am decreeing that there be a $50 tent fee to stay here and a 3 candy bar toll to pass through. Our little stretch of Trail going through the center of town is now the Mouseville Turnpike. Katie says "Sounds like a plan!," so with a majority vote the motions carry. Now to lay in wait in our sleeping bags for new victims, oops, I mean new citizens and travelers.

8:20. Mouseville now has four residents, three of them women. It even has a female psychiatrist!

-Mayor Mouse

Tuesday, April 06, 2004
Destination: Fontana Dam
From: Cody Gap Campsite
Today's Miles: 10.2
Trip Miles: 163.1

Boo Hoo! My beautiful new hamlet is a failure! The mayor tore down her house and moved away about 7:20 this morning and word is that after that all the other residents quickly left too, leaving Mouseville deserted. Oh well.

Now I am sitting outside Fontana Dam Visitors Center. Or at least as close to it as the Department of Homeland Security will allow, which is across the parking lot in the meager shade of a thigh high wall next to a large sign that sternly admonishes "No Packs Beyond This Point." I got here about 1:30, after a hard finish to the day's hike. From Highway NC28 a mile and a half ago to the dam the map profile had looked flat but it had lied and there was actually a steep nasty ridge. The Trail planners were determined that the Trail go over every possible bump of the high ridge, lest we feel cheated by walking on too much level ground. I am beginning to realize that no matter how flat the profile looks, on the Appalachian Trail there is always another mountain before you get to where you are going.

Back at NC28, a note had instructed anyone wishing to stay at the Hike Inn Motel to come here and call them on the pay phone. So I dutifully dig quarters out of my pack, leave it nervously at the designated pack-approved spot and look for the phone. Hopefully none of the pack thieves I have been warned about will grab my pack while it is out of my sight. The phone is on the far side of the building. I put the quarters in and dial the number. A recorded voice tells me to first dial 1 or 0. I try again dialing 1 first. The voice tells me to first dial 1 or 0! I try it with 0 and get a recording saying welcome to Sprint Long Distance and to dial 0 to talk to an operator. He tells me to try it again without putting money in first. So I try again and am relieved to hear a recorded voice instruct me to put in 50 cents. I comply only to hear, you guessed it, the voice telling me to dial a 1 or 0 first!

This is starting to be like a puzzle at beautiful Flood Control Dam #3 in the computer game Zork! Trying not to babble insanely, I try with 0 again to get an operator and explain that I have dialed every possible way without getting through and am stuck here at a pay phone in the middle of nowhere and could she PLEASE get me through? She offers to put through a collect call. I agree dubiously, not knowing if the motel will accept. Miraculously the Hike Inn does!

Only to tell me that not only are there no rooms left for tonight, they can't find the bounce-box of supplies and equipment I sent them three weeks ago. Isn't civilization wonderful?

Gnashing my teeth a little, I trudge back to my pack to get my calling card and return to the phone to try calling the Fontana Inn. After needing two tries to get the card to work, I realize the Inn has a 1-800 number and I didn't need the card. Hmmm, maybe I AM starting to babble insanely! Finally I get through and they say they DO have a room and a shuttle will be out to the dam in 50 minutes.

The Visitors Center is locked up, so I cannot pass the time there. Philosophically, I pull out my Pocketmail, settle down in the little patch of pack-approved shade, and catch up on my journal. Now the shuttle should be here in five minutes. Looking over at the locked up Visitors Center, I wonder if there is a little back room with 3 buttons like in the game Zork....

My attention is distracted by a bumblebee the size of a helicopter gunship hovering near my shoulder. After a few ranging passes, it makes a firing run towards my head! I jump up and scramble out of range. It follows as I dart here and there about the parking lot. Looking behind me I discover several flowering trees with squadrons of additional bees waiting in reserve. Well, it looks like I won't lack for something to do while awaiting the shuttle. Excuse me while I run for cover!

-Mouse

Wednesday, April 07, 2004
Destination: Hike Inn Motel
From: Fontana Dam
Today's Miles: 0.0
Trip Miles: 163.1

One thing you learn on the Trail is that given a little time, nearly every difficulty works itself out. The hill is surmounted, the storm passes, the injury heals and the lost is found. Last night I ended up in a nice comfy room at the Fontana Inn with an AYCE buffet right down the hall. Once I got settled I called the Hiker Inn about my package. The Post Office had just sent it over and they would come pick me up to spend my second night there. What could be nicer?

Another thing is that often those difficulties don't smooth away all by themselves. They have help. The Appalachian Trail is lined with thousands of people who make every thruhike possible and they deserve full credit. Everyone from fellow hikers who share encouragement and supplies to Trail Angels performing countless acts of Trail Magic to Trail maintainers and ridgerunners to towns absolutely full of hospitality to just plain ordinary people being really nice. My thanks go to all of them. In this case to the efficient hospitable innkeepers who made my troubles vanish.

Now to prepare for the Smokys. It is the highest part of the Trail, at 70 miles one of the longest between towns and known for difficult weather.

The Hike Inn costs more than hostels at $40 a night and with only 5 rooms it is best to reserve in advance from NOC. But I found it a great place to stay. It is cozy with a capital C, with homey decor, thick comfy quilts and soft linen, and kitchenettes.

It has nearly everything a hiker could want. They took my mountain of dirty laundry and brought it back before supper all clean and folded, shuttled us into Robinsville for meals, ATM and buying supplies at a real grocery instead of just a camp store picked over by hoards of thruhikers, provided free shuttles to and from the Trail and even had a supply of the backcountry permit forms required to enter Great Smoky Mountains National Park.

I got my warm Patagonia R3 fleece jacket from my bounce box and put into the box my used disposable camera, spare eyeglasses and everything else I thought I could spare to compensate for the added weight of the jacket and the six days worth of food I expect to need to get to the other side of the Smokys at Davenport Gap.

Tomorrow I get to lug it all from the Dam up to the high spine of the Smoky Mountains.

-Mouse

Thursday, April 08, 2004
Destination: Mollies Ridge Shelter
From: Hike Inn Motel
Today's Miles: 11.0
Trip Miles: 174.1

Well, somewhat to my surprise I made the whole 11-mile ascent from the dam to the first shelter up on the spine of the Smokes, heavy pack and all. And I got here before 3:30, less than seven hours. It has been perfect hiking weather, cloudy and cool. By noon the lower valleys and hills were blanketed in the mist that gives the Smokes their name, but up on the heights it stayed nice. Then the Trail here is graded for horses, so no four-foot high steps or rock scrambles to slow one down.

The wildflowers up here have gone crazy. Before, they were scattered about. Here the ground between the trees is absolutely carpeted with little pale purple flowers. Against the green and brown undergrowth they look white, so the ground looks like it did when blanketed with snow but now it is flowers.

There is something mysterious up in the mountains. For days now, from time to time I hear a deep thumping sound. It has exactly the quickening cadence and fadeout as a rubber ball bouncing but much deeper; thump thump thump thump thumpthump umpumpump... I wonder what it is. Some atmospheric acoustic fluke? Reverberations of grade-school recesses all over the world conjoining here? Giants playing jacks? Or maybe the war drums of the Ents, calling the trees to battle?

This park is famous for its bears and as soon as I got to the shelter I was greeted by a sign warning sternly "No cooking or eating in or near shelter." Sounds like my main meal might be at midday for now, away from shelters.

I was the second person to arrive, meaning that I ought to have a space in the shelter. Smoky Mountain Park has special rules. In theory only the first 4 thru-hikers at each shelter are assured a space. Section hikers reserve in advance and get priority for the rest of the spots. So if the shelter is full and another section hiker arrives, a thruhiker has to move to their tent. To make things more confusing, you are not allowed to tent if the shelter is not full, even though you are required to tent if it is full.

My feet are a bit sore, but nothing like before I got the new insoles. The rest of me is happy as ever.

-Mouse

Friday, April 09, 2004
Destination: Derrick Knob Shelter
From: Mollies Ridge Shelter
Today's Miles: 11.7
Trip Miles: 185.8

A warm night and got going at 7:30, the day nice and clear as predicted.

The first 5 miles was easy on horse-friendly trail. Then it got more rugged. It was worth it though. The balds here are finally balds with great expanses of thick grass making for comfy rests and great views. The view from Rocky Top was especially nice. You could see almost forever.

It was tempting to go on to Silars Bald Shelter 5.5 miles away. But that would mean over 17 miles for the day. My feet are tired and this terrain is not the place for setting records.

In the Park Hikers are required to stay at the shelters and the spacing is awkward, forcing either a too-long day or a too-short one, as well as causing the hikers to clump together into large groups instead of spreading out like before. It is 14.5 miles to the shelter past Clingmans Dome and 7.2 to the shelter this side of it. I think I will get the earliest start I can tomorrow, and when I get to the nearer shelter I will look at the time, the weather and my feet then decide whether to tackle Clingmans or take a short day.

-Mouse

Saturday, April 10, 2004
Destination: Mt. Collins Shelter
From: Derrick Knob Shelter
Today's Miles: 13.5
Trip Miles: 199.3

Well, I made it over Clingmans Dome. I also made my longest day's hike yet at 14 miles.

The day started nice and clear and not too cold, then clouded over.

I got to Clingmans Dome at about 1:15 in the afternoon. As I approached, the broadleaf trees were replaced by pines. In recent years there has been a major die off and few mature pines are left. So I was glad to see lots and lots of young trees about 12 feet and smaller. I hope they live to replace the ones that died.

I decided to go up the long ramp to the top of the tall concrete observation tower to enjoy the view. It was the first time I had met large numbers of tourists and they were full of questions about thruhiking like where we sleep and how much my pack weighed. Someone offered me some cheese and without thinking about it I said no thanks. Imagine a thruhiking Mouse turning down cheese! It will take a long time to live that down.

Descending Clingmans Dome, the trail was covered with slushy snow. Three miles of that quickly soaked my boots and felt like hiking barefoot in ice water. In the shadows of the pines the overcast sky made it seem late evening instead of mid-afternoon and I could not wait to get to the shelter. Other than that, it was perfect hiking weather.

Expecting the shelter to be full of non-thruhikers with reservations, I went ahead and set up my tent, finishing just as the long-predicted rain arrived. It was just a shower (so far, that is) but now my tent has officially been rained on while on the Appalachian Trail.

I have also made it halfway through the Great Smoky Mountains National Park before getting any rain. Since much of the Trail I have passed through here has been a deep rut worn in the ground by so many park visitors that becomes flooded like a river when it rains and since Clingmans is known for being really nasty in bad weather, I am just as happy to have escaped rain until now. I am also just .7 of a mile short of having hiked 200 miles on the Trail.

Now I have to decide whether to hike just 8 miles tomorrow or go on to the next shelter and have to hike 17 miles. I guess I will let my feet decide when I get to the first shelter tomorrow. Most of the others are going into Gatlinburg tomorrow to eat and resupply. But my food is holding out and Gatlinburg means hitchhiking 16 miles, so I will skip it.

-Mouse

Sunday, April 11, 2004
Destination: LeConte Lodge (off the AT)
From: Mt. Collins Shelter
Today's Miles: 7.3
Trip Miles: 206.6

What a day! The good news is I got to a shelter long before I expected. The bad news is it is on a totally different trail and I am over 5 miles off course!

But at least I got lost with style. I unerringly erred to a shelter with a lodge next to it with hot food and a little store right in the middle of nowhere!

My day started normally enough. I left Mount Collins at 7:30. The trail for the first hour was clogged with alternating rocks, snow, slush, mud and water. I was getting grumpy and Gatlinburg was starting to sound better and better.

Then out of nowhere I heard voices. I came upon a parking lot and a woman said "Happy Easter! Are you a thruhiker?" In less than no time Trail maintainer and Trail Angel for the day Louisiana Lou had me seated out of the rain on the tailgate of her pickup truck with my feet dangling happily off the hard ground. Then I had a nice ham sandwich, cherry tomatoes, banana and can of coke while she filled me in on the weather and told trail maintaining stories. Happy and ready to face the world again, I was strapping on my pack when the next hiker appeared and Lou yelled "Happy Easter! Are you a thruhiker?"

After that I flew happily to the parking area at Newfound Gap without a thought of Gatlinburg left on my mind. I dumped my trash, used the first flush toilets I had seen since Fontana and topped up on water from the faucet. Then I headed onward. Soon I ran into two Easter Bunnies who gave me candy. Honest! All right, it was really two women wearing pink bunny hoods. Euphoric with all the goodwill and extra calories I floated up the Trail and just before 12:30 came to a sign that said "Icewater Springs Shelter .2 Miles." Wow, there was so much of the day left I could surely make the 7.8 miles to Pecks Corner Shelter well before dark. Since Icewater Springs seemed to be on a side trail, I did not bother stopping in, I just headed on.

I was a bit puzzled that no sign for Charlie's Bunion appeared when expected, but otherwise things were going great. The Trail surface had turned to gun-metal gray metallic looking pebbles that were well drained, even and well graded. I strode along, eager to make all the time I could while the surface was so nice. A light rain was falling but I was warm and happy in Capilene, Polartec and Gore-Tex. The trail ran on the top of a ridge and the views were nice, of mist-shrouded hills and a hint of clearing in the distance.

Then I passed a saddle and the geology changed. It was a different type of rock and not so well drained. Still the wet trail did not dampen my spirits.

The trail began to rise and started to turn ugly! It clung to a steep hillside, almost a cliff. Snowdrifts clogged the trail, making footing really bad. I was almost relieved that fog was setting in, so I could not see just how bad the drop was. At one point I saw the tip of a tall dead pine looming out of the mist a few dozen feet away below my eye level and realized there WAS a cliff right off the edge of the Trail. Feelings of acrophobia wafted gently across my consciousness and I grimly glued my eyes to the Trail trying to gain control over my senses. The snowdrifts slopped sideways towards the edge making footing quite dangerous. Every step and pole placement had to be made carefully lest I slip and get shot right off the edge over the cliff into space. Twice there was even a steel cable bolted to the rock to serve as a rude handrail. The first time it was just in a scraggly patch of broken rock devoid of vegetation like an old landslide. But the second time was in a snow-clogged section with a yawning void on the side of the Trail and I took the hint and clung like death to the cable. I could not imagine how Rocket and Bono negotiated this hazardous mess last winter on snowshoes towing their gear behind on a sled.

Things were getting really bad and the Trail climbed ever upward into the Fog. I kept at it, knowing at some point that the Trail HAD to descend out of the snow to Peck shelter a few miles away at a more temperate 5,200 feet. Finally it made a switchback and continued up the opposite direction. At least I now had a gentler slope in the loop of trail between me and the cliffs! Relieved, I headed on, looking for the trail to turn downward.

Then I came to a sign. "LeConte Lodge .7 Miles." I decided I'd better check where I was and pulled out my map. To my puzzlement, there was no such place on the Appalachian Trail. Along came a jogger who informed me that I was MILES from the AT. YIKES! He added that the lodge was reservations only but there was a shelter along the way.

I checked the map and eventually realized what had happened. The ".2 Miles" to the last shelter had not been a side trail at all but the AT. I had turned off the AT and hiked happily north on the Boulevard Trail over five miles out of my way before discovering my mistake.

Knowing I could not possibly get back to the Appalachian Trail before dark, I decided to camp at the shelter before hiking back in the morning. It would put me one day behind schedule and with the reserve food and all the day's trail magic I should still just make it. I dropped my pack at LeConte Shelter and went for water before setting up camp. On the way back I ran into a group of hikers who insisted I come along to the nearby lodge just in case there was room.

I had stumbled right onto what has to be the best-kept secret of Great Smoky Mountains National Park. LeConte Lodge, it appears, is perched 6,593 feet up a mountain, miles from the nearest road, with guest cabins, kitchen and dining room and even a tiny little store. It is run sort of like the Huts in the White Mountains. Staples are airlifted in by helicopter and perishable food packed in by llama!

The man at the desk, former thruhiker White Pine, 1995, said there were no cabins free but I could stay at the shelter. He also let me call the Park Rangers just in case I was missed. Apparently I was not the first AT hiker to stumble in here, but he said I was the first to manage it this year. Then one of the guests introduced himself as Steve Nelson and said he'd reserved for two but came alone and would be happy to give me the empty space for dinner. Talk about Trail Magic!

I set up my bed, then went back to the Lodge to sit in the nice warm reception room to catch up on my journal until suppertime. I also took the chance to buy 4 Snickers bars to stretch my food, a disposable camera to document my new adventure, and a "LeConte Lodge, I hiked it in 2004" patch to sew on my pack in memory of my experience.

Over dinner I learned Steve Nelson is a familiar guest, having been here over 30 times. He is a police officer for the University of Tennessee. Several of the guests knew other thruhikers and wished me well. The Lodge believes in comfort food and I had soup, roast beef, mashed potatoes, greenbeans, stewed apples, hot chocolate and two chocolate chip cookies. Still, despite eating sparingly I barely got the second cookie down. I wonder if my stomach is shrinking from the sparse Trail diet? Then warm and satisfied I went off to bed after a very eventful Easter. LeConte Shelter is one of the big new improved ones and I had it all to myself for the night.

I have a lot to be thankful for today!

-Mouse

Monday, April 12, 2004
Destination: Pecks Corner Shelter
From: LeConte Lodge (off the AP)
Today's Miles: 7.6
Trip Miles: 214.2

I had a restless night, alternating between lots of nightmares inspired by the sheer drop-offs on the snowbound trail yesterday and worries about the slushy trail freezing overnight into an impassable icy mess. Had that happened I might have been stuck here until it thawed. It was dangerous enough in the snow; ice would have been simply too risky. No matter how much I told myself that I could always try another Trail down or wait for a thaw then resupply in Gatlinburg, my rattled nerves would not settle into sound sleep. To add injury to insult, the shelter mice chewed big holes in the tops of my socks! To my immense relief it did not freeze. I got going at 8:00 am to give more time for the snow to melt still further. The Trail was not nearly as bad as yesterday and within half an hour I was through the snow. Thank Goodness.

After two hours I ran into six hikers coming the other direction who greeted me with "You're going the wrong way!"

"No kidding!" I replied, and told my tale of woe.

"But this IS the Appalachian Trail" they responded. I managed to convince them they were really on the Boulevard and got them headed back so the Lodge would not get six more unexpected guests. Then I hiked along behind them back to the AT. I had a quick lunch of gorp at the shelter where I ran into Rod, whom I had last seen just after Fontana Dam.

All day it was foggy and wet with a fierce chill wind blowing wet mist across the Trail. It gave an air of the wild Scottish moors instead of the American woods, especially when the trail perched high on the ridgeline with nothing but fog on either side. It was the same sort of hiking day that Bilbo Baggins and the dwarves took refuge in the cave full of orcs. Whenever I realized I had not seen a white blaze in a while, I nervously scanned the trees until the next blaze would come mercifully into view. This was no weather in which to get lost again!

Finally just after 3pm the sign appeared for the sidetrail to Becks Corner Shelter. To my surprise, there was no one there yet. Checking the log I found there seemed to be few visitors. Odd since it is one of the nice improved ones, just like LeConte Shelter last night. I guess most thruhikers prefer to go on 5.5 miles to the next one that is right on the AT. But I was wet and cold and tired, my feet hurt and I was glad to stay.

About 4:45 Zipcode showed up and found there was still a fire from last night in the fireplace. He coaxed it to life and then four more hikers showed up. They had all spent the night in Gatlinburg and started this morning from Newfound Gap. Some had been at Mount Collins Shelter with me two days ago. So I have not lagged behind EVERYONE who knows me, despite my getting lost.

-Mouse

Tuesday, April 13, 2004
Destination: Cosby Knob Shelter
From: Pecks Corner Shelter
Today's Miles: 12.9
Trip Miles: 227.1

It looks like the Appalachian Trail weather goddess has decided to re-adjust our thinking as to what constitutes a wet day. A thunderstorm started up at midnight and it has rained like crazy all night.

I lay in bed until 8:00 am, a record late morning for me but I was still the first one up. I had enough ambition to put moleskin and tape on yesterday's sore spots then fetch my food bag from the bear cables outside and cook oatmeal before retreating again to the warmth of my sleeping bag. The rain had moderated, but now at 9:00 am the sky darkened over and it started pouring again.

If it eases before 10:00 there would still be time to get to Cosby Knob Shelter as I had planned. That makes 10 miles to the hostel outside the park, my next resupply. But if this keeps up it is no weather for going over Guyot Mountain at 6,200 feet.

Even at noon there is time to make for the nearest shelter, Tri-Corner Knob. That will get in 5.5 miles. I have food to stay at both shelters or take today off and go to Crosby tomorrow. I will probably go at least to Tri-Corner; that gives me the most options with the food I have left.

I left at 10:30. At first the clouds started to break and in half an hour I stop to take off my Gore-Tex top and bottom. I can finally see the distant mountain ridges. Vapor rises from the trees exactly like the smoke from a forest fire I saw at Lake Tahoe last year. Larger clouds rise from the rivers far below. Instead of the roar of wind from the ridge tops, the roaring I hear now comes from below, water rushing in rain-swollen mountain streams and rivers.

Then I feel a chill gust on my back. I look over my shoulder and see a towering white cloud bearing down on me. Hastily I stop and put on my Gore-Tex top then rush on, scrambling to reach shelter before the oncoming storm breaks. A ridge top is no place to be in wet weather, both from the risk of lightning and from hypothermia. In my haste I slip on a log waterbar and go down, wrenching my left shoulder before my poles fly free. I sit a moment and rub it carefully, checking the damage, then get up and rush on. Eighth inch hail starts falling from the sky as I get closer to the Tri-Corner shelter.

I scramble gratefully into the shelter fully expecting to stay the night there. The weather is turning bad and I really should dry off and let my hurts heal. It is also 2:00 pm, rather late to start the 7.7 mile leg to Cosby Knob shelter. Zipcode, Mojo, Hitch, Andrew and Zipdrive from last night are already there, having passed me on the Trail, as well as another hiker I had not met before. They say they are going on after some lunch. Zipdrive and the new hiker leave and shortly after that the hail increases and is joined by a downpour of rain. Two Cents arrives looking bedraggled from the wet.

I comment that it is looking like we will all be stuck here for the night. Then I pull out my mattress and sleeping bag and start getting myself organized to spend the night. Joking about my reputation for early starts, Andrew says "Don't worry Mouse, we won't let anyone know you had a late start and took a short day."

Then during a lull in the rain a man and three boys arrive from the north.

"How is the trail north of here?" someone asks them and they reply "A short steep ascent right after here, then the rest is like an avenue all the way to the Pigeon River."

Galvanized by that encouraging report I quickly repack my pack, don my Gore-Tex coat and grab my poles.

"Mouse, what came over you?" Two Cents asks, awed by my sudden action after all my talk of staying.

"I've lost my mind" I reply and head for Crosby Knob.

-Mouse

Wednesday, April 14, 2004
Destination: Standing Bear Hostel
From: Cosby Knob Shelter
Today's Miles: 10.4
Trip Miles: 237.5

The Smokys had one more trick before we escaped their clutches. This morning at Cosby Knob Shelter there was an inch of snow on the ground. When I got up, my boots had frozen so stiff I had to force my feet into them for the short walk to get my food bag. The row of socks hung to dry over the shelter fireplace were stiff as boards and dusted with snow. Having gotten my food, I pulled off the frozen boots and retreated again to my sleeping bag.

I took my boots into my sleeping bag with me to thaw a bit. Necessity is the mother of invention and I first inverted the sleeping bag stuff sack and put the boots into it then. That kept the sleeping bag and the inside of it's stuff sack protected from the boots' mud and wet so I could thaw the boots while keeping everything else clean and dry. Next I ate Poptarts, spooned cold-stiffened peanut butter into my mouth for extra calories and waited, hoping another early riser would leave before me so I would not have to break trail through the snow-covered Trail.

Despite my best efforts to procrastinate, I was still the first to hit the Trail. It was foggy and a cold wind blew tiny snowflakes about. Soon I was covered in snow and a stray lock of hair hanging from my balaclava slowly became coated with rime. My ice and snow framed face would have made a great photo, but there was no one to take it.

At first the snow began to drift ominously but as I lost altitude it slowly began to relent. By Davenport Gap Shelter I was finally below the snow and the world turned green again.

I hiked on past the Gap, out of Great Smoky Mountains National Park. It had been a nice visit. I was glad to have seen so many of the moods of the Smokys: calm and clear; overcast; icy; wild mist and wind; thunderstorms with hail; and cold and snowy.

I hiked onward to Interstate 40. An odd sight, being the first freeway I had seen since Atlanta three weeks ago. A mile past that, I reached Standing Bear Hostel, my first taste of civilization since Fontana Dam.

Located on an old farm in a hollow, it is a bit primitive: bunkhouse with wood burning stove, outdoor showers, mouldering privy like the ones at trail shelters. But it has everything a hiker coming out of the Smokys could want.

Shower, laundry, a warm dry bed, frozen pizza, burgers and other food to feast upon and assorted trail-friendly food to resupply for the next leg to Hot Springs.

-Mouse

Thursday, April 15, 2004
Destination: Brown Gap Campsite
From: Standing Bear Hostel
Today's Miles: 10.1
Trip Miles: 247.6

Yesterday I found I had painful raw spots worn through my skin at my left Achilles tendon, probably from a seam in my boot, and on both heels. So I slathered them repeatedly with Neosporin, kept off them and gave them as much air as possible during my hostel stay.

Today I limited my miles to 10, camping between shelters all by myself at Brown Gap. Nearly everyone else is headed for Max Patch, a bald that is said to be very pretty camping on clear nights like tonight, but it is four miles further, too far on my damaged feet. From the looks of my tendon, even ten miles was pushing it, but had I stopped at Groundhog Creek Shelter after only seven miles it would have meant a longer hike tomorrow.

I'm slathering on lots of antiseptic and hoping my injuries do not get infected. The ground is a lot drier and that is a big help. Most of this foot trouble started in the Smokys from long mileage in wet boots and socks.

I spent this morning climbing out of Davenport Gap up Snowbird Mountain. True to its name, it was covered with snow from yesterday's storm. But the weather is clear and warm for a change so it was not too soggy.

I finally got to see the mysterious spaceship on the top of Snowbird Mountain. It looks like a shack with a wide overhanging circular roof whose edge is lined with what look like large fluorescent desk lamps and with a giant bowling pin rising up from the center. There are hiker tales of it being a UFO or a secret nuclear missile.

Actually it is just a VOR homing beacon for aircraft navigation. The bowling pin is the main transmitting antenna and the desk lamp looking things are receiving antenna used to calibrate the signal. But I am sure hikers will still tell tall tales about it.

-Mouse

Friday, April 16, 2004
Destination: Walnut Mountain Shelter
From: Brown Gap Campsite
Today's Miles: 10.2
Trip Miles: 257.8

    Well, Max Patch is as good as advertised. Not just the top, but the entire mountain was cleared. That means a breathtaking view from the top, (and people like me NEED to take a breath after getting up there). The Trail is marked with white blazes on posts since there are no trees. It looks very incongruous in the southern forestland, as if a mountain from the Yorkshire dales were transplanted here.

    I added up the calories of the meals I had planned and found I had less than 1500 per day. So I'm eating my emergency stocks to make it up. I had my spare breakfast of oatmeal when I got to the shelter and will have my spare supper too. I also mixed half a pack of Jell-O mix with cold water to drink. I had brought it to mix with hot water for treating hypothermia but with warmer dry weather I am surely not getting hypothermia between now and tomorrow so can afford to eat it. The gelatin bits taste just like the pulp in fresh-squeezed orange juice. I plan to gobble up everything in my food bag, then start eating real food when I get to town. I see the next leg is about 70 miles too, so I need to plan my food more carefully. Wow, I'm starting to think about food, maybe I am starting to get the insatiable hunger thuhikers are known for.

    My heel looks a bit better. It ought to last 13 miles tomorrow and then I can take a day off to let it heal.

    Cuppa-Joe, Steve and Little Chicken have arrived so the shelter is starting to fill.

    This seems to be the shelter of walking wounded. Stretch has arrived and out of the five of us four have foot or leg problems. The other one, Steve, is an older local man accompanying Little Chicken, who had to take a week off for leg problems from going too far each day. Every able-bodied thruhiker has already rushed ahead to attend the Trail Festival in Hot Springs.

    -Mouse

Saturday, April 17, 2004
Destination: Hot Springs, NC
From: Walnut Mountain Shelter
Today's Miles: 13.1
Trip Miles: 270.9

    This was the first day since Clingmans Dome that I actually hiked on dry ground! It is also the first day in I don't know when that I did not see snow on the ground. What a novelty! Much of the day was spent hiking long gentle downhills so as an experiment I tried carrying my poles in one hand instead of using them. It is a bit easier on the Trail and changes which muscles get used a little.

    The world is getting more and more green. The leaves are even starting to peek out of their buds. That is a good thing, since it is getting warm enough for some shade to be in order.

    I could see Hot Springs long before I got there, nestled by a river in a valley far below. Who needs aerial photos when you have the mountains! The downside of the view was the descent; my knees were popping by the time I got down to the street level.

    I came right into the middle of TrailFest so the town is crawling with hikers. There were booths and music and events. I ended up tenting at a campground at the far side of town. All sorts of people are here, Little Tree and The Walking Stomach, Crash-Bang, Andrew, Two Cents who shuttled up from Standing Bear to see the festival and others I have not seen in weeks. Checking my email I found my old companion Danny had rushed ahead and was all the way to Erwin.

    After living on Poptarts, Snickers bars and peanut butter fortified ramen noodles I was happy to see the outfitter's well-stocked organic section. For the 70 mile leg to Erwin I stocked up on yummy nutritious things like textured vegetable protein, instant hummus, instant vegetarian chili, instant pea soup, Bear Valley pemmican bars and even calorie-drenched halvah bars. I'm in hiker heaven! Of course by the time I get to Erwin I might be so sick of healthy food that I switch to a diet of slim jims and donuts or something.

    Then I got a quart of milk and a pint of chocolate milk and sat down to overcome my 10 day dairy deprivation and enjoy the music.

That done, I carried my loot back to camp and lay in the shade under the trees on my air mattress typing and giving my feet some air. The hurt spots are all pink instead of angry red, so another day of exhaustingly strenuous lying around doing nothing should get them in shape to hike again.

-Mouse

Sunday, April 18, 2004
Destination: Hot Springs, NC
From: Hot Springs, NC
Today's Miles: 0.0
Trip Miles: 270.9

Well, I found something to do even more strenuous than lying in my tent. After a wonderful $5 AYCE breakfast that finished off the TrailFest I went to the Hot Springs Spa. A hundred years ago there were big hotels here and people came from all over the US and Europe to "take the waters." There is still a little spa. So I went and was led to one of a row of fenced off enclosures under shade trees along a beautiful creek. There I sat for an hour in a Jacuzzi full of hot mineral spring water. Then I had an hour long massage. It made a new Mouse of me!

Next I went to the Paddlers Pub for a half pound hamburger and a goat cheese-walnut-granny smith apple salad. In an hour I saw more bikers come through on their motorcycles than I had seen hikers the entire weekend. I gather that there is a twisty road near here that motorcyclists like to ride.

-Mouse

[After Hot Springs staying warm was replaced as a concern by a need to get in miles. I had volunteered to work on the stage crew of a women's music festival in central Virginia. That meant I needed to get far enough north that they could come pick me up without too much driving. At first I had hoped to get to Waynesboro by May 25 but it became more and more clear that I could not make it. I changed my goal to US Highway 60 and even that was a challenge. During this time the weather evolved from a pattern dominated by passing warm fronts into a time of mild partly cloudy days with afternoon thunderstorms every day. Foliage increased and I saw far more bumblebees than I had seen in my entire life! They seemed to be looking for nesting sites]

Monday, April 19, 2004
Destination: Spring Mountain Shelter
From: Hot Springs, NC
Today's Miles: 11.0
Trip Miles: 281.9

Last night at dark two women named Lonesome Dove and Coyote and a man named Saltlick moved in next to me. They had gone to Gatlinburg when it snowed on the day I left the Smokys, then have hiked such long mileage they caught up with me.

This is the first Ibuprofen Day in a long time. When I first lifted my pack this morning my arches were popping. I went to the Post Office to send post cards and while there I did some pack-trimming. I mailed home my R3 fleece jacket and the sleeping bag cover I got at Neels Gap, cutting my load by over two and a quarter pounds. Hopefully it won't get too cold for my remaining things.

That seemed to help a lot. But as soon as I made the climb up to Lovers' Leap and started walking on level ground the trouble started. Every time I put weight on the inside of the ball of my right foot and flexed it, OUCH! So I spent the day plodding cautiously, careful to keep the weight on the outside of my soles or on my heels. That helped, except for the occasional mis-step. Then as the afternoon went on my back started aching too.

Gee whiz, shouldn't I be used to this by now? I will cook my heaviest meal tonight and hope the drop in pack weight solves the problem.

Other than that, my high point for the day was meeting Jan Liteshoe going the other direction. I did not know until I passed Barbara and she told me who it was.

This day finishes my first month of hiking. Suitably enough, I am at Spring Mountain, NC, since a month ago I was at Springer Mountain, GA. Keeps things nice and tidy.

Barbara arrived about 5:00 and at 6:00 Hitch and Mojo showed up with a surprise, their dog Dexter. I had not realized they had a dog because I met them in the Smokys where dogs are forbidden. So Dexter had stayed in a kennel until they reached the other side.

-Mouse

Tuesday, April 20, 2004
Destination: Jerry Cabin Shelter
From: Spring Mountain Shelter
Today's Miles: 15.4
Trip Miles: 297.3

Wow, I actually made it. 15.4 miles, my farthest day yet.

The day started nicely, a bit overcast and not chilly. I did 8.6 miles by noon. Then there was a shower. I tried my Gore-Tex jacket but soon its inside was wetter from sweat than the outside was from rain.

I had just dried out when the Trail sprang a surprise. First the geology changed. The soil began to resemble fireplace ashes and the trail began to be strewn with rocks to step on and over. Then I came to a sign. In white it pointed to a path marked "Exposed Ridgeline." In blue it pointed to another and said "Bad Weather Route."

"Exposed Ridgeline" was an understatement. It led up to a ridgeline that was more rugged than anything I had seen since Georgia! Rude stone steps and scrambles went up and down for nearly a mile. It was the sort of place that makes me think of orks and trolls. The view was great until it started raining again. Then fog set in and hid everything but the rocks I was clambering over. It seemed to go on forever.

Finally the trail got a bit more normal and then rejoined the bypass. By now I was ready for the shelter to appear. My feet were beginning to feel the effects of the long miles, scrambling and dampness. At last the roof of the shelter popped into view.

Who should I find there but Kat! She had been ahead of me but took a laundry day and had things hung inside the shelter to dry. After a bit Chigger and someone else from last night arrived but all three plan to hike on.

Four more men have arrived. Because of the bugs, they decided to build a fire. One of them proceeded to give the most unusual demonstration of how to build a fire I have yet seen upon the Trail.

First he fetched a pile of large rocks, breaking the largest ones into smaller pieces. Next he disassembled the entire existing stone fire-circle which clearly had sufficed for uncounted fires. The stones he considered too small he threw off into the woods, placing those that passed muster in a pile to one side. Then he took his trowel and scooped aside all the ashes. He proceeded to build a new circle, smaller than the first but with the stones stacked twice as high. Then he carefully sealed the gaps between the stones with ashes. Only then did they pile tinder and kindling and light it.

It turned out they rebuilt the firecircle everywhere they stopped as a way of giving back to the Trail.

-Mouse

Wednesday, April 21, 2004
Destination: Hogback Ridge Shelter
From: Jerry Cabin Shelter
Today's Miles: 14.7
Trip Miles: 312.0

Wow another 15 mile day! Or maybe I should say "Ow!" instead of "Wow"! Oh well, the important thing is that all of me arrived at the shelter.

Both my feet are sore, the ball of my left foot especially so. Oh well, with luck now I can get to the Erwin Post Office before it closes Saturday so it was worth the extra wear and tear.

The Trail changed character in another way today. Up to now it has run through federally owned wilderness areas. Now it is more a thin corridor through privately owned land. That means seeing more barns close to the Trail, going through stiles in fences from time to time (Three today), once hearing a gunshot disconcertingly close to the Trail, and seeing more signs of human settlement. Going up a beautiful ravine with a fast stream tumbling down it, I saw a rather dilapidated barn, an even more dilapidated house, an old junk pile, and a picturesque tumbled-down log cabin and log shed. After that the Trail ran right along a fence line up a high ridge, marking both the edge of the federal land and the border between Tennessee and North Carolina.

So far, at 645 Poppins and his dog are here. I loaned him my little Swiss Army knife to cut up an onion and gave him some olive oil to cook it in. I just made my best trail meal ever. 2/3 of a pot of boiling water with one package ramen and half a package of vegetable chili, a large dash of oil for calories, then TVP until the pot is full. It soaked up all the liquid making an entire pot of rib-sticking supper. Yum! Poppins gave it a thumbs-up when I offered him a taste hoping to taste his sautéed onions in return. It worked and the onions were great!

Now it is 7:30 and Mojo and Hitch and Dexter, Kat and Treefrog have arrived. An older man was here looking for a young hiker, then left again. Kat informed me it was multiple thruhiker Warren Doyle. You never know who you will meet on the Trail.

-Mouse

Thursday, April 22, 2004
Destination: Whistling Gap Campsite
From: Hogback Ridge Shelter
Today's Miles: 13.4
Trip Miles: 325.4

A hard but pretty day. The first two miles led down to Sams Gap where the Trail crosses US Route 23. Then it went up a ridge, over some crests, including one bald whose grassy patch looked like a misplaced golf course.

Then it went aggressively up 5,516 foot Big Bald. My feet were aching by the time I got to the summit but the view was wonderful when I joined Poppins, Skirts, and Mansooka at the top. We could see a 360 view of the surrounding countryside. The day was cloudy and cool with a stiff breeze at the summit.

Big Bald Shelter was a mile on and it was tempting to stop and make it a ten mile day. I decided to cook my supper early and hike on to be sure I would get to the Erwin Post Office. I took off my boots and socks to give my feet a rest, dangling them while I sat and cooked and ate. Poppins stopped to cook too, then took a nap. Skirts and Mansooka just took a short rest and went on, hoping to get to the next shelter nearly 10 miles away.

A little after three I left and went about three miles further to a campsite with water at Whispering Gap. That means 14 miles left until Erwin, so tomorrow I have a choice of camping just outside if I find a spot or going all the way.

Mojo and Hitch stopped to cook supper before heading on to another campsite about two miles further on. Poppins arrived after his nap and their dogs got to play together. Poppins decided to go to the further site as well, as did Treefrog when he got there. By 7:20 I was alone and will probably spend the night by myself for a change.

Camping alone does not bother me too much, especially since I am over two miles from the nearest road. I suppose there are always the bears, but one is not really safer camping in a group than alone as far as bears go.

-Mouse

Friday, April 23, 2004
Destination: Erwin, TN
From: Whistling Gap Campsite
Today's Miles: 13.5
Trip Miles: 338.9

After lunch at No Business Knob Shelter I fell in with Poppins and Skirts and we hiked almost nonstop the remaining 6 miles to Erwin arriving a nice early 1:30 pm.

Most of the day the Trail was fairly level, a welcome change from the climbs of yesterday. The view from several overlooks of Erwin and the river were incredible, even better than those of Hot Springs. Another of those unexpected gifts the Trail brings.

I started walking the 3.5 miles into the center of town but soon a passing pickup stopped and the driver offered me a ride to Miss Janet's House. The beds were full, but I got the last bit of floor space. Poppins and Skirts arrived later having waited for a shuttle from the bridge.

Next I went to the Post Office for my bounce box, then the three of us went to Erwin Burrito for lunch, one of those legendary must go to eating places for thruhikers.

Miss Janet's has the usual hostel bustle with its own flavor. I helped carry in sheets of drywall for a renovation project and everyone watched a video of "Harry Potter and the Chamber of Secrets." One of the night's guests was a professional chef who cooked up some scrumptious lasagna for supper, which we ate out back by candlelight sitting at a long patio table. Then I grabbed a space of dining-room floor to sleep on. After weeks of shelters, sleeping on the floor in my sleeping bag was second nature.

Of course I also got a shower and laundry. For a change there were lots of choices of shampoo and even conditioner so my hair washed out without a single tangle, let alone the mats I've gotten used to undoing. And my clothes were the softest and fluffiest ever. Miss Janet knows how to get the important things right!

-Mouse

Saturday, April 24, 2004
Destination: Erwin, TN
From: Erwin, TN
Today's Miles: 0.0
Trip Miles: 338.9

This morning after a communally prepared and eaten breakfast traditional at Miss Janet's, I mailed my bounce box to Damascus, then walked to the grocery and bought food for the next leg. I had a lot of leftovers from the last leg; new items are summer sausage and dates for lunch and snacking. Sometime I want to try granola and powdered milk for breakfast but not on a long leg when pack weight is critical.

I rested most of the rest of the day. In the afternoon Poppins brought his mother, who will be hiking 10 days with him. She is about my age and we had a nice talk. She mentioned an interest in attending library school and concern about entrance requirements. I could not resist taking her to the computer and finding what library schools were near her home and showing her how to find out their admission requirements. I guess once a librarian, always a librarian.

Then I went to a local diner for a catfish supper and got organized to leave tomorrow. Tonight I get a real bed instead of the dining room floor.

-Mouse

Sunday, April 25, 2004
Destination: Deep Gap Campsite
From: Erwin, TN
Today's Miles: 12.0
Trip Miles: 350.9

    I got up about 6:30 and went to help with breakfast. I made coffee, cracked three dozen eggs, peeled and sliced three bunches of bananas and sliced strawberries. Chef was making a cross between bread pudding and French toast topped with apples banana and caramel with fruit salad and bacon. Yummy!

    I love how Miss Janet gets everyone to share in the work. She has been both a mother and schoolteacher and draws on the skills of both as well as being a very good delegator. It gives a nice sense of community and lends a good flavor to staying there.

    Next I loaded my pack. Checking the hiker's box of castoff supplies for hand sanitizer I stumbled across a bottle of violet nail polish. It had to be the most impractical thing imaginable for thruhiking, so of course I could not resist putting it on my nails as a memento of my stay at Miss Janet's House.

    It was a pleasure staying at Miss Janet's but at last the time came to return to the Trail. I was the only one going back from the house today but Janet shuttled Coyote and Saltlick from a motel to the trailhead as well.

    Nearly everyone else in the house was going slackpacking: hiking a day's section of the trail with just water and lunch in a daypack, then going back to the house for the night. That cuts down on the effort needed to get to the next resupply point, but I was eager to get back on the Trail.

    Janet took one last picture of the three of us and Catdog with her dog Wags, who were also at the trailhead ready to leave. They had been brought to the trailhead by Catdog's husband.

    By 10:30 I was hiking again. It was 4 miles to the nearest shelter and 16 miles to the next shelter. Neither was a good distance, so I compromised and stopped to tent at Deep Gap just after a rather pretty bald called the Beauty Spot.

    Catdog stopped at the first shelter to let her dog acclimate to hiking and Coyote and Saltlick headed on to the second. But I was joined for the night by the Honeymooners and Rob, all of whom I had met earlier.

    There were thundershowers predicted for today and tomorrow but so far there has only been a sprinkle.

    -Mouse

Monday, April 26, 2004
Destination: Clyde Smith Shelter
From: Deep Gap Campsite
Today's Miles: 13.1
Trip Miles: 364.0

It is 7:00 a.m. and raining steadily. I lie in my dry warm sleeping bag and debate whether to become one with that wet world out there.

I finally decide to get moving. With my tent as a cocoon I begin the metamorphosis from warm dry human to rainy day hiker. I stall by trimming my toenails, then pull on my socks. I pull out a pack of Poptarts for breakfast and some snacks for during the day. Sausage and dates go into my pack, energy bar and papaya into the pocket on my pack strap. I put my sleeping bag into its sack, then in two plastic bags, then deflate the mattress and stow it in its sack. Starting with the sleeping bag I squeeze all the stuff sacks into the pack and strap down the top pocket and add the pack cover. Finally I put on my Gore-Tex suit and boots.

Only then do I unzip the tent door and step out into the rain. I pull out my pack, remove the poles, shake all the water off the tent, stuff it in its bag and strap it to the side of the pack. By 8:15 I am hiking.

I got to the next shelter at 10:45 and found Coyote and Saltlick still warm and comfortable in their sleeping bags. It was tempting to stay, but if I took a short day every time it rains I might not get to Katahdin before it is closed on October 15. So I ate some sausage and headed for the next shelter nearly nine miles away.

It seemed to take forever, perhaps because of the rain. Along the way I unwisely topped off my filter bottle with cloudy runoff water. I had done this several times with no problems, but this time the prefilter clogged with silt and I could barely get water through it. Refilling later with clear water, wiping the prefilter and even scrubbing with gravel did little good.

Almost by surprise the sign for the shelter appeared about 4:00 p.m. It fits 10 and there are about 3 spaces left. The group I ran into before Clingmans Dome were there. Right after claiming a bed space I attended to my filter. The nail file on my Swiss army knife was too recessed to be much help. But the edge was sharp enough to scrape off the ridges from the prefilter and scrape the rest of the surface. That improved the flow somewhat. If I get really desperate I can remove the prefilter altogether and hope the main filter element does not clog between here and Damascus.

-Mouse

Tuesday, April 27, 2004
Destination: Overmountain Shelter
From: Clyde Smith Shelter
Today's Miles: 12.9
Trip Miles: 376.9

What a great day!

It started in the 40's, clear and windy. It was the first time in days that I slept wearing my balaclava and fleece top to stay warm.

At first the temperature rose, getting nearly to sixty, but as I made the 2,500 foot climb up Roan Mountain it got colder and even windier. As I neared the top the trail plunged into a pine thicket. The wind began gusting and great dark clouds drifted overhead, turning the pine grove into gloom and raising worries about thunderstorms brewing up. Nothing like the thought of getting caught on an exposed peak in lightning to lend excitement to one's hike! It does not happen often, but hikers do get killed in those conditions and that knowledge spurred me on. I pushed up to the top as fast as I could. At the top the chill high altitude air turned the weather system to snow flurries instead of thundershowers and I relaxed a bit.

I took a chilly moment to admire the site of the hotel that once stood on the summit, then went to Roan High Knob shelter for lunch. It is the highest shelter on the AT and once was a firewatch cabin.

The Smokys gang were there as well but after lunch quickly hiked out of sight. They tend to go faster but take long breaks so we end up with about the same mileage.

The real bonus of the day came after Roan Mountain. I came upon three huge balds in a row, nearly 6,000 feet high. It was wonderful hiking over one great dome of grass in the sky after another. The cloud ceiling had risen enough that the view was incredible. The spine of the Smokys had made me feel remote from the world with little to see but more Smokys whereas this made me feel on top of the world perched high above peopled valleys watching cloud shadows drift across the landscape. The chill gusty wind only added to the atmosphere. I had no film left, but I doubt any camera could do justice to the magnificent vistas.

I ended the day at Overmountain Shelter. I had thought the name just meant it was a mountain away from the highway, but a sign explained that the "Overmountain Men" were Revolutionary War militia from beyond the crest of the Appalachians and that the gap the shelter was located in is where the AT intersects the route they took on the way to winning the Battle of King's Mountain.

The shelter itself is a converted barn with lots of room. At first I was going to stay downstairs where there was light and a nice view, but the cold wind drove me up to the dark but more sheltered loft.

One of the Smokys bunch showed me what ramps look like, those two-leafed garlic-tasting onion-like plants that grow in the mountains which are a thruhiker delicacy. So I was finally able to pick some ramps and slice them to add to my supper.

Didi, whom I had seen at Miss Janet's, had just left there that morning and said good weather was predicted but that it was supposed to freeze in Erwin tonight. That means it will be even colder here. So I put my groundsheet and a spaceblanket under my mattress for extra insulation. I also emptied my filter bottle so it would not leak and put it into my sleeping bag to keep the filter element from freezing and cracking.

Speaking of the filter, at an earlier stop I disassembled it and rinsed out the grit that had accumulated in between the primary and secondary filters. After that it was its old happy self again! That is one less worry.

-Mouse

Wednesday, April 28, 2004
Destination: Mountaineers Falls Campsite
From: Overmountain Shelter
Today's Miles: 17.1
Trip Miles: 394.0

Wow, 17 miles, my longest day ever.

The day started clear and a little below freezing. I got going about 8:15, heading uphill to climb Little Hump and Hump mountains. It was a nice crisp day, perfect for scaling balds. The downside was that the frost-covered mud was slippery. I fell hard going downhill, covering one thigh of my pants in mud and more seriously, bending one of my poles. Now I will have to be careful with that pole until I reach Damascus and can get a new section. It was my sixth fall since leaving Springer Mountain.

At the top of Hump Mountain, The Other Five, as the Smokys bunch like to call themselves, caught up with me. They passed me after their break, then I caught up with them at Apple House shelter at lunchtime.

After that came the section after Highway 19E. This is an odd section. First, the land the Trail is on was taken not too long ago from its prior owners by eminent domain. So there is still said to be local resentment against the Trail and hikers. Then much of this section was rerouted recently. That meant my map was not accurate and the landmarks given in my trail guide were not very helpful.

So from the time I crossed the highway I had no idea where I was. I could say I was on the Appalachian Trail but little else. I had two choices: go about 17 miles and go to Dennis Cove Road tomorrow, or go about several miles less and spend tomorrow night in the woods as I had originally planned.

By 5:00 in the evening my feet were killing me and I decided I had better stop short. But I had little idea of where I was and when the time I expected to reach the nearer campsite passed there was no sign of it. All I could do was keep going. Finally I saw the umbrella belonging to one of The Other Five leaning against a tree at a side trail. I guessed it was a sign for their slowest member Pokey, who was behind me, that they were camping here. Sure enough, there they were. I had gone the whole 17 miles without realizing it!

-Mouse

Thursday, April 29, 2004
Destination: Kincora Hostel
From: Mountaineers Falls Campsite
Today's Miles: 15.2
Trip Miles: 409.2

The morning dawned nice and temperate, a pleasant change from the frigid sort of morning that makes you not want to leave your sleeping bag at 6:30 a.m.

It is strange how forgiving the body can be. Last night my feet were so raw that it was hard to find a position to sleep in that did not hurt them. Yet when I looked this morning to see what parts needed moleskin, my feet just looked up cheerfully and said "Raw? We aren't raw! Let's go hiking!" Strange.

The trail was also strange. After a couple of easy miles it twisted, turned, rose and fell with no rhyme or reason. Add that it was not on the map and there were no landmarks and the landscape was just as random, and it seemed like something from purgatory. All I knew was that if I kept following the white blazes I would reach Moreland Gap Shelter in about nine miles. Or I thought I knew at least. To add to the fun, no water sources were noted until the shelter so I carried extra water only to find a stream every ten minutes. The trail would dive into a ravine, cross a stream, climb a ridge, then repeat the process infinitely. Half a dozen streams are pretty; dozens start to get maddening.

Finally I got onto the ridge the shelter was on. For the first time in 24 hours I actually knew about where I was. Just when I got there the Other Five caught up with me and we stopped for lunch.

The afternoon was a high ridgewalk, strenuous but at least I could see where I was going. Then a long foot-bruising descent to Dennis Cove Road. A half mile one direction was a campground with everything and Kincora Hostel was only .2 miles the other. I let my feet decide and went to Kincora.

It was full so I had to tent out back and I only barely got a shower in time to ride to Elizabethtown to eat and buy groceries. Most of us ate at the Chinese buffet.

I made gorp again, unlike the last two legs. I also got powdered milk, instant pudding and granola, as well as my usual indulgence of chocolate milk. When I lose some weight I might switch to Ben and Jerry's but the scale at Miss Janet's house said I had not lost an ounce in over a month of hiking.

Socially Kincora was a good choice. The Other Five were here and I met Little Tree and The Walking Stomach for the first time since Hot Springs, as well as Mojo, Hitch and Dexter, Crash-Bang and others I remembered. I also caught up with Heidi Hobbit and Holly Hobbit, a pair of twins whose journal entries I have been reading since Springer.

-Mouse

Friday, April 30, 2004
Destination: Watauga Lake Shelter
From: Kincora Hostel
Today's Miles: 10.6
Trip Miles: 419.8

This morning I hiked through Laurel Gorge. The rock steps were hard, especially right after resupplying. But the gorge and river were beautiful and well worth it, especially Laurel Falls.

The next event was climbing 2,000 feet over a mountain between the gorge and Watauga Lake. I did most of it with my friends Little Tree and The Walking Stomach. There were two rain showers along the way, but things dried out before the top. Then down to the lake and along the shore to the shelter. The trail coming down the mountain was very well graded with a nice smooth surface. That made my knees and feet much happier than coming down to Dennis Cove.

Another shower started just after I reached the shelter so I was glad to get a space. Dave, Crash-Bang, Little Tree and The Walking Stomach, and Scholar also arrived, making a full house. Many of those who had been at Kincora were slackpacking so as to attend a Gaelic celebration there this evening.

Lying on the floor of the shelter looking out is a treat. The trees are covered with leaves and everything is green. It is a refreshing change from the higher altitude shelters where spring is only just beginning. Everything here is brimming with life.

-Mouse

Saturday, May 01, 2004
Destination: Iron Mountain Shelter
From: Watauga Lake Shelter
Today's Miles: 13.7
Trip Miles: 433.5

Another nice day. One rain shower just before noon, just enough to keep the day cool. I tried a lightweight poncho but it was wet, clammy and rattled like I was wrapped in Saran wrap. One more good idea that did not work so well. Maybe I will try Frogtogs, a brand of lightweight breathable raingear.

During one of the sun's brief appearances it made climbing a slope hard. I had stopped to catch my breath when The Walking Stomach came surging past. When I expressed my envy she said it was from not using poles. She thinks they waste energy by all the upper body motion. So since the trail surface was good today, I tried not using my poles. I am not convinced they waste that much energy, I think Stomach is just one strong hiker. But I suspect using poles all the time may make some leg muscles less strong than they might be. So I will try to remember not to use them when the ground is good.

Yesterday we had five women and only two men at the shelter. So far tonight it is five women and one man. Not only that but three of the women are twins! Heidi Hobbit and Holly Hobbit just arrived and I am a fraternal twin. Navigator jokingly wrote in the shelter register "Six women and one man. I'm TENTING. HELP!"

This shelter is not as green as the last one. I guess up here on Iron Mountain it is a bit colder than down by the lake. The views up here are nice though. First on the right there was the lake, wide at first then diminishing into meandering channels that faded into a long beautiful valley of green fields and farm buildings.

Then there was the entertainment! Even before dark we began to see large well-fed mice scampering along the top of the shelter wall. It was the first time I have actually seen a mouse on the Trail. It was either mouse races or a mouse chorus line, I'm not sure which. I had been sure the shelter's nice concrete block and plywood construction would not be as attractive to mice as the log shelters. I had used the top ledge as a convenient shelf for my pot and utensils awaiting breakfast. Now my cupboard had become a mouse freeway. I spent part of the night listening to them and wondering if they were chewing into my kitchen stuff sack before finally falling asleep. Fortunately all the mice did was poke around.

-Mouse

Sunday, May 02, 2004
Destination: Abingdon Gap Shelter
From: Iron Mountain Shelter
Today's Miles: 16.3
Trip Miles: 449.8

A wet but fast day. The footpath was good and no really high mountains to go over, so I only took 3.5 hours to go 8 miles in the morning and went nearly as fast in the afternoon.

The rain started with showers. But just before 3:00 we got an honest to goodness downpour complete with tree-swaying wind gusts. It was like a thunderstorm without lightning. I later heard nearby Virginia had tornadoes.

I hastily stopped to put on my rain suit, then hurried along, worried about not getting a space at the shelter. First Little Tree and the Walking Stomach passed me, then three more hikers and I knew the Hobbits and Navigator were not far behind. But the three hikers kept on for Damascus ten miles away. So we ended up with the same group as last night, at least so far.

Even under my Gore-Tex suit I was wet, though not as utterly drenched as I would have been without it. This was the first time I arrived at a shelter so wet I had to change completely into dry clothing. I hung all the wet things up, hopefully to dry by morning.

This evening for entertainment we had a reading of the chapter from "The Hobbit" in which Bilbo and the dwarves get caught in a mountain storm and take refuge in the goblin cave, courtesy of Navigator and the Hobbits. It left more than one of us listening to the rain hammering on the shelter roof and wondering like Bilbo why we had ever left our warm dry hobbit holes.

Heidi and Holly Hobbit are very entertaining. They remind me of the twin daughters of a friend of mine. Like those twins the Hobbits are silly and giggle a lot. Being only a fraternal twin I only giggle half as much and am even sillier but like having them around.

-Mouse

Monday, May 03, 2004
Destination: Damascus, VA
From: Abingdon Gap Shelter
Today's Miles: 10.0
Trip Miles: 459.8

The morning dawned damp, foggy and cold, about 40 degrees. Funny how on mornings like that I want to just hide in my sleeping bag. Still, I roused myself and managed to get going, after Little Tree and Stomach but before the Hobbits.

It warmed just a bit so as I hiked through the fog I stopped to remove first my Gore-Tex coat and then my balaclava and Capilene bottoms. The high point was reaching the Virginia State line. At last, a new state after weeks of going back and forth between North Carolina and Tennessee! I will be in Virginia for a long time; it is the longest state on the Trail at over 450 miles.

Four miles later I was in Damascus, "The friendliest town on the Trail." At the outfitters I got a room at their hostel across the street. They also replaced my bent pole section at no charge, which was nice of them.

While I was at it I bought a new bandana and a set of Superfeet insoles for my boots. People either swear by them or at them. The only way to tell is to try them out so I decided to get a pair.

I also got my bounce box from the Post Office, had lunch at the Sidetrack Cafe, another famous hiker hangout, took a shower and toted my clothes to the laundry. I am writing this while waiting for my clothes to dry. Crash-Bang was at the laundry having arrived earlier and Andrew came in having arrived a few hours after me.

It is cold here, too cold for the shorts and t-shirt from my bounce box. So I wore my dirty long pants and fleece top over them to the laundry, then took them off and put them in the washer. It is warm in here but in a moment I will go out into the chill to send these entries over the phone.

The hostel has no heat, so I feel little inclination to take a zero day to rest. I will be warmer out on the Trail hiking.

-Mouse

Tuesday, May 04, 2004
Destination: Bear Tree Gap Campsite
From: Damascus, VA
Today's Miles: 11.7
Trip Miles: 471.5

Last night I went to the Sidetrack Cafe's nightly AYCE supper for hikers. Guest cooks are welcome and the meal was prepared by a hiker with the trailname of William Wallace. It turns out he was Scottish and he chose that name because it seemed the only Scot that Americans know, courtesy of Mel Gibson's "Braveheart." Talking with him, I noted there is also Rob Roy, then asked where in Scotland he came from. It turns out he was from Perthshire and so is my housemate's family, so I have been there! He knew of her home village and we talked about its landmarks. So I was happy to let William Wallace know at least one thruhiker knew of his corner of Scotland.

For some reason I had trouble falling asleep even though I had a nice quiet hostel room all to myself. I ended up reading old National Geographics until 3:00 a.m.

Next morning I went with Little Tree, The Walking Stomach, Scholar and Crash-Bang to the Sidetrack Cafe for an AYCE breakfast. Then I started getting organized to leave; packing, preparing my bounce box and mailing it to Pearisburg, getting last minute supply items and so on. I weighed my pack and found it was 35 pounds, the heaviest it has been, partly from a week's food and also needing a spare stove canister. I have been using the same canister of fuel since Fontana Dam and it cannot last much longer. Finally I said goodbye to the Hobbits, who had arrived at the hostel, and got back on the Trail.

It was a wonderful day for hiking, cool and sunny. Much of the route went along a beautiful fast-flowing river and green hills. The Superfeet did seem to help my feet handle the extra load but the hard heel cups made my heels raw. I was glad to arrive at Saunders Shelter where I found Crash-Bang having supper before he headed for the next shelter six miles away.

I took off my shoes and socks and had supper too as others began arriving, mostly section hikers. I decided to go to a campsite two miles further. That way, a 16 mile day tomorrow would put me at the Thomas Knob Shelter near Mount Rogers. From Saunders I would either have to go 18 miles or spend an extra night on the Trail.

I got to the site about 7:00 p.m., a pretty clearing in a pine grove next to an old ruined dam. Just before it at Bear Tree Gap trail junction were some flowering trees that smelled heavenly! I do not know what they were, perhaps honeysuckle?

I am beginning to grasp that keeping a pace that will get me to Mount Katahdin before it closes for the winter pretty much means raw sore feet every night. That seems to be what everyone is experiencing right now. As long as they seem to recover by morning I can live with the discomfort.

-Mouse

Wednesday, May 05, 2004
Destination: Thomas Knob Shelter
From: Bear Tree Gap campsite
Today's Miles: 16.3
Trip Miles: 487.8

I got going today a little after 7:00, winding my way past the tents on the far side of the pond with their sleeping occupants. This section has registers at road junctions as well as at shelters and in them I learned The Other Five were a few hours ahead of me.

I caught up with Sanguine and Pooja at Buzzards Rock. Again it was one of those cold windy days with clouds racing by, the perfect weather to ascend the high grassy balds. On the other side of Whiterock Mountain we found the strongest gushing spring we had seen yet, overlooking a valley far below that looked just like Tolkien's painting of The Shire. Of course we had to take pictures of ourselves with the "Shire" for a background.

As I said, the mountains are full of surprises. After crossing the gap at Elk Garden I had climbed partway up Balsam Mountain when I heard a loud roar behind me. I turned and saw a steeply banked C-130 shoot low through the pass. Then more like a fighter jet than a big transport it straightened its wings and dove down into the valley beyond Mount Rogers heedless of the strong crosswind and unforgiving hillsides. It must have been thrilling and I think would have cost a civil pilot his license but for the C-130 crew it was probably just practice at tactical flying in mountainous terrain.

A little later came a different sort of surprise. I was overtaken by a couple. The woman had a blanket draped down her front and when they got closer I realized she was carrying a baby, high up the side of Mount Rogers. Unimpressed by the terrain, it was sleeping soundly.

I seemed to wind around Mount Rogers forever when I finally caught sight of the shelter. Even more exciting, I saw shaggy wild ponies dotting the hillside behind the shelter. I did not expect to see ponies until tomorrow at the Grayson Highlands.

In the shelter I found three of The Other Five inside. Jon and Indy had detoured onto easier trails for a bit. They told me the water source was inside the pasture and that the ponies would walk right up to me. It was just like My Little Pony, with the ponies nuzzling me and their long shaggy manes and tails blowing in the wind. There were even three little baby ponies. Sanguine and I took turns taking each other's picture with a mother and her foal. They are very cute. Imagine, a petting zoo 5,400 feet up a mountainous wilderness miles from anywhere and you have to backpack to get there!

My old stove canister finally ran out after lasting nearly a month from when I bought it at Fontana.

-Mouse

Thursday, May 06, 2004
Destination: Old Orchard Shelter
From: Thomas Knob Shelter
Today's Miles: 11.0
Trip Miles: 498.8

[Written at Wise Shelter] Oops, trouble. There has been a lot of rock hopping going at Mount Rogers and again today. It is hard to find level footing and both feet and legs get a lot of jarring. By 3 miles or so the outside of my lower left leg was hurting. I slowed way down the last 1.5 miles to Wise Shelter and have stopped to give it a rest.

If I am lucky it is just a shin splint or sore muscle. If I am not lucky, it might be the start of a stress fracture, although it does not have that broken bone sort of pain. I am going to rest here until 1:00 p.m. and see if it gets better. If not I might stay the night here instead of going the 6 miles to Old Orchard Shelter as I had planned.

Always Another Mountain

I had been wondering whether to hike longer than 12 mile days, camping on the trail instead of sheltering to save a day getting to my next resupply. But my leg seems to have made that decision for me. No extra miles for now.

I fed myself two Ibuprofen, used my water bladder like an ice pack to cool the sore part and am giving it a good rest.

The weather has been beautiful, with a brisk wind. It was above the ceiling in the morning, walking through racing clouds until I got far enough from Mount Rogers to get away from the mountain-generated clouds. Then it turned to scattered cumulus clouds, a fine day.

Early in the morning I ran into more Mount Rogers ponies grazing or laying in the grass. Two even came right up to nuzzle me. That was just as well, since Grayson Highland Park's +100 ponies seem to be hiding away from the trail. Still, I got a proper dose of pony gazing, so I am content.

[Written at Old Orchard Shelter] Well, it is evening and I made it. At Wise Shelter Pooja consoled me with a handful of candy conversation hearts. In gratitude I gave her my extra water. At first she could not find her Aqua Mira purifying chemicals to treat it. So I filtered more water into my spare water bottle to give her in case she had lost it. Fortunately she found her Aqua Mira, leaving me with a nice bottle of water to make Gatorade with.

I started off slowly and carefully and my leg seemed better. At the campground at the Scales a woman dayhiker who thought I looked tired talked me into accepting three hostess cupcakes and a pack of mini-muffins. Yum!

I did all right until the descent from Pine Mountain into the shelter. It was quite rocky, as bad as the section that I got hurt on in the first place. I was extremely glad to see the shelter come into view. I shared two Hostess Cupcakes with Pooja for being so supportive at noon. She will hitch into Troutdale tomorrow for supplies so I might not see her for a while.

Now I plan to stick to 12-mile days until my resupply at Groseclose to try to keep my leg from getting worse.

-Mouse

Friday, May 07, 2004
Destination: Trimpi Shelter
From: Old Orchard Shelter
Today's Miles: 14.1
Trip Miles: 512.9

Mouse has her groove back!

I got going this morning and found the footpath much better but within 3 miles my leg and ankle were starting to go again. On sudden inspiration I stopped and replaced the Superfeet insoles with my old Spenco insoles, which I still had in the bottom of my pack. End of problem! I found myself striding with my old bounce, despite lingering traces of the leg soreness the Superfeet had caused. There were roadside trash cans and I got rid of my trash, including the empty stove canister. The Superfeet went in as well, in a ceremonious bit of pack-lightening.

The soreness faded as the day went on and I got to Raccoon Branch Shelter 12 miles away in barely five and a half hours, including three stops to dig through my pack. That restored my optimism a bit! There was no promising camping past the next shelter only 3 miles away so rather than hike in the heat of midday I rested there for an hour and a half reading the last part of a novel someone had left. Then I hiked to Trimpi in just over an hour. If my feet hold out like this, I can start getting in more mileage. It is frustrating how nearly everyone I know has either forged ahead or fallen back.

There is an older man traveling with a younger woman named Hobbit whom I have not seen before.

I was just about to start supper when a young man came to the shelter and asked "Remember me?" It was Danny Ashman, whom I last saw over a month ago when I turned back in the snow at Winding Stair Gap! He, Sylke and I had hiked for days together before we were separated. I thought he was far ahead of me.

The Trail has its surprises and today it was a familiar face. It seems he went back to do 30 miles that he had skipped after the Smokys and then he took several zero days so now here he was.

-Mouse

Saturday, May 08, 2004
Destination: Chatfield Shelter
From: Trimpi Shelter
Today's Miles: 17.7
Trip Miles: 530.6

This morning I saw a deer on the path from the shelter back to the Trail. Later the Trail went over a stile and through a wide grassy meadow full of cows who gazed at me as I passed.

Much to my surprise I arrived at my original goal for the day, Partnership Shelter, over ten miles away in less than five hours.

Stopping there and then going only 12 miles to Groseclose the next day seemed lazy; the Trail beckoned me onward. Partnership is the famous shelter with hot water and a nearby phone you can order pizza from. So I took a nice shower, did my laundry in the sink behind the shelter with Dr. Bronners soap, and set it out to dry. I changed into shorts; I would pack away my trusty long nylon pants that I had worn from Springer to here. Next I went to the adjacent park headquarters and ordered a small Hawaiian pizza and a Greek salad with a two liter bottle of Dr. Pepper. I ate the pizza and drank most of the soda then waddled satiatedly back to the shelter to check on my laundry.

By 2:30 I was all packed up with the remaining soda filling my spare water bottle and the salad container nestled on top of my pack under the buckle-on top pocket. I headed for Chatfield Shelter 7 miles away.

Within an hour there was the rumble of thunder close behind me. I was off the bare high ridges but still I really did not want to get caught in a thunderstorm. Fueled by pizza, two liters of Dr. Pepper and by adrenaline I stampeded up the Trail like a mad elephant. I made the 7 miles in record time with narely a twinge from feet or legs. Maybe I ought to o.d. on pizza and soda more often?

At the shelter I ran into two fellow members of the Womenhikers mailing list named Leapfrog and The Old Grey Goose. After a nice salad for supper they played trail angel and treated me to hot chai with whole milk and a fortune biscotti. My fortune read "The world belongs to those who DARE and DO!"

-Mouse

Sunday, May 09, 2004
Destination: Knot Maul Shelter
From: Chatfield Shelter
Today's Miles: 18.4
Trip Miles: 549.0

    Last night a thunderstorm came at 9:00 p.m. and rained about two hours but this morning was dry and clear.

    I got to I-81 about 8:45 and within an hour and a half had resupplied, eaten a nice breakfast at the diner and was back on the trail. I saw a couple deer as well as walking through a herd of cows.

    Today went over ridge and valley geology so the trail went up and down all day. Many of the valleys were pastureland, sometimes private. That meant a lot of fences with stiles. Stiles are things that let people over or through a fence but not animals without using a gate that could be left open accidentally. Stiles come in different styles. My favorite has rails forming a sharp V-shaped path through the fence. A human can turn the corner at the point of the V but an animal is too long. Those are easy to get through. Then there is a kind with a ramp running parallel to the fence on both sides. You walk up one side, step to the side of the ramp on the other side of the fence and walk down again. I guess animals can't turn around at the top of the ramp, so they are stuck on one side. The worst is a ladder type and I had to go through nearly two dozen of these today. They have two pairs of boards nailed in an X shape set next to each other over the fence. Other boards are nailed between the bottom legs of the X's to form a sort of ladder on either side of the fence. The top legs of the X's serve as handholds to steady yourself as you go over the top. So you climb one side to the top of the fence then down again on the other side. That can be a job when the rungs are eighteen inches or more apart and you have a heavy pack. I found it helped to turn around at the top so I went down facing the fence. Still, after enough stiles in one day it can get a bit much.

    To add more fun, someone said they had met a southbound hiker who had reported a ten mile stretch with no water. So I started off being very sparing with my water and getting rather thirsty only to find no less than eight water sources in that ten miles.

    Finally I got to the last ridge and it seemed to take forever to get to the top and then to the shelter. There was another woman alone and a couple; everyone else had gone on to a camping area four miles further on. But after 18 miles I was happy to stop. The register said a bear had been sighted a few days ago so for the first time in weeks I hung my food from a tree rather than the mouse protectors inside the shelter.

-Mouse

Monday, May 10, 2004
Destination: Davis Farm Campsite
From: Knot Maul Shelter
Today's Miles: 16.0
Trip Miles: 565.0

What a day! First of all, it is official, I am not Superwoman. I have been doing high mileage lately but I see I have my limits. I had to stop 3 miles short of the shelter and I am TIRED!

It started nicely with a smooth well graded footpath up and over a couple ridges. Then it headed 2,500 feet up really high Chestnut Ridge. Even in 70 degree weather in less than no time I was drenched in sweat. I had to stop again and again to catch my breath. Finally the path became a bit less steep but still climbed relentlessly.

Eventually it reached the spine of the ridge then broke into open meadowland. The view of the country I had covered the last few days was superb and I could pick dandelion leaves for some badly needed green vegetables and roughage. Trail food is sparse on both. The Trail went alternately through meadows and shaded clearing but it still climbed pitilessly.

At last I reached Chestnut Knob Shelter 4,407 feet up and threw myself on the grass exhausted. The couple who had spent last night with me were there finishing lunch. The woman consoled me by noting that this is the very last shelter above 4,000 feet until New England.

While I had a lunch of peanut butter spread on buns various hikers I knew came through going the other direction. They were slackpacking out of the motel back at Groseclose; being driven ahead and hiking back carrying only water and snacks. It lets you stay an extra day in a nice soft bed with lots of food and is easier and faster, but it costs more and is not quite the same satisfaction as hiking straight through. Off to the north was Burkes Garden, a large depression with gorgeous farms spread across its flat floor. It was nicknamed "God's Thumbprint" for its shape and beauty.

At 1pm I started on again for Jenkins Shelter 10 miles away. It quickly became clear that this would be no gentle descent along the ridge from Chestnut Knob. The trail bobbed up and down over crest after crest and the ground was usually too steep or too rocky for fast hiking. There was one spot with water two miles in, then no more until Davis Farm Campsite five miles further and that was a full half mile off the Trail.

As time went on and I got more and more tired it became clear I was not going to reach Jenkins Shelter and would have to make the side trip to Davis Farm Campsite. But the ridge seemed endless. Right when I thought I ought to start descending into the gap before the turnoff I came upon YET ANOTHER high steep crest in front of me. I could have burst with frustration. I dug out my last square of semi-sweet chocolate and ate half to regain some energy, then plodded on. Thunder began rumbling off to my right but I was too far gone to hurry. A rustle swept through the trees that I could not tell was wind or approaching rain. Hastily I stopped and put the rain cover on my pack, finished the other half of the chocolate, and plodded on.

Finally the gap appeared. I ought to have about a half mile to the turnoff. But now thunder rumbled on my left as well as my right and it started raining. Fortunately it was just light enough so my broad brimmed hat was sufficient cover and I did not start getting soaked. But the turnoff seemed to take forever to arrive. I began contemplating setting up my tent at whatever flat spot I could find and catching what rainwater I could to stave off thirst until I could go on to Jenkins Shelter in the morning.

But at last the sign came that read Davis Farm Campsite. I turned onto the sidetrail and began to descend the side of the ridge in wide switchbacks. Each time I turned into the wind I would start to get more wet, robbed of the shelter my tall backpack gave when walking downwind. Finally the rain eased and I saw a fence that had to be the campsite. As I came into it, all I could think was "My God, that is beautiful!" As if to punctuate that thought, the sun suddenly came out and bathed the scene in light.

The campsite was a twenty foot square terrace built into the side of the ridge with log retaining walls. It overlooked an absolutely incredible view of the east end of "God's Thumbprint" and framed in the center of the vista was a picture-perfect farmstead.

While the remains of the storm rumbled off to the east I pitched my tent, got water and cooked supper. Miniaturized by distance, tiny Holstein cows wandered the hills below, grazing. I could tell by tracks that they even wandered up here when they were in the mood. I was high enough for a good view but not too high to hear the cows lowing, a tractor rumbling, and dogs barking in the distance.

My trials of the day had been well rewarded. Like my adventure to LeConte Peak, this is one of those treats that most thruhikers never see. Only the lucky, the tired, or those too desperate for water to go another three miles to Jenkins Shelter stumble upon this incredible view. So far this evening, I have it all to myself.

About 9:00 p.m. another storm rumbles and it starts to rain. But I am already snug in my tent. The big open awning of my Wanderlust Nomad forms a picture window, letting me lie in my sleeping bag and watch the lights twinkle on in the valley below and the flashes of lightning up in the sky.

-Mouse

Tuesday, May 11, 2004
Destination: Bland, VA
From: Davis Farm Campsite
Today's Miles: 14.5
Trip Miles: 579.5

Well, it finally happened. For the second morning in a row when I started hiking my stomach said "So what's for breakfast?" as if it hadn't just been fed. This time it was more insistent. By the time I reached Jenkins Shelter my stomach was growling audibly. I had to shovel in an extra 700 calories to subdue it.

It looks like I am finally developing The Hunger; that ravenous thruhiker appetite that astounds tourists and is the despair of All You Can Eat buffet operators. In any event I am discovering I cannot hike 15-18 miles a day on the same food intake I had when doing only 12 miles.

It became clear that my food would not last to Pearisburg and I would have to hitch into Bland to fill both my stomach and food bag.

About 11:00 I ran into Andrew hiking the opposite direction. I had last seen him at Partnership Shelter about to get picked up by a local friend. He had been dropped off at Bland and was hiking back so he could get a ride from Partnership to the annual Trail Days festival this weekend in Damascus. Most hikers around here seem to be arranging to go. He also gave me two donuts and let me know a Trail Angel had left a cooler of juice near the next road.

The afternoon is everything yesterday was not. The Trail is well graded and smooth, placed on the shady northern side of the ridge and the weather cooler and more overcast.

Almost as soon as I reach the road to Bland a pickup pulls up to drop off two hikers, then the driver offers me a ride to town. I check into the motel and find it is across the freeway from the town proper. There is just a truckstop and Dairy Queen for food here. I will hike into town tomorrow and hopefully mail my winter clothing home to save weight, then head back to the Trail.

Still, I got some food, a shower, and hand washed my t-shirt and a pair of socks in the sink of my motel room. I also got a chance to catch up on news in the outside world and sleep in a real bed for the first time since Fontana.

-Mouse

Wednesday, May 12, 2004
Destination: Jenny Knob Shelter
From: Bland, VA
Today's Miles: 12.1
Trip Miles: 591.6

This morning I had to walk the whole 3.5 miles from the motel back to the Trail since no car stopped to give me a lift. On the good side, I mailed home 2.5 pounds of winter clothing and equipment. I sent off my midweight Capilenes, my lightweight Capilene bottoms, the fleece vest, my trusty balaclava, gloves and the heat packs I had brought for emergency warming. I kept my Gore-Tex for now, fleece top, lightweight Capilene top, long pants, shorts, two t-shirts and three pairs of socks.

The Trail was good again today except near the end but ran mostly on the sunny south side of the ridge instead of the cool shady north side. Still I got in 16.5 miles including the walk from Bland by 3:30.

So far no thunder today. Someone said today's forecast has a front moving through around Saturday that might cool things up.

During the night at Jenny Knob Shelter an older male hiker showed up at 10:30, after everyone else had gone to bed. Next thing I knew I heard a scratching sound near my ear. To my consternation it was not a mouse, but the man's hand sliding out of his sleeping bag toward my head. I hastily grabbed my boots from the edge of the sleeping platform and used them to shove the hand back where it belonged, then set them there as a barrier. But it was little help. The rest of him started moving toward me like a tide. I squeezed right up against the hut center post as far away from him as I could get, but his sleeping form kept spreading over my air mattress. He was sleeping like he was in a king-sized bed at home, not a three foot space between two tired hikers! I ended up spending most of the night wide awake shoving back anything that crept too far.

Next morning he had the nerve to laugh at my discomfiture and treat it as a big joke. I was revolted. Every other male hiker has been very considerate whether awake or asleep. I have never encountered rudeness like that before on my hike and hope never to again. *[This did turn out to be the only such incident during my entire hike. Weeks later I ran into him again and he apologized.]*

-Mouse

Thursday, May 13, 2004
Destination: Stealth Camp
From: Jenny Knob Shelter
Today's Miles: 16.0
Trip Miles: 607.6

Today around noon there was an interesting suspension bridge taking the Trail over Kimberling Creek. Just after that was Highway 606. Off to the left a half mile or so was a grill and general store where nearly everyone stopped for lunch. When I got there it was out of hamburger so I had a Philly cheesesteak instead and a quart of chocolate milk.

We had the usual thunderstorms starting at 3:00 only closer and louder than before. I was getting sprinkled on when I arrived at Wapiti Shelter.

I really did not want to spend another night in a shelter with the man from last night and also I hoped to get to the post office in Pearisburg tomorrow before it closed. So I fixed my supper and waited for the thundershower to pass, then got back on the Trail. It led upward on an old logging road and I looked for a likely campsite. After nearly an hour of climbing I reached a spot where the trail left the road and cut up a ridgeline. Just past that point the roadbed had a flat spot where I could set up my tent out of the way of any late night hikers. It would give me privacy, save me an hour of steep climbing in the morning and put me nearly two miles closer to the post office.

-Mouse

Friday, May 14, 2004
Destination: Pearisburg, VA
From: Stealth Camp
Today's Miles: 14.4
Trip Miles: 622.0

I got going early at 6:15 a.m. The morning was damp and humid but cool enough for good hiking.

I have been seeing one or two deer a day, usually in the morning. If you hold still they seem unable to decide what to make of you. One even kept making sudden movements to try to get a reaction from me that it could use to decide what I was. I also saw my second black snake on the trail. The first was before Hot Springs. That one just lay still pretending to be a rattlesnake while I stepped carefully over it. This one abruptly slithered away before I got near, getting twenty feet away in seconds.

The rain started early today at 1:30. I got a good soaking just before getting into Pearisburg. It also made the ground slick. A Trail Angel left a cooler of Coke and beer near the road into town. I was holding an open can of Coke in one hand and my poles in the other when I slipped on the last few steps. I went down hard, spilling half my Coke, jabbing a support post hard into my hip and entangling my pack so it took a while to free myself. The Trail Angel was at the road and kindly drove me to the Post Office to pick up my bounce box and summer sleeping bag and then to the Plaza Hotel.

Once there I managed to get my bounce box and winter bag ready to mail off before the Post Office closed. That means I won't have to wait for it to open tomorrow before I can leave town. I bounced every ounce I could ahead to Waynesboro. I sent all my cooking equipment except my spoon, the top pocket off my pack, my fleece top and mailed my Gore-Tex suit home. I got a 2 liter Platypus water bag from my bounce box to increase my water capacity.

On the way back to the Post Office I ran into Sanguine and a friend. They invited me to go off to Dairy Queen for some food and we got caught up on what had happened to each of us since we got separated. Sanguine had left Groseclose when I did but even though she slack packed all the way to Pearisburg she got here a half hour after I did carrying my pack the whole way.

Tomorrow early I start the next leg.

-Mouse

Saturday, May 15, 2004
Destination: Symms Gap Campsite
From: Pearisburg, VA
Today's Miles: 12.2
Trip Miles: 634.2

I ended up getting out a little slowly and it was after 8:30 before I checked out.

I had been more than a bit tempted to follow Main Street until I met the Trail, skipping the section between there and Cross Street where I had gotten a ride. After all, there were some sections I had hiked three times and then there was that excursion to LeConte Peak. But rather than have something to regret, I dutifully trudged up the hill to where I had left the Trail, getting there at about 9:30.

I was just as glad I did. That section was steep, slippery and overgrown with poison ivy. It would not have been fair for everyone else to endure it and not me.

That ethical dilemma solved, I headed over the bridge across the New River and into the woods. Next came the hard uphill slog to the top of Peters Mountain. It was made all the harder because the guidebook notes on water sources were a bit vague so I carried more than usual. The source at Pine Field Shelter was half a mile away down a steep slope, my guidebook lacked details on the next source a mile and a half up the Trail so it might be as bad, and the next official source was nearly ten miles away. So I topped off at a spring two miles before Rice Field, drinking all I could, filtering water into the 2 liter Platypus, filling up the filter bottle, lugging it all up the last of the climb up the mountain.

At the shelter I met first one, then five more southbound section hikers. While I had an early supper thunder rumbled and I was sorely tempted to stay the night there.

But that would have been only 7 miles and I needed to average at least 15 miles a day to reach US Highway 60 by the 26th. I am getting picked up from the trail to work on the stage crew at a women's music festival then. I want to get at least to Hwy 60 so they won't have to drive far to get me.

So I packed up and headed for Symms Gap five miles away where there was supposed to be a campsite or at least a meadow free of poison ivy. After just a mile and a half I found there was indeed a spring at a campsite as the guidebook had hinted. The thunder was getting closer and again I nearly set up my tent to avoid getting soaked, but headed on toward Symms Gap.

I ran into the rather incongruous sight of a work crew right next to the Trail installing a cell phone tower. One of the workers had a small black poodle with her. I asked if it was the Foreman. They all laughed and she said the dog was to scare away the bears.

About an hour away from the Gap the rain caught up with me. The sun started shining at the same time, making me think it was just the edge of the storm. Sure enough, it just sprinkled for a bit then stopped.

Finally I started passing tent-worthy grassy clearings and could see what had to be the Gap with a rainbow in the background. I stopped to take a quick photo of the rainbow but a large dark cloud was moving in from the west and I knew soon it would rain for real.

In the Gap I found first the small pond mentioned in the guide and then the campsite with two tents already there. It was Toe Break and Homeboy. Toe Break generously offered to hang all our food bags on his bear cord so we would not have to string cords. He noted that the cell tower crew had said a bear had been into their garbage last night. I guess we are back in bear country and I have to give up keeping my breakfast in my tent and stop using mouse hangers in the shelters. I set up my tent and not long after at about 7:00 p.m. the thunderstorm arrived.

It is only the second real storm with wind gusts my tent has been in. The last time was at Angel Island in San Francisco Bay where I first tried it out. That time it nearly tried to fly away like a kite with me in it. I had had to move it in the dark to the shelter of trees.

The wind direction shifts about in thunderstorms so it had been hard to decide what direction to face it. I faced the open end north, hoping to get some shelter from both the east wind that was blowing and from the west if the wind shifted. Sure enough, soon the wind shifted to the west. The awning keeps inflating like a parachute but nothing worse so far. It is raining fairly hard and the ground is rocky making driving stakes difficult so I don't want to move the tent unless I really have to.

-Mouse

Sunday, May 16, 2004
Destination: Potts Mountain Campsite
From: Symms Gap Campsite
Today's Miles: 16.4
Trip Miles: 650.6

Wow, if this weather pattern keeps up, I'll have to change my trailname to Mouse Who Dances With Thunderclouds.

We had at least three thunderstorms last night. At lunch in Pine Swamp Shelter one got close enough to sprinkle. As I climbed the steep hill to Bailey Gap Shelter another one moved in. I got to the turnoff to the shelter's water source, dropped my pack and went down to refill my Platypus. As I was filtering the first bottleful the thunder got closer and closer and more frequent. I quit at one bottleful, hastily refilled the filter bottle for good measure, then scampered back up to my pack and made for the shelter. A flash of lightning followed in less than a second by a loud thunderclap drew an involuntary yelp and sent me frantically flying up the Trail. More lightning followed before the shelter finally came into view. I had just enough time to introduce myself to a section hiker resting there before the sky opened and it started pouring. And now this evening I just finished making camp and got into my tent and another one is bearing down on me! Here comes the rain....

Speaking of meals, my no-cook menu is working pretty well. For breakfast I have a packet of hot chocolate mix shaken up with cold water in my spare water bottle (a Gatorade bottle I saved) along with one or two packets of Poptarts. Then peanut and dried cranberry gorp for morning snacks. Lunch is a bagel spread with cream cheese. I got the cheese in two 4 oz sealed plastic packs that last two days in hopes that it will stay good longer than one 8 oz package. Afternoon snacks are Balance Bars carried in the pocket on my shoulder strap since I am usually too busy dodging thundershowers to open my pack and get out the gorp bag. Supper is a packet of ramen noodles eaten raw out of the pack like crackers and a 3oz foil packet of Albacore Tune. I discovered the 3oz Albacore has nearly as much protein and calories as a 6 oz can of regular tuna. And my bedtime snack is another serving of hot (not!) chocolate. I find I tend to eat supper or at least part of it at the last shelter before where I camped, giving a nice rest before the last five miles or so.

It is getting pretty quiet out here aside from the thunderstorms. Most thru-hikers have gone off to the Trail Days festival down in Damascus. Homeboy and Toe Break are the only two I have met and they went on to the next shelter so I have not seen them since this morning. I am camping alone tonight. And after the Mount Rogers area I have been hiking through fairly nondescript mountains. But the day after tomorrow I should start coming to Famous Stuff again.

I had better be careful about the extra mileage. I learned in a shelter log that Mansooka did a thirty mile day, injured his shin and had to limp painfully to the next road and hitch to town. And he is just one in a long string of hikers who pushed too hard, hurt themselves, and had to leave the Trail.

-Mouse

Monday, May 17, 2004
Destination: Sarver Hollow Shelter
From: Potts Mountain Campsite
Today's Miles: 15.9
Trip Miles: 666.5

Wow, I should not have mentioned thunderstorms yesterday!

I got to Laurel Creek Shelter for lunch and the thunder started rumbling about 1:30. Being an incurable optimist I set out for Sarver Shelter 6 miles away. As I entered a wide rolling meadowed valley the rain began. I tried out my newest downpour avoidance scheme: place pack on ground waterproof cover down, put on cheap plastic poncho, sit quietly on pack until downpour abates. I reasoned that staying still would avoid getting hot and sweaty and prevent the Saran wrap sound which had annoyed me last time I had tried a plastic poncho. I sat for ten minutes and stayed relatively dry but water still found its way in through a bad seam near the hood and through the upwind armhole. As time passed I realized I was hot and sweaty despite sitting still and the cool rain outside seemed almost inviting. Then there is a certain problem with sitting out in an open field during a lightning storm. This fact was punctuated by a bolt from an unexpected direction.

The rain had diminished quite a bit, so I got up, put the poncho away, put on my pack and started out confidently in the remaining drizzle.

Then the storm cell off to the north whose fringe had just passed over me turned me over to a new dancing partner, a nice large cell coming right at me from the west. This one introduced itself with a renewed downpour and made light conversation by sending down frequent lightning bolts. It was sort of like the thunderstorm scene in the movie "Fantasia" except there was not a convenient Greek temple nearby to hide in.

The foot-wide dirt path that formed the Appalachian Trail here in the meadow quickly flooded, becoming more like the Appalachian Barge Canal complete with tiny weirs and locks to maintain the water level. At first my boots sought out the towpath alongside but that disappeared and they had to settle for being barges, cruising through the water. In less than no time my Nikwax treated Gore-Tex lined boots gave up and filled with water.

My attention was diverted from my wet feet by the frequent and fairly close bolts of lighting. There is something a bit unnerving about being the highest object in a hundred yards during a thunderstorm. As I reached the road and the center of the valley a new adventure awaited. There was fence after fence each with a stile to clamper over. I could visualize what a nice electrical conductor a fence would be and how it ought to multiply the risk when near it for long enough to climb up and over the stile. I even debated in my mind whether to toss my aluminum trekking poles over each fence rather than hold them in the air.

I scampered into the dubious cover of trees on the other side, only to have the trail lead me into yet another meadow full of cows all staring at me as if I had lost my mind for hiking in this weather. Then more stiles and finally the woods on the other side of the valley.

The storm went on for three hours. Near the end, things seemed to be quieting down when I nervously made my way under a high-tension line. As I got clear a loud flash up in the sky and a deep boom that started like the report of a fireworks aerial bomb then rippled overhead reminded me there was still plenty of storm left. At last as I finished the 2,000 foot climb up the ridge the rain died out and I made my way along the ridge to Sarver shelter.

I know, the chances of getting struck by lightning on the Trail are pretty low. But the knowledge it CAN happen certainly spices up one's afternoon!

All that excitement nearly made me forget everything else about today.

The climb in the rain was the second 2,000 foot climb of the day. During the first one before the storm hit I was thinking for the umpteenth time that I seemed pretty out of breath for a marathoner who has been hiking for two months. I resolved to try getting more meat in my diet and probably an iron supplement. I have been slightly anemic for several years and the hiking and sparse diet might be making it worse.

Then at a road crossing just before the top I ran into two big coolers filled with beer and sodas. Floating in one was a nice big juicy tomato! After that and an orange soda my mindset had changed enormously for the better. This big piece of trail magic was courtesy of Big Dave from Martinsburg, Virginia. Thanks Dave!!! I can't begin to say how much trail magic boosts hiker morale.

I was also so busy dodging lightning that I completely forgot the first of the famous things coming up on the trail. Just past the road with those stiles was the second largest oak tree on the Appalachian Trail and I went right past. It would have been hard to take a picture in the rain anyway. Oh well.

-Mouse

Tuesday, May 18, 2004
Destination: Pickle Branch Shelter
From: Sarver Hollow Shelter
Today's Miles: 15.9
Trip Miles: 682.4

Today I started off running along the crest of the ridge I climbed yesterday. In many spots the trail ran right over canted rock slabs broken off in a jagged edge at the crest. I was right on the spine of the Appalachians. The left side of the ridge drained to the Mississippi and the right side to the Atlantic. That ridge will be the last time I will be in the Mississippi basin. After it the Trail stays in the watershed of rivers draining to the east into the Atlantic.

I had lunch at Niday shelter and it was a repeat of my Fontana bee experience. After getting out my food and popping off my boots and socks I discovered there were bees everywhere! I inched to the very back of the shelter to get away from them. Fortunately the only things they were not interested in were shade and bagels with cream cheese. So as I ate they buzzed about my pack, my boots; everything but me. After finishing eating I gingerly crept forward and retrieved my boots and socks and put them on then slowly inched over to the rest of my gear, gathered it up and retreated to a safe distance to repack everything.

After crossing a valley and climbing 1,500 feet up another ridge I came to the next attraction on the trail, the Audie Murphy Monument. The most decorated veteran of WW2, he died in a plane crash in 1971 near the site of the monument. The monument is a simple stone slab engraved with his story.

Then along that ridge. My feet were starting to hurt despite my pack weight getting down to around twenty pounds. I am going to have to hang on until Daleville and go to the outfitter there and get some lightweight shoes with more cushioning. I tried a trick I had read about, loosening the lower laces, tying an overhand knot to hold the slack, then lacing the upper part normally. That helped a little but not enough to really correct things.

Finally I got down to Trout Creek where I found a Trail Angel had left sodas at the bridge. A grape soda helped forget how much my feet hurt and gave energy for the climb to the shelter. Just as well, because just as I got turned onto the .3 mile side trail to the shelter it started to rain. I dashed down the trail like I was possessed to avoid another soaking.

-Mouse

Wednesday, May 19, 2004
Destination: Campbell Shelter
From: Pickle Branch Shelter
Today's Miles: 16.1
Trip Miles: 698.5

What a great day!

It did not start out so promising. I woke up with a flat air mattress. Either I did not close the valve all the way, or it has a leak. I will find out tonight.

I got started early at 6:30. Three miles away was the next attraction, the Dragon's Tooth, and a road to a store three miles after that. I figured in about 3 hours I'd be eating real food.

WRONG! That was the hardest six miles I have hiked. The Dragon's Tooth is a towering rock pinnacle at the end of a two mile ridge thrust out into the lower end of the Catawba Valley. The ridge is made of sandwiched strata of rock canted nearly vertical, about 75 degrees. So hiking the crest of the ridge meant going along the irregular jagged edges of the upturned slabs, a lot of difficult scrambling. I began to doubt I'd make the 16 miles I needed to stay on schedule for my pickup.

At the end of the ridge a side-trail goes to the Tooth itself. I was too tired and hungry to go all the way. Instead I just got a picture of what looked like the Tooth and went back. Anyway, it is best photographed with a swarm of hikers clambered up it and I did not have a swarm of hikers handy.

I figured now I'd have an easy downhill walk to the store and my reward. Wrong again! The trail down followed jagged ledges formed by layers of the steep rock that had broken away. It was the most serious rock climbing I have seen on the trail so far. It was strenuous and had to be done carefully. A fall could easily mean broken bones or worse.

It was nearly noon by the time I got to the store. I ordered a sub and soft drink for there as well as 12 ounces of bologna to pig out on today and ramen, tuna, energy bars, Poptarts, a half pound of cheese and two fruit pies to feed me for the next 3 days, assuming I would need an extra day to get the 25 miles to Daleville the way things were going. The thunderstorms started early today and it rained as I ate my food on the store's covered porch. It is amazing what a big infusion of calories does to both your energy level and mindset. I made good time after lunch and it looked like I would make my original schedule after all.

As I crossed VA.311 big dark clouds were billowing again and I put on speed to beat the rain. I got to Johns Spring Shelter just before the next thundershower hit. I waited out that shower there, then hiked on to Catawba Mountain Shelter, arriving just before yet another thundershower. I was having good luck today at dodging thunderstorms!

McAfee Knob is a famous ledge at the top of a 4,000 foot mountain, no place to get stuck in a thunderstorm. I had a mile and a half to go from Catawba Mountain Shelter with a thousand foot climb so I was convinced I'd have to stay the night at the shelter and climb the Knob tomorrow. That would likely cost an extra day getting to Daleville.

Miraculously, the weather cleared. At 6:00 p.m. I started for the Knob and the weather held!

McAfee Knob was spectacular. The ledge thrusts high over a valley hundreds of feet below with an incredible view. There was no one there to take a picture of me in the classic thruhiker pose seated at the edge of the ledge like you see in books. But I took lots of pictures anyway.

So I got to see everything and kept to my schedule despite the rough terrain and thundershowers. I was one happy hiker when I got to the shelter tonight. The rain just came again at 9:30 p.m. but I am snug and dry.

-Mouse

Thursday, May 20, 2004
Destination: Daleville, VA
From: Campbell Shelter
Today's Miles: 15.4
Trip Miles: 713.9

Another nice day!

Hoping to get to Daleville in time to get to the outfitter, I got going at 6:15 a.m. I got to Tinker Cliffs at 9:30. It turned out to have a precipitous overlook rather like McAfee Knob. Just as I got there I met a man and woman, Junior and L.L. Fuzzy, who took my picture to make up for missing one at Mcafee Knob. The view is incredible; you can see the length of the Catawba Valley with both McAfee Knob and the Dragon's Tooth in view. The pictures done, I scooted a prudent distance from the edge and settled down for an early picnic lunch. They sat right on the edge with their legs dangling casually in space. The apparent sheer drop of hundreds of feet is largely illusion, the actual height of the cliffs is probably less than fifty feet before meeting the sloped mountainside, still it made me really nervous to see them right at the edge.

After that the Trail turned away from the cliff edge south and went along the southern arm of Tinker Mountain, overlooking Tinker Creek of Annie Dillard fame. It descends and then crosses Tinker Creek before reaching Daleville. For fun, I scooped up a bit of water in my filter bottle and drank it in memory of Dillard's book "Pilgrim of Tinker Creek."

Yesterday chafing was becoming a problem for the first time and today by the time I got to town I had raw spots and an angry rash. After checking into a motel

I got to the outfitter only to find they had no suitable shoes or a repair kit for my mattress. I settled for new insoles. I also got insect repellent, as yesterday I saw the first biting mosquitoes of the hike.

-Mouse

Friday, May 21, 2004
Destination: Bobblets Gap Shelter
From: Daleville, VA
Today's Miles: 18.5
Trip Miles: 732.4

Ooooooh! Today is definitely an Ibuprofen day. The insoles helped but only so much. The good news is that today was both the farthest and the heaviest for this leg. I brought along a pound of liverwurst, half a pound of pastrami, and half a pound of carrots to gobble up today to try to get some more nutrients into me.

Today I reached the Blue Ridge, which the Trail now follows all the way to Harpers Ferry. And the Rhododendrons here are in bloom, the first I have seen. They are big bright clusters of purplish pink.

There was the usual thunderstorm but I only got the fringes of it. It rained hard for about ten minutes. I sat on my pack under my poncho for that part with a little more success than last time, then hiked through the remaining drizzle. A shower, a night in the cool dry motel air instead of a clammy sleeping bag, clean clothes and Neosporin seem to have helped my rash troubles and now my skin is clear again.

On the other hand my feet were really sore, especially the arch and top of my left foot. That made it impossible to find a position that did not make them hurt, so I had trouble sleeping. To add to things a man next to me was a prodigious snorer. My summer bag does not have a zippered pocket to keep my earplugs in like the winter one did, so I had to rummage through my backpack in the dark to find them. After that I finally dropped off to sleep.

-Mouse

Saturday, May 22, 2004
Destination: Bryant Ridge Shelter
From: Bobblets Gap Shelter
Today's Miles: 13.3
Trip Miles: 745.7

My feet were still sore this morning. I was debating in my mind whether to go to the nearer of the two possible sites to stop at tonight when events made the decision for me.

Three miles into today's hike I was going at a brisk but not reckless pace on a straight smooth downhill stretch when I suddenly felt a sharp pain knife through my right knee. The leg buckled and I went crashing to the ground. After 735 miles of every sort of terrain imaginable with hardly a twinge, my loose knee cartilage had chosen this moment to shift out of place. It had happened many times since high school but not recently and never before while backpacking.

I struggled free of my pack and sat up to assess the damage. Everything in the joint had snapped back into place once I had fallen and the weight was off it, and nothing seemed to have been hurt too badly this time. After waiting for the pain to subside I gingerly got back to my feet and carefully hoisted my pack into place then cautiously started walking. The ligaments and muscles may have been stretched enough to let the cartilage pop out more easily so I had to be careful.

Within a few minutes I reached the road crossing at Bearwallow Gap. A Trail Angel had left sodas and snacks. Gratefully I sat down with some peanut butter crackers and soda and took out my map and guidebook pages to take stock. Weeks of hiking had convinced me that my knee would not cause trouble and now that sense of security had been badly shaken. I decided to try for Bryant Ridge Shelter and then play it by ear. After yesterday's high mileage I could afford a shorter day. A rest would be good for my feet as well as my injured knee. When I get to the James River tomorrow I will decide whether to get off there and go to Glasgow or go all the way to Highway 60 as I had planned.

I did the three miles to Cove Mountain shelter, where I had some food and made a note in the register about my knee so others would know I was having a problem. Then I headed on to Jenkins Creek. Things went well until the descent to the Creek made my knee tender from the strain. But it was worth it. At the VA 614 bridge was a popular swimming spot in the creek. I popped off my boots and socks, sat on a rock and put both legs into the soothingly cold water. After that I filtered enough water to make a pint of milk and had that and a 7 oz pack of tuna.

All that improved things enough that I found myself catching up with and passing a group of boy scouts headed for the same shelter. I had to remind myself to take it easy.

The shelter is one of the largest on the AT and I found it very fancy with covered decks and a loft with balcony. I could imagine the scouts taking to it like a jungle gym when they arrived and the shelter register entries warned of lots of mosquitoes and tiny biting flies called no-see-ums. But there was no quiet spot where I could put my tent. So I filtered a supply of water for the night and started up the trail again hoping for a private flat spot where I could nurse my hurts in peace.

I went up past a pretty waterfall and within half a mile came upon a trail junction with a small campsite. Perfect! By 4:00 p.m. I was in my tent relaxing. My decision to stop had worked out; neither feet nor knee were more than a little sore. In the privacy of my tent I could remove my sweaty clothing and give my body some air to keep the chafing at bay. A nice cool breeze would have been nice, but you can't have everything, at least not when you want it.

Around 5:30 thunder started rumbling in the distance, the first in an unusually calm day. It was feeling uncomfortably hot and muggy with no breeze. I almost hope for rain to cool things down.

Hwy 60 is just over 45 miles away. Despite the mishap I am still on schedule and can still make it on time if things go well.

-Mouse

Sunday, May 23, 2004
Destination: Marble Spring Campsite
From: Bryant Ridge Shelter
Today's Miles: 17.2
Trip Miles: 762.9

Woohoo! My knee held together and I got as far as I hoped. Now I am 29 miles and two days from US HWY 60. My feet are sore but it was worth it.

There have been so many times the last three weeks I was sure I would not be able to keep up the pace. The most recent was just this morning on the 2,000 foot climb up Floyd Mountain. I was SURE I would not get here and was mentally looking forward to bailing out at Glasgow and justifying it in my mind.

Pessimism is endemic on this part of the Trail. There is even a term for it; the "Virginia Blues." It seems a combination of fatigue from being so long on the Trail plus discouragement at being in Virginia for so very long and according to some, depression caused by the onset of malnutrition as the body's reserves begin to be depleted. I am a firm believer in the last factor after seeing first hand what a challenge it can be to plan and carry an adequate balanced diet, especially on five and six day legs. The more you carry the more calories your body burns carrying it.

Having to stick to a daily mileage quota can be hard and force skipping things you might see at a more relaxed pace. I guess the flip side is that it gave me something to focus on and has gotten me that much closer to Maine.

-Mouse

Monday, May 24, 2004
Destination: Saltlog Gap Campsite
From: Marble Spring Campsite
Today's Miles: 15.1
Trip Miles: 778.0

I woke up about 5:00 a.m. crawling with what looked like fleas! Long ago another hiker had mentioned getting fleas in a shelter that presumably had been brought by a hiker's dog but it had seemed a remote threat at the time. Now it did not seem remote at all!

I got up and shook out everything as thoroughly as I could, then doused myself with insect repellant. The good side was that by 6:00 a.m. I was packed and on the trail. I consoled myself that tomorrow night I should be at a motel with a laundry and could decontaminate everything.

The first part of the day's hike led through a section where the broken slate trail surface and the way the trail clung to steep shrub-covered slopes reminded me fondly of the Pine Ridge Trail in the Ventana Wilderness of Big Sur. Then the Trail descended relentlessly down to Matts Creek Shelter where I had lunch and then to the James River, which is the first of the really big long rivers the Trail crosses.

I followed the 625 foot long footbridge across then went to the Johns Hollow Shelter. First I had a second lunch; I seem to be having two more often than not. Then I went to the fast-running stream near the Shelter and found a spot like a cold water Jacuzzi and put my sore feet in. While the swirling water soothed away the pounding my feet had gotten from the long descent I filtered enough water to make a quart of Gatorade to fuel me on the long climb back up into the mountains.

The afternoon proved overcast and breezy, making the climb much easier than it might have been. I found myself hurrying the last mile or so lest a storm blow up, but there was no rain or even a distant rumble of thunder. I arrived at the site I had planned about 3:30 and set up camp, aside from my sleeping bag. I left it in its stuff sack and triple plastic bags, preferring to sleep cold rather than open it and possibly find a flea circus.

Now I am a scant 14 miles to Highway 60 where I expect to get a ride to Buena Vista. I will spend tomorrow night there getting cleaned up then get picked up the next day to work at the festival.

-Mouse

Tuesday, May 25, 2004
Destination: Buena Vista, VA
From: Saltlog Gap Campsite
Today's Miles: 14.0
Trip Miles: 792.0

I spent an interesting night with my legs tucked into my backpack instead of a sleeping bag and using my pack cover as a blanket for the rest of me. I trust the fleas spent a hungry but comfortable night bundled up in my sleeping bag. Yesterday they had invited me to spend another night with them but I respectfully declined.

The next attraction was a thunderstorm at the unusual hour of 4:00 a.m. The wind was particularly strong and I found myself recalling first hand stories of near misses from falling limbs. I REALLY hoped nothing would fall from the trees above me.

Little did I know that the morning excitement was just beginning. As I lay contemplating a late start to let things dry out, I heard the scuffling of a small animal outside my tent. I had brought my food bag in when the rain started so I assumed it was a raccoon and yelled "Get lost!" in a loud voice. To my horror, a black and white streak disappeared into the shadows. I had yelled at a skunk!

I was feeling relieved that it had left without spraying me when back it came. It clamped its teeth on the door zipper, grabbing hold of a hiking boot inside as well. I gently pulled the boot away and it let go of the fabric only to scratch away at the wall and try to burrow under the floor.

"Please go away" I pleaded, to no avail. Soon it was starting under the floor. I carefully used the boot to shove it gently out again but it tried again. Again and again the skunk tried to get in, from every side; getting underneath, chewing at the door, clambering up the wall and gazing at me through the mesh. Meanwhile I fended it off as best I could, but never too forcefully lest it decide to spray me.

It became clear the skunk was not after my food or my boots and did not care that I was there, it just wanted IN! It would keep it up as long as the tent was there, so during a lull in the action I started packing. At first I followed my usual neat orderly packing but when it returned to chew at the door zipper and would not let go for anything I just threw things in willy-nilly. When the skunk let go to run around and try its luck on the tent rear I snuck out the door and brought out my pack. I turned to pull the stake for the front awning and start taking the tent down when behind me I heard a scuffling of fabric.

"Oh no" I moaned, "Not inside!"

Not exactly. When I looked in I saw a skunk-sized mound in the floor. While it was exploring the basement I gingerly reached over the wriggling mound and plucked out the last few items. Then I cautiously removed my trekking poles holding the tent up. Taking no chances, I picked up everything I had so far and carried it a prudent distance away. Then I went back to pull the stakes and ever so cautiously pulled the tent off the skunk. At first it seemed about to grab a stake loop before it got out of reach and play tug-of-war. But it noticed the groundsheet and started worrying and burrowing at that while I took the tent to my pack and stuffed it into its sack. Finally I went back and got the groundsheet. Only then did the skunk give up and shuffle into the underbrush. Worried that it might return, I grabbed my pack and dashed, not even stopping to adjust the trekking poles to the right length for walking until I was a quarter mile away.

How I escaped getting sprayed, I'll never know.

The rest of the day was almost an anticlimax. But I will always remember what I saw on the top of Bluff Mountain at a monument to a 4 year 11 month old child who wandered from school in 1890 and froze to death on the mountaintop. On and around the stone tablet were flowers, toys, a teddy bear, little dolls that hikers had brought along as mascots and left there, as well as a large pile of pennies. I burst into sentimental tears at these gifts and burrowed in my pack to leave all the pennies I had.

About 3:00 I finally arrived at US Highway 60. Waiting there were Gadget who hiked in 2002-2003 and his wife BCC (Base Camp Coordinator). They were there to pick up a slack packing couple with the trailname "CNN" (Charles N Nancy) and to dispense trail magic. They had a whole table of food and drink. I told my skunk story on videotape. Everyone decided it either wanted in out of the rain or it had fallen in love with me. They kindly offered to give me a ride to Buena Vista.

Once at a motel, my first step was to run my bug-ridden sleeping bag through the washing machine! Then a shower and laundering my clothing and I was ready to go to the festival the next morning.

-Mouse

Monday, May 31, 2004
Destination: Hwy. 60 Stealth Camp
From: On Break
Today's Miles: 1.0
Trip Miles: 793.0

I am back on the Trail again.

It was a pretty strenuous break. I spent two days helping prepare for the music festival. Then I spent the three days of the festival itself running around 16 hours a day with a radio headset solving all the off-stage problems of sixteen music groups along with lending a hand backstage and tarping the speaker stacks whenever it rained. I was ready for the quiet life of the Trail. Still, it was a nice change of pace and my feet and knees benefited from the break from hiking.

On my wrist is my festival worker wristband, a souvenir to add to the bits of violet nail polish still remaining on two nails from when I put it on way back in Erwin, TN and two beads I picked up from the trail after they were dropped by other hikers and a feather that looks like those from my pet cockatiel back home.

The music reminded me of home, and being with my significant other and everything else that one leaves behind when thruhiking. More than once I had to find a quiet spot backstage and blink away the tears before rushing back to work.

But who knows if I will ever get the chance to thruhike again, so I am willing to make the sacrifices to keep hiking. Especially with so many people from all over the country giving me moral support, from my former co-workers back in California to family to fellow hikers and even just people who stumble across my journal.

I did not get away until nearly 4:00 and it took until well after 6:00 p.m. to get food, ride to the trailhead and get organized to hike. It quickly became obvious I would have to hike until dark to reach the nearest shelter over four miles away. I was already exhausted from spending most of the day helping disassemble and load a truckful of heavy sound equipment. So when I reached a fire road junction with a poison ivy-free spot next to the roads, I decided to go ahead and camp even though I had gone barely a mile.

-Mouse

Tuesday, June 01, 2004
Destination: Sealey-Woodworth Shelter
From: Hwy. 60 Camp
Today's Miles: 13.0
Trip Miles: 806.0

During the day I crossed two more balds maintained by mowing. I love hiking on those high mountain meadows with their views but these may be the last balds I see, I do not believe they exist up north.

I arrived at the shelter by 3:00. For a shelter it had quite a library: two new testaments, an adventure novel and the latest issue of the New Yorker. I was reading happily when a hiker from Canada named Rocket arrived. A bit later Andrew arrived! I had not seen him since Damascus, so we did a lot of catching up. About 6:15 Slowpoke showed up as well.

It was unusually chilly. I put on my long sleeve top and retreated to my sleeping bag to stay warm.

-Mouse

Wednesday, June 02, 2004
Destination: Harpers Creek Shelter
From: Sealey-Woodworth Shelter
Today's Miles: 14.3
Trip Miles: 820.3

Last night was chilly with wind and rain. For the first time in weeks I tucked my head into the hood of my sleeping bag and rolled my body into a ball for warmth. Oddly, the chill vanished when the sun came up. On the good side, it did not rain a drop today and it felt cooler and less humid than past weeks.

I noticed this morning that Rocket has the male version of my pack, the Mountainsmith Auspex. I asked him how he liked it and was a bit surprised to hear he was having neck and back pain from it. I offered to try to adjust it for him. It seemed like the attachment point for the shoulder straps were too high for the loadlifter straps to work properly on him. I raised the lifters as far as they would go to try to get them closer to the proper 45 degree angle but there was little else I could do. It was a bit surprising to see how different the geometry was from my Chimera, which has given me nice service under all load conditions.

Today's hike was slow because of the climb up Priest Mountain followed by a foot-jarring 3,000 foot descent to the Tye River and an 800 foot climb to the shelter. It felt wonderful to pop off my shoes near the wobbly suspension footbridge over the Tye and soak my feet in the cold river.

At mid day I ran into Stretch, whom I went through most of the Smokys with and last saw at Hot Springs. He had had to take a five day break there with shin splints. It is nice to run into people I know so quickly after getting back on the Trail.

At the shelter I found two section hikers. We all ended up tenting because of mosquitoes. It was only 530 but I felt so tired it was tempting to skip supper and just curl up in my sleeping bag. Finally after a short nap I got myself to eat. I don't want that pound or so of food in my pack when I start tomorrow with a 2,000 foot climb.

-Mouse

Thursday, June 03, 2004
Destination: Humpback Overlook Campsite
From: Harpers Creek Shelter
Today's Miles: 15.3
Trip Miles: 835.6

The day was cool, dry and breezy just like yesterday. That was good, seeing that the day started with a 2,000 foot climb up The Three Ridges. The Trail may be a bit lower here than further south, but it is just as strenuous. Instead of high peaks it is the deep gaps in the Blue Ridge that keep us working; 3,000 feet down and back up again. Whatever the "easier" part of Virginia is, this is not it!

I had lunch at Maupin Field Shelter where I met a thruhiker from last year out for a section hike. He gave some useful advice on where to find water and on how to find things in Waynesboro. Reading the register I could still find no entry from The Walking Stomach. I did find my timing was bad for Trail Magic. A day before I reached the Tye River the Sierra Club was handing out hamburgers and two days after I pass Reed Gap another club will have a free breakfast for thruhikers. I guess the Trail Goddess wants me to work off all the food I ate at the festival.

I went on to my old friend the Blue Ridge Parkway, which the Trail follows for a bit. At the end of that section I topped up on water at Dripping Rocks Parking and headed on. There were campsites just inside the woods but I wanted further from the road and closer to Rockfish Gap. So I decided to hike on and see if there was a site near the overlook on Humpback Mountain.

According to the guidebook the Trail bypasses the rocks along Humpback. So I was surprised to find it climbing uncompromisingly up a huge pile of large boulders. Perched atop the heap I ran into three day hikers coming south. They said there were indeed campsites at the overlook.

Next I ran into a blue-blazed trail that had to be the route through the rocks. I can't imagine how impressive they must be if they are worse than the pile I had already scaled. On top of the signpost was a ziplock bag with a copy of the novel 'Ishmael,' a Snickers bar and a packet of Welch's Fruit Snacks. The book was too heavy and I had had enough Snickers but the fruit snacks caught my fruit-and-vegetable starved interest. I took them and left a Balance Bar in return, since I had some leftover.

About 4:30 I got to the overlook. The view was breathtaking, though not quite as much as Tinker Cliffs or McAfee Knob. It dwarfed the ridge the Parkway ran on. On the right was the Shenandoah Valley, on the left was the Three Ridges with the Priest off in the distance.

Going past some trees to another section of the overlook I was surprised to see two turkey vultures perched on the brink of the cliff not ten feet from me. I slowly set down my pack and got out my camera. They perched calmly, every now and then giving a look in my direction as I took several pictures from different angles with the vultures in the foreground and the different landscapes in the back. I put my pack back on, said "Bye Bye, Birdies" and made my way along the overlook. In the woods at the other end I found a firecircle and tentsites.

I put up my tent and took my Pocketmail and food bag back to the overlook to write my journal and eat. Why sit in a hot tent when you have a stunning cliff top view to enjoy? Two more vultures had joined the first two and we sat together until one by one they spread their wings and soared off. Later I will go back with my camera to watch as the sun slowly slips behind the mountains on the far side of the valley.

-Mouse

Friday, June 04, 2004
Destination: Waynesboro
From: Humpback Overlook Campsite
Today's Miles: 12.0
Trip Miles: 847.6

It starts raining at 500 a.m. and keeps up. By 6:30 I know my hopes for an early start are drenched. With just a cheap poncho with a hole in it I am disinclined to venture out, at least not until it warms up.

By 7:30 I venture out. A couple with a dog come into view. Naturally the dog wanders over to me and shakes the water off its drenched coat onto my legs.

"Come on, Town's calling" the woman tells me. I retrieve my food bag from its branch and retreat to my tent.

With Rockfish Gap only 12 miles away I can afford to be patient, but the rain seems relentless. I begin thinking about duct-taping the hole in my poncho and using my long-sleeved top under it to give some warmth and avoid the cold wet plastic feel. I check the map and it is downhill nearly the entire way. No sweaty climbs inside a clammy poncho. If the rain lasts all day there will be a nice motel to dry off in. There is even one right near the Trail in case no one wants to drive a drenched hiker to Waynesboro.

I begin breakfast. Next I repair the poncho, then methodically pack everything away. By 8:30 I am hiking.

Even in the rain there are things to see. I heard a hissing and flutter of wings in the underbrush. It is my first grouse attack! If you come too close to a nest the mother usually tries to lead you away by pretending to have a broken wing. If that fails she ferociously attacks the intruder to protect her young.

A bit later I saw what at first seemed a very wet cat or coyote. It turned out to be a small fawn. It stumbled awkwardly to the side of the trail and stood regarding me with wide eyes. I spoke gently to it in a soothing voice as I passed, near enough to touch it if I wanted. I hoped its mother found it before my vulture friends did.

Later still was a box turtle walking along the Trail. With all the wet and the ferns crowding the underbrush I half expect a dinosaur to appear, it looks more like their world than our current one. I was glad I had not tried to outwait the rain. It rained all day, for only the second time in my thruhike.

I got to Rockfish Gap and the Information Center there. The man there, Mike Soloman, had me try to hitch a ride for five minutes as it might be faster than calling for a ride. I tried it, but fog was setting in and no one stopped. He called and fairly quickly found someone to take me to the outfitters and also set up a reservation at a motel. If I did not get a ride from the outfitter he also offered to come get me after he got off work.

At the store I finally got a new pair of lightweight Merrell Chameleon shoes to replace my heavy Asolos, some Aqua Mira water purifier to save my filter elements, a new photon flashlight as my old one had failing batteries, and a water repellant windbreaker to replace the cheap plastic poncho. A woman who had section hiked most of the Trail was there and offered to take me to my motel.

I had an AYCE seafood buffet and bought food for my next leg then rested up for tomorrow.

-Mouse

Saturday, June 05, 2004
Destination: Calf Mountain Shelter
From: Waynesboro
Today's Miles: 7.0
Trip Miles: 854.6

My motel was so far from downtown that I decided to check out and take my whole pack to the Post Office rather than bringing my bounce box to the motel. I went through the box and got another box to mail my old boots to Harpers Ferry in case the new ones did not work out. I also put in my leaky mattress. I had dipped it in the motel sink a bit at a time until I found the leak; it was in an awkward spot near the valve that would be hard to patch reliably. I barely got both boxes sealed and addressed and to the counter before the post office closed.

That done, I walked back to the outfitters and bought a Ridgerest pad. It was only half the weight of my mattress but MUCH bulkier. I might cut it down to my width and height to reduce the size a bit. I really wanted a Z-rest but they had sold out a few days ago.

I hitched a ride to the Trail and was hiking by noon. It was not actually raining but was still damp, cold and windy so the new jacket came in handy.

The landscape varied between wet foggy forest that reminded me of Jurassic Park and fog shrouded meadows with high grass and brush that nearly hid the trail. Despite reports of the trail being easier, so far I have seen as much boulders, rock ledges and steep climbs as elsewhere.

I seem to have left my hat somewhere, probably in a car as well as leaving the map for the first section of Shenandoah National Park, so it was not the best of town visits.

On the other hand the new shoes seem to be working so far. I might try to go 20 miles tomorrow or the next day and see how that works. Like the Smokys, there are restrictions on where you may camp. That makes for limited choices on how far to hike.

The shelter tonight had about 16 people in and around it. Some are section hikers who thruhiked last year. They had lots of stories to relate.

It was so chilly I went straight to my sleeping bag and only came out when I had to. It has not been like this in over a month. The funny thing is, the Weather Channel forecast for the coming week is the same 84 degrees partly cloudy and thunderstorms we have had for weeks, just as if this damp cold spell had never happened.

-Mouse

Sunday, June 06, 2004
Destination: Loft Mountain Campground
From: Calf Mountain Shelter
Today's Miles: 20.4
Trip Miles: 875.0

TWENTY MILES! Woohoo!!!

Once I got into the Park proper, the Trail really was flatter and smoother. Between that and the lighter shoes I was moving a lot faster. My feet may be sore tomorrow but it was worth it. I got a real shower and some real food at the camp store. But the laundry and restaurant were too much of a walk, they will have to wait until next time.

The deer here seem fearless! I passed three close up that did not bother to run away. One was standing on the Trail nibbling at the undergrowth. It looked at me, stepped off the trail to let me pass, then went right back to resume nibbling.

Just before the campground I ran into Gaiter Woman, who slept next to me last night. She is a nurse from Vermont. We ended up sharing a campsite with Fire Marshall and Hotrod.

Fire Marshall, Gaiter Woman and I went to look at the store and restaurant. We found the restaurant was a mile further and closed soon so we settled for buying food. I got corned beef, canned mixed vegetables and chocolate milk for tonight and ham, crackers and an apple for later.

Then we went and tried the showers. It was an odd type I have not seen before where you put in four quarters for five minutes.

Tomorrow I think I will go to the next shelter 14 miles away to give my feet a bit of a break.

-Mouse

Monday, June 07, 2004
Destination: Hightop Hut
From: Loft Mountain Campground
Today's Miles: 14.0
Trip Miles: 889.0

Last night was like a Wanderlust Tent convention. I counted five and until now the most I had seen besides my own was one. They were all of different years so I could see the gradual changes in the design.

This morning several of us slept in so as to arrive at the restaurant after it opened at 9:00. Gaiter Woman, Fire Marshall and I had breakfast together. At the store I found a wide-brimmed hat with an adjustable chin string almost like the one I lost for only $7.00. It is stiff instead of soft but I think a few trips through washing machines and some trail time should fix that. Amazingly, it is even plain with no touristy logos.

It was mostly damp and foggy today but no rain. We saw another fawn right by the Trail. Apparently it is normal for the doe to leave them for a bit and they stay motionless until she returns. That makes me feel better about the fawn I saw before Waynesboro, now I know it was probably not hurt or abandoned.

The shelter tonight was the most crowded I have seen since the Smokys with both shelter and tentsites packed. There are over a dozen women, the most I have seen in one place on the trail, and nearly as many men. This is my first stay at a shelter inside the Park boundaries and it is an adventure. In Shenandoah the shelters are called "huts" to distinguish them from picnic shelters. Instead of the bear cables seen further south they have poles with hooks at the top. You are supposed to lift your food bag up to a hook using a long pole with a u at the top. The catch is that the pole is heavy pipe that is very hard for most women to lift upright. Even some of the men found it a challenge. Watching each other learn how to use them is as much fun as when we first learned to toss a rope over a branch to hang food from.

One thing I really like here is that instead of the wooden signposts scattered on the rest of the trail that sometimes are too rotted to read, there is a concrete post at every trail junction and road crossing with metal bands with embossed letters giving the location and distances to other places. They are very durable and make navigating very easy without having to consult a map or guidebook.

One thing that is annoying is that you can only camp in certain spots and like in the Smokys the spacing is inconvenient. I checked and I can either do about 20 miles tomorrow, then 19 the next or I can take an extra day and do about 12, 12 and 15. Either two long hard days back to back or three too easy days. No other choices. I will wait until the twelve mile point tomorrow to decide which to do.

Speaking of annoyances, my new Ridgerest and I are not friends. Because of its bulkiness the only way to carry it is strapped to the back of my pack where it sticks out and gets in the way. Even cutting it down to my height and width only helped a little. But its worst failing is that it just does not match a self-inflating air mattress for comfort. It is not TOO bad on soft ground, but on a wooden shelter floor it may as well be a sheet of plywood as far as I am concerned. The Ridgerest's light weight does not make up for those failings.

-Mouse

Tuesday, June 08, 2004
Destination: Big Meadows Campground
From: Hightop Hut
Today's Miles: 20.4
Trip Miles: 909.4

Oooooh, my feet! I did the 20 mile option. Now I have 19 tomorrow but at least it will speed me on my way north.

We are all getting a bit desperate to get to Harpers Ferry and out of Virginia. Virginia is so big it makes one feel like being on a treadmill getting nowhere, and that is discouraging. I am also bothered especially by knowing that it will take more than 3 months to get to the halfway point. I had hoped to do the whole hike in five and a half months and had taken the lightest gear possible to be able to do so. But my feet just have not cooperated. My biggest mistake was not getting lightweight boots back in Damascus. Still, I went faster the second month than the first and am going even faster now so I really should not worry. But having a slow first half still makes me anxious. Speeding up makes me feel better so I decided to try the two long hikes if I could.

I made the 12 miles to the camp store at Lewis Mountain at 11:15 a.m. My feet had new blisters on my toes from the socks and my heels a touch raw but not getting worse so I decided to keep going. I bought two days and a night of food to last until Elkwallow Wayside and a can of peas, half pound of salami and pint of chocolate milk for to eat for lunch. I am finding it is a good idea to get non-trail food when I can get it. By noon I was on my way.

Pilot and I kept passing each other on the 8 mile trek to Big Meadows. She suggested that she, Gaiter Woman and I share a campsite there. I got there first, so found a site, paid and registered, then left a note so the other two would know where to go.

Pilot joked that it was the "All woman, all Nomad tentsite" because we all three have Nomad tents.

First we all had showers and combined our laundry to make a load. It felt great to be clean again and have clean clothes. Then we went to the Lodge dining room for supper. It was sort of surreal coming from a hut in the wilderness that morning and now being in a full-service restaurant. It was the best meal I have had on the Trail. I had steak with all the trimmings. All three of us were too stuffed for dessert.

-Mouse

Wednesday, June 09, 2004
Destination: Pass Mountain Hut
From: Big Meadows Campground
Today's Miles: 18.8
Trip Miles: 928.2

Yow, another long day. Near the end was a long downhill on badly washed out trail whose uneven rocky surface was the worst thing possible for sore tired feet. Fortunately the last mile was a gentle uphill on mostly smooth trail that actually felt soothing after all the rocks. The good thing is that we have zipped through the whole central section of the park in just two days. We were not too rushed to stop in at the dining room of the Skyland Lodge at midmorning. I was a little behind and had to settle for a box lunch as the dining room had closed, but everyone else got to pig out on the generous breakfast menu.

We did not have the same luck at the next stop at Thornton Gap. We knew the restaurant there had shut down but there was still a store with snacks. It had a big "OPEN" sign but there was a handwritten note on the door saying it was closed Tuesdays and Thursdays! Hmmmph!!! Not even a soda machine. Even the drinking fountain was broken.

But everything evens out. The '03 Gang, trail alumni out for a reunion hike, showed up at the shelter that evening with two pizzas from a nearby town and gave one of them to the rest of us. Andrew is here to, as well as the group I have been keeping pace with. He had said he would take a zero day in Waynesboro so I was surprised to see him. The bugs are bad here, so I am hiding in my tent.

It gets a little thin at the ends but I guess it is true that in the middle part of the Smokys you can eat your way through. More than half my meals lately have been at stores and restaurants. That is just as well, for it let me conserve my food supply. If the wayside store at Elkwallow is closed like the one at Thornton was, I have enough food to last until I am out of the park.

A few days ago the Trail was badly overgrown and had a fair amount of poison Ivy. I tried to avoid it but apparently not well enough. I am getting little patches of rash here and there on both my arms and my legs. Now I have some nice bug bites to go with them. I have not gotten nearly as many chigger bites as further south but the ivy makes up for it and I am as itchy as ever. For now, all I can do is try not to scratch and bear it as best I can.

-Mouse

Thursday, June 10, 2004
Destination: Gravel Springs Hut
From: Pass Mountain Hut
Today's Miles: 13.1
Trip Miles: 941.3

Today is relax day. Only 13.5 miles to the hut instead of 20 or so.

The path was smooth enough that I arrived at Elkwallow Wayside at 10:30. Most of the hikers at last night's hut had passed me and were already at the picnic tables outside, eating away and relaxing. It was not lunchtime yet, so I ordered two breakfast egg muffins and a blackberry shake and joined them. It was nice to be able to linger over lunch and relax instead of hurrying onward.

Someone at the campground said her husband had been harassed by a problem bear right near Elkwallow. It had not gone away until the man charged it! Fortunately today I saw no sign of it. I really don't want to have to play chicken with a bear!

I got to the hut at 2:00 p.m., so like everyone else I could sit around the rest of the day doing nothing. That may sound a bit decadent. But downtime is incredibly important. It gives a chance for all the hurts and strains to heal, leaving the body ready for more the next day. What really causes problems with high mileage days is that it takes so long that the body has no time to recover. Day after day of that invites an injury. I have heard of hiker after hiker, some of whom really ought to know better, go flying up the Trail only to have to leave the Trail with shin splints or some other injury. The trick is to keep pushing north, but not too hard.

It turned out to be an eventful night. Register entries warned of a raccoon that could climb the bear poles. I was having trouble sleeping because the Ridgerest foam pad I bought felt nearly as uncomfortable as the hard floor. About 10:30 p.m. I heard what sounded like a chain rattling and claws popping through food bags. "Has anyone got a strong flashlight?" I asked out loud. Fire Marshall groggily listened to my explanation and skeptically shined his headlamp towards the bear pole. We could see two big green eyes reflecting brightly from the top of the pole. Grabbing a trekking pole and the headlamp, I ran to the pole and chased off the raccoon. Almost immediately we heard the same tell-tale jingle of a chain from the pole placed at the tentsites. By then others had gotten up and like a posse in the movies we rushed over and chased it off.

Someone whimsically suggested Vaseline on the bear pole to make it too slippery to climb. I offered up my half tube of Neosporin ointment. Someone else had a tube as well, and we slathered three feet of the bear pole and the pole used to put food bags up, then wound the chain up out of reach. We went back to bed, but first I dug out my tiny photon flashlight and put it in easy reach.

About 11:30 I heard the chain at the far pole rattling. There was only one bag there but it seemed unfair to leave it to the raccoon. I grabbed pole and light and went to chase it away. I found the heavy bag perched atop the crosspieces. The raccoon had hoisted it up to work on getting into it. I prodded it down, unhooked it from the pole and took it to the shelter where I hung it for the rest of the night.

At midnight the raccoon was back, this time right into the shelter and up on the picnic table to try to grab the rescued bag. By now we were all jumping at the slightest sound. Shortly later Fire Marshall shined his light at the table and instead of the raccoon we found a little mouse! Terrified by the light and commotion, it ran frantically back and forth, behind and over the water bottles on the table looking for a way to hide or escape. It had us all laughing by the time it jumped to the ground and skittered for safety.

"I hate this shelter" commented Gaiter Woman.

"I hate camping!" someone added facetiously in a pretend whiny-child voice.

But the excitement was still not over. At 4:30 the raccoon came again. Then Fire Marshall heard another noise and found a mouse in Gaiter Woman's pack. He poked and prodded trying to get it to leave before giving up and just leaving the zipper open for it to find its own way out.

Bleary-eyed from lost sleep and heartily tired of the wildlife at this hut, we all were glad to hike away as soon as possible in the morning.

-Mouse

Friday, June 11, 2004
Destination: Terrapin Hostel
From: Gravel Spring Hut
Today's Miles: 9.6
Trip Miles: 950.9

Today was a short 10 miles to the Terrapin Hostel run by 1995 Thru-hiker Mike "The Grateful Greenpeace Guy" Evans. I thought about going further but there was simply no place further on that did not mean a string of twenty mile plus days and I had had enough of that.

Being run by a thruhiker meant it had everything, from soft beds with real sheets and pillows with pillowcases to the bins of assorted sized clothes to borrow after showering to let you wash ALL of your clothes instead of having to keep out something to wear.

Mike drove us into Front Royal for shopping, food and even a movie! I got a full length 3-season lightweight Thermarest to replace the Ridgerest that had worked out so poorly. After supper we all went and saw "Harry Potter and the Prisoner of Azkaban." I had been worried I would not be able to see it before it left the theaters, so that was a special treat.

-Mouse

Saturday, June 12, 2004
Destination: Manassas Gap Shelter
From: Terrapin Hostel
Today's Miles: 14.5
Trip Miles: 965.4

    I was one of the first ones up but my hopes for an early start were dashed by a health problem. I had serious constipation, one of the hazards thruhikers face from eating a trail diet low in roughage and eating unaccustomed foods when in town. Before all was resolved I think I burst a hemorrhoid. For a while the amount of bleeding was alarming and I feared I would have to go see a doctor. Fortunately it tapered off and I decided to go on. Because of the delay I did not get on the Trail until after 10:00 am. I had not lost TOO much blood but I still felt weak and shaky from the ordeal and was very worried about an infection developing.

    After leaving the park boundary the trail got rougher just as it had been at the south end. Along the way I picked all the dandelion greens I could find in hopes the roughage would help get my digestive system back in order. It was 3:00 p.m. when I got to the Jim and Molly Denton Shelter. I felt drained and it is one of the fanciest on the Trail so I was tempted to stop early. But that would mean either another short day tomorrow and getting to Harpers Ferry a day late or a twenty mile day. So more from lack of options rather than energy, I headed on to my original destination, Manassas Gap Shelter.

    I was just as glad I did! I found the first ripe raspberries of my hike. Then at Manassas Gap I found two big coolers full of Trail Magic from Aloha Ann herself. The log showed The Walking Stomach had passed through today. I had not seen her since Damascus!

    At the shelter the only one there was Rex, a woman who had decided she would end her hike at Harpers Ferry. She told me The Walking Stomach, Little Tree, Aloha Ann, and several of their friends had been through only an hour earlier, slackpacking. I had just missed them! Maybe I will catch up soon.

    -Mouse

Sunday, June 13, 2004
Destination: Hwy. 605
From: Manassas Gap Shelter
Today's Miles: 17.1
Trip Miles: 982.5

The start of today was less than promising as it started raining at 6:30 but it turned out very well.

I got away at 7:30. By then the rain had stopped but it was still cold and wet. I hiked the 5 miles to Dick's Dome Shelter where I stopped for early lunch. While I was there, who should appear but Little Tree! Before leaving, she said The Walking Stomach probably had skipped the shelter but was not far ahead.

I quickly finished purifying a refill of water and gathered my things. Then I flew up the path as fast as my legs could carry me. I had not seen Little Tree and The Walking Stomach since Damascus.

It took me more than a mile to catch up. They were slack-packing with Stomach's friend Ann and Aloha Ann, who had hiked the Trail in 2001 and 2003. I had read her journal but had never met her.

They invited me to join them and we hiked together to Hwy 605, two miles past Rod Hollow Shelter where I had planned on spending the night. It was a nice opportunity to get caught up. Aloha Ann and I got a chance to talk and get acquainted. I liked the advice she had and it was nice to hear her say she thought I had what it took to get to Maine. Between that and meeting old friends my aches pains and doubts seemed to evaporate. Even the weather cooperated by turned sunny but cool.

For weeks now my right fingers have stiffened up whenever they are not moved for any length of time and become painful to move. It has gotten steadily worse, especially at night. At first I feared arthritis was setting in, until my left hand began to be affected as well. That made arthritis seem less likely. I discussed it with Aloha Ann and she thinks it is from clutching my trekking poles all day. She suggested I try using the wrist straps to take the load so I do not need to grip the poles so hard. I hope she is right. The pain has been wearing me down.

We were met at the road by Aloha Ann's friend Shar, who drove us to Ann's car. Then Stomach, Ann, Little Tree and I had supper and drove to an AYH Hostel in Maryland for the night.

So I got to see old friends, meet new ones, find a better supper than cold ramen and tuna and then had a warm comfy bed for the night. What could be better? The chance to stay at a hostel for several days is particularly opportune after the health problems I had at the Terrapin Hostel. Cleanliness is my best hope to avoid an infection.

-Mouse

Monday, June 14, 2004
Destination: Snickers Gap
From: Hwy. 605
Today's Miles: 6.8
Trip Miles: 989.3

Today I joined The Walking Stomach, Little Tree and Ann for a day of slackpacking. So I left the heavier things behind and just took water, snacks and map in my pack.

It was a long drive to the trail so we did not get to hiking until 10:30. Already the weather was hot and humid, making for slow hiking. So we ended up going just 7 Miles to Snickers Gap.

We have entered the area the Brood X cicadas are in. The forest hummed with them, sounding like an invasion of flying saucers. The ground was littered with cicadas both living and dead. It is a pretty unusual sight, one that will not recur like this for another 17 years.

The infamous Roller Coaster does not seem very hard. It is a section where the Trail is off the crest of the ridge so it goes up and over 10 side ridges in 13 miles. The humidity slowed us down a lot more. It may intimidate day hikers but there are much worse sections of trail than the roller coaster. I actually liked how there was a stream crossing every mile or so. That meant lots of water whereas the ridge top is often dry for miles at a time.

Once we got to the road, we called the hostel and hostel keeper Ray picked us up and drove us back to Ann's car. Stopping at the Dollar Store for supplies I finally got around to buying iron supplement tablets. It was nice to discover that those huge heavy-looking bottles that had intimidated me for weeks were really filled mostly with cotton, with just a thin layer of pills on the bottom. We rounded up the day with a nice spaghetti dinner at the hostel.

Slack-packing gives less time to hike because of all the shuttling but it does give my feet a break by reducing the load on them. The lighter load also let me use just one trekking pole. That should give my right hand a break. I need to be careful because there are a lot more miles to go before the end of the Trail.

-Mouse

Tuesday, June 15, 2004
Destination: Keys Gap
From: Snickers Gap
Today's Miles: 13.5
Trip Miles: 1002.8

Today the four of us got an earlier start and were hiking before 7:00.

It was hot and humid again but it was a good section of trail. First, we finished off the Roller Coaster. Then, joy of joys, WE FINALLY CROSSED THE BORDER OUT OF VIRGINIA! 535 miles in one state is a LONG time. I heard a yell up ahead and found The Walking Stomach and Ann standing by the border sign with big smiles on their faces. Of course we had to take lots of pictures.

The next event was coming to a stone on the footpath on which was written "1,000 miles. Congratulations!" I have now hiked 1,000 miles since Springer Mountain. That meant lots of hugs and picture taking in honor of the occasion. Just for fun I bent down and kissed the stone for good measure. Stomach and Little Tree still need to finish 19 miles of Shenandoah Park before they reach 1,000 miles and finish Virginia but that won't take long.

On the drive back to the hostel we looked at the huge billowing cumulus clouds with awe and felt thankful they were heading away from us. But when we stopped at a Wal-Mart for food another cloud was bearing down on us and the sky was darkening ominously. The storm broke as we were about to leave the store. We sat on a bench just inside the door and waited. And waited. The storm lasted quite a while and got very severe. We watched with fascination as a woman opened her umbrella, went out the door and made for her car. She had trouble hanging onto the umbrella, then it blew inside out and nearly took her away like the nanny applicants in the movie "Mary Poppins." Finally she got into the car but had to wrestle with the umbrella for nearly a minute before she managed to get it inside and close the door. The wind was so strong we could see spray streaming over the roof past the rear window like the smoke trails in a wind tunnel or as if the car were on a freeway in the rain.

I was glad I had decided not to try to hike all the way back to the hostel today because if I had I would be out in the storm. Soon fire engines were going everywhere. Again and again the rain seemed to slacken and one of us started to get to the car only to have it come down with renewed force before she could get to the door. When we finally got away the traffic on the road to the hostel was stopped to let rescue workers deal with an overturned car. Right near the hostel a blowdown tree blocked half the road and fallen branches were everywhere.

Little Tree had tented last night and left her tent up while we were hiking. By some miracle the tent was still up and her sleeping bag inside was dry, much to her relief. I suspect there will be a lot more fallen trees across the Trail tomorrow.

-Mouse

Wednesday, June 16, 2004
Destination: Harpers Ferry Hostel
From: Keys Gap
Today's Miles: 9.4
Trip Miles: 1012.2

We got up extra early because Ray had another shuttle to the Amtrak station he was combining with our trip.

Little Tree made us all yummy tomato and cheese sandwiches to carry for lunch (except for The Walking Stomach, who does not like cheese) and scrambled eggs with toast for breakfast. Then at 6:30 a.m. we got into the van. After dropping the other hiker off, Ray took us to Keys Gap and we were hiking by 7:30.

The air was very damp from the previous days' storm and much of the trail looked like a model river. It had rapids, sandbars, meanders with an oxbow lake or two. It even had a floodplain with evidence of a recent flood!

After trying to avoid the wet spots for a while, Little Tree quipped "Become One with the water!" and started wading right through, disappearing ahead of us.

I had a bit more success at keeping my feet dry. Not for the first time, I was thankful the Gore-Tex lining and leather uppers in my new boots did their job of keeping the water out. I had fretted over the extra weight when I bought them, but it has paid off.

Picking my way through the puddles I suddenly found myself confronted by a wall of branches instead of Trail. Two trees had come down, not merely across but along the Trail obliterating it with their foliage. I picked my way around them through the poison ivy. Shortly after I came to an even larger blowdown. This one was a big mature tree with a tall 18 inch trunk and huge limbs laying along the trail. Clearing it was sure to be a job. The Walking Stomach and Ann were both maintainers up in Connecticut so I waited for them to hear their reaction. "Now aren't you glad you didn't try to do 20 miles yesterday and were at Wal-Mart when this came down?" asked Stomach. No kidding!

We found Little Tree waiting for us at the end of the ridge and descended down to the bridge across the Shenandoah. Along the way the trail went past a waterfall raging from the recent rain. Then we crossed the bridge into Harpers Ferry.

At AT Headquarters we signed the log and posed for the traditional pictures for the hiker album. I am northbound thruhiker #328 to pass through this year.

Next was the post office for my bounce box and a mail drop of anti-seizure medication for the second half of my hike. I was glad to see that! I would have had to find a doctor willing to write me a prescription had it been lost. While there I ran into Fire Marshall who arrived yesterday and Stretch who arrived a little after we did.

Little Tree had already left for the hostel when I met the other two at ATC Headquarters. We stopped at Jefferson Rock for lunch then descended into the lower town past the Engine House to the bridge to Maryland. Another state finished!

There was a pigeon sitting right on the railroad track. We guessed it must feel the vibration of approaching trains because it seemed quite unconcerned about perching on the rails. On the C&O towpath across the Potomac there were dozens and dozens of downed trees from the storm. It looked almost like a tornado had been through. Fortunately the park service had done an incredible job of clearing away the debris in record time, but the trail clearly had been completely blocked with fallen logs. Again Stomach asked "Now aren't you REALLY glad you were at Wal-Mart and not hiking?" I was awed at the evidence of the storm's fearsome power and was indeed glad to have missed it.

Back at the hostel we relaxed before fixing a nice dinner of steamed broccoli, zucchini and carrots, lentils and rice followed by cookies and Ben & Jerry's ice cream.

Ann solved a mystery that had puzzled me for months. Remember that eerie thumping sound I heard in the mountains during the first month or so? It turns out it was GROUSE! It is almost unbelievable something as small as a bird can make such a deep penetrating sound. But it is the mating call of male grouse, produced by drumming on a log. Amazing!

Tomorrow I am on my own again, with my full pack when the others go back to finish the last part of Shenandoah Park. It has been a nice time hiking with Little Tree, Ann and The Walking Stomach. I hope we run into each other later on the Trail.

-Mouse

Thursday, June 17, 2004
Destination: Dahlgren Backpack Campground
From: Harpers Ferry Hostel
Today's Miles: 14.3
Trip Miles: 1026.5

I got up in time to bid my friends farewell at 5:45 a.m. before they drove down to finish 19 miles in Shenandoah Park. We had hugs all around and I could not help feeling a little teary. They will not head north until after the weekend and since they will be going slow to spare Stomach's feet I may not see them again on the hike. The Walking Stomach and Little Tree and Ann have been great company and we had a wonderful time hiking the past few days. I will miss them.

I stayed around for the AYCE breakfast before leaving at 8:30. I made good time, stopping at the Edward Garvey Shelter and Gathland State Park to eat. The park is the site both of part of the Battle of South Mountain and of a monument to war correspondents.

About 1:30 the sky clouded over and thunder began rumbling. Most seemed behind me so I guessed that if I hurried I could avoid the worst of the storm. Then a lightning bolt struck some ways in front of me. "No Fair!" Still there was little I could do but hurry along, mindful of the recent severe storm. Suddenly there was a bright flash ahead followed almost immediately by a loud thunderclap. YOW! That one got a yelp out of me and sent me scrambling for cover. Yup, I was frightened! It had to be within a quarter mile of me. From next to a log I gathered my wits. It was not going to protect me from lightning and I really could not predict where the next bolt would hit. I decided to get up and keep moving. The sun broke through and there seemed a lull. That sent me scurrying even faster, as there was a cluster of three towers ahead and I wanted past them before any more lightning showed up. By then I was drenched but I had been too busy with the lightning to pay attention to that.

Fortunately another thundershower did not follow and I and the Trail slowly dried out on the way to Dahlgren Backpack Campground. This is a neat spot with about six tentsites and hot showers and flush toilets. All for free! Even better, just .2 miles away was the Old South Mountain Inn restaurant.

I signed the register and took a quick shower and changed into my clean long pants and top. Then I headed to the Inn for supper, taking my pack for safe-keeping.

While waiting for the Inn to open for dinner I read the signs scattered about detailing the Battle of South Mountain. One in particular got a laugh out of me:

A resident of Frederick described the Confederate soldiers as follows "I have never seen a mass of such filthy strong-smelling men. Three in a room would make it unbearable, and when marching in column along the street the smell from them was most offensive... The filth that pervades them is most remarkable... They have no uniforms, but are all well armed and equipped, and have become so inured to hardships that they care little for any of the comforts of civilization... They are the roughest looking set of creatures I ever saw, their features, hair and clothing matted with dirt and filth, and the scratching they kept up gave warrant of vermin in abundance." Another observer described the Confederates simply as "a lean and hungry set of wolves."

Skip the part about being armed and substitute mosquitoes and poison ivy for vermin and it makes a remarkably accurate description of AT thruhikers!

The Inn goes back to colonial times and was a favorite haunt of Henry Clay and Daniel Webster. I had a nice prime rib dinner and a slice of berry and rhubarb pie for desert. It was fun to have such a nice restaurant in the middle of nowhere right next to the Trail!

While there I ran into Stretch. He and I ended up having the campground to ourselves. It was just a bit creepy because there were shattered trees about and every now and then a big limb would come crashing down in the woods. Fortunately the tentpads were in a large clearing safely clear of the falling lumber.

-Mouse

Friday, June 18, 2004
Destination: Cowall Shelter
From: Dahlgren Backpack Campground
Today's Miles: 13.9
Trip Miles: 1040.4

I met Fire Marshall and Palm Tree as I reached Dahlgren Chapel. They had stayed at the shelter a few miles back. I could not resist telling them about the nice dinner they missed.

Next stop was the Washington Monument. I spent about 20 minutes looking for the phone before a ranger let me know it had been moved from where the map shows to near the museum. The monument itself was up a hill and consists of a stone tower shaped rather like a giant milk bottle. Did George like milk? Wait, milk bottles did not exist in 1827, so it must be a coincidence. Anyway, it was made that year by the citizens of the nearby town of Boonsboro. You can climb spiral steps inside to a viewing platform at the top with a view of the valley to the west.

Much of the trail here looks like a country lane, a nice change from the often overgrown stretches I found in Northern Virginia. There seemed less poison ivy and undergrowth in general. Alas, the raspberries seem further away from ripening too. Will I ever come to those magical acres of berries past thruhikers write of gorging themselves upon? I hope so.

In compensation, some sections were packed with rocks and boulders. I would either step between them on the flat ground if there was any or pick my way carefully along on the top of the rocks using my poles to keep my balance. At Annapolis Rocks I stopped to rest and had around 20 girl scouts arrive. They were the first I had seen on the Trail and the largest group of any sort. One of their leaders asked my trailname and said she had done about 1,000 miles in 2000.

It was a humid day and even though only 80 degrees felt very muggy, especially in the sunlit patches. By the time I neared the shelter I was chafing in the usual places as well as some new ones, like my arm under the sleeve of my t-shirt, so I was more than ready to stop for the day.

My one concern was that the shelter was near a road and it was a weekend so locals might come to party. So I was expecting to be prepared to leave and camp on the trail. But a youth group with several adults showed up to tent as well as a thruhiker and a section hiker so it seemed populated enough to not worry.

White Stag, the section hiker, was a librarian from City University of New York. He had lots of information on the trail to the north. But I wonder, are two librarians in one shelter a little much? After all, most shelters don't even have a library!

-Mouse

Saturday, June 19, 2004
Destination: Deer Lick Shelters
From: Cowall Shelter
Today's Miles: 14.1
Trip Miles: 1054.5

The day started with three miles of relocated trail. An entry in the register complained about it being "all rocks and mud" but it seemed to have no more of either than most sections of trail. The two things I noticed most were that it looked like a footpath through the woods again instead of the wide country lane appearance I have seen so much of lately, and the soil has not had time to wash away so most of it was LESS rocky than usual.

The cicadas are still here but their eerie sound is more intermittent. Now it sounds like the fleet of alien spaceships are practicing parallel parking, constantly engaging and disengaging the engines instead of the constant hum that they had before.

I took a short side trail to High Rocks, a stone overlook of the Cumberland Valley with one of the highest sheer drops off the edge I have seen so far. Apparently it is even used as a launch point for hang-gliding. I could see traces of an old masonry foundation of some sort with large stone piers.

Then down a rock jumble. As is common with rock jumbles it was a bit of a scavenger hunt sorting out where the trail went through all the boulders. Fortunately it was long enough to be interesting but not too long. Scrambling over boulders mile after mile gets difficult. Though, if rumors of northern Pennsylvania are true, I had better get used to it!

Next came Pen Mar Park. In the 1870's an old time railroad amusement park was here, complete with rides and big fancy hotels. It closed in 1943 but in the 70's the site was restored as a public park. It has an overlook offering a splendid view of the valley with a pavilion that is apparently a popular site for weddings. A little museum has pictures and memorabilia from the park's past. There I learned the stone ruins at High Rocks were once the foundation of a three story observation tower.

I checked my email and found my friend Jane from DC wanted to come out and see me. Jane left her cell phone number but her phone must have been off. I called and sent emails for four hours trying to get hold of her but never succeeded. Finally I sent a last message that I had to move on but would be at Caledonia State Park tomorrow and got back on the Trail at 3:00 p.m.

I did not mind the delay though. A band of showers passed through and it was nice to be able to duck indoors. More importantly there was a reunion of soldiers from nearby Ft. Richie and one of them was a Trail maintainer and was offering food to thruhikers. All those times I had missed trail angels' free meals and now I stumbled right into one. Life DOES work out sometimes! I had two big sausages on buns and baked beans and root beer and a can of V-8 and he even talked me into taking an apple for the road. Mmmmmmmm!

Leaving the park I crossed the Mason-Dixon Line. Woohoo, another state! What is more, I have passed from the Appa-latch-in Trail to the Appuh-lay-shun Trail; from the South into Yankee territory. Having just moved to Philadelphia, I am even in my home state. Ahhh, Home sweet home. As if to welcome me, right across the state line were all those ripe raspberries I had been dreaming about. I picked and ate handful after handful and for a while my pace slowed to a crawl. Yummy!

Halfway to Deer Lick I caught up with Ponderer, an older man that I had met in the Shenandoah Park and last saw near Front Royal, and we hiked the rest of the way together.

Deer Lick is one of several spots in this area with two small adjacent shelters instead of one normal sized one. I'm not sure what the reasoning of that is, but it does add variety.

-Mouse

Sunday, June 20, 2004
Destination: Quarry Gap Shelter
From: Deer Lick Shelters
Today's Miles: 15.8
Trip Miles: 1070.3

I got going at 6:00 a.m. and by 7:00 was passing through tents full of sleepy boy scouts waking up near Antietam Shelter. I signed the register there and at Tumbling Run with a greeting for Little Tree and The Walking Stomach.

By then Ponderer had caught up with me and starting off together we hit a steep upgrade. Checking my map I found it was a ONE THOUSAND FOOT CLIMB! Hey, no Fair! Who said there were mountains in Pennsylvania? Oh yeah, I guess there is some mention. Sigh... I guess I have to go up it.

I stopped for a break and Ponderer was quickly long gone. It was a nice day for climbing mountains at least; cool and dry instead of the recent mugginess. The alien spaceships or cicadas were still humming away but a bit more sporadically than before.

At the unusually late hour of 9:00 a.m. I heard the bugle notes of "Reveille" from a PA system somewhere up ahead. Someone sure believed in starting the day late. Shortly later I came upon a road and near the Trail was a sign that said "VisionQuest" outside a fenced-in compound with people marching around in gray sweat suits. That was what I had heard. Hikers had mentioned it, a court-ordered program for juvenile offenders that is a cross between boot camp and Outward Bound.

I came across a doe acting strangely. It made an odd squeaking noise, took a few steps away, come back and repeated the process. It was the first time I had heard a deer make a sound, I thought they were silent. Then there was a thrashing in the undergrowth nearer to me and I saw a fawn scramble towards the doe. The mother deer had either been trying to get me away from the fawn or the fawn away from me. It was refreshing to see deer timid again instead of the fearlessness I had seen in Shenandoah. Just a bit later I saw a mother grouse pacing back and forth like a bull, glaring at me furiously and deciding whether to charge. I guess I was not close enough to be a threat because it stayed where it was.

Then whoever planned the Trail decided we needed some boulder hopping because it led up to the ridge top and through a long stretch of rocks. Finally I got across Hwy 30 to Caledonia Park.

I checked my email and found my friend Jane from the DC area planned to meet me at the park and would be awaiting a call from me. Digging out my calling card I dialed her cell phone only to get no answer. Oh No, Deja vu! I was just about to walk through the park when Jane came walking up.

United at last! I was sure glad to see her, she was the first non AT-hiking friend I had met in three months aside from the music festival. She had asked the rangers what phone I was most likely to go to from the Trail and went there to find me. It turned out her phone had no signal in the park and yesterday it had had a dead battery. All's well that ends well.

We went for lunch outside the park, then Jane loaded me with snacks and we returned to the Trail. We hiked together to Quarry Gap Shelter. There I showed Jane what the shelters are like and explained the register and so on. She could even bask in the aura of thruhikerdom since dayhikers assumed we were both thruhiking. Then I saw her down to the trail back to the park and we hugged each other farewell.

Back at the shelter I discovered the hiker who had been napping when we were there was none other than JoAnn, whom I had last seen at Fontana when we stayed at the Hike Inn and shared a shuttle into town for supper. We got caught up over tea and crumb-cakes. An older man, Wonder-Lost, was there and Ponderer arrived before dark.

It was an interesting shelter. It had two sleeping shelters side by side with a covered eating area in between. It was neatly kept and well painted and there was a park bench and even four hanging baskets of flowers! I thought it was a very nice touch. "Innkeeper," the caretaker, said once he had even put in solar powered accent lights to light the way to the privy, but the ATC had said they were not in keeping with the primitive nature of the Trail and made him take them away.

-Mouse

Monday, June 21, 2004
Destination: Pine Grove Furnace
From: Quarry Gap Shelter
Today's Miles: 17.4
Trip Miles: 1087.7

Last night was the coldest in weeks. I dug out my long pants and long sleeved top and still slept cold. But it made for good hiking today, as did long stretches of smooth level path covered with pine needles.

According to thruhiker tradition, Jun 21 is Hike Naked Day. Some go all out, the more timid celebrate it more privately on isolated stretches of trail or not at all.

But all that was forgotten when I saw a couple poking around the underbrush. They were picking BLUEBERRIES!!! I had finally come to Berry Heaven! Blueberries, blueberries, blueberries! The bushes closest to the ground were full of ripe berries and the higher bushes were packed with even more not yet ripe, promising berry feasts in the coming days. I was so busy picking and eating that my pace slowed to a crawl. It was a miracle I ever got to Pine Grove with all those berries to eat. Finally I had to remind myself that one reason the South lost the Battle of Gettysburg was that their solders had eaten themselves sick on berries as they marched into Pennsylvania. I had better not do the same and besides, I really ought to leave some for other famished thruhikers.

I was feeling buoyant at being nearly half finished. I was the happiest I have felt since I ran into those Easter Bunnies back in the Smokys! At one point near the end I took a suggestion Aloha Ann had that I try jogging short stretches to give my legs a break by using them differently. Only I jogged for more than a mile, rather excessive with a heavy pack after 15 miles of hiking!

Today is also the day I reached the halfway point on the Trail at Pine Grove Furnace State Park, the site of the remains of a colonial era blast furnace that remained in operation over a century. Now the ore pit where iron ore was mined is a lake with a beach. The mansion of the furnace owner is an AYH Hostel where I am spending the night. And the stable is now the park store and home of another thruhiker tradition, The Half-Gallon Challenge. Any hiker who can eat an entire half-gallon of ice cream is awarded a wooden ice-cream spoon that says "Member, Half Gallon Club."

I had resolved to be sensible and not try it, but by the time I arrived about 3:00 p.m. the temptation was almost irresistible. I wandered into the store, looked at the flavor choices and wandered back out again. How would I feel skipping a time-honored ritual? Would it really be worth the risk of serious indigestion or worse? But the hostel did not open for two hours, what a great way to use the time!

My mind resolved, I went in and bought a carton of vanilla. I had read that it was the easiest to get down because of its bland flavor. Two other thruhikers, Hobbs and Flipflop, watched solemnly as I got my trusty Lexan spoon from my pack, opened the carton, noted the time, and began.

I started around the edges, looking for the parts that had softened and were less cold, taking small bites to avoid a headache from freezing the roof of my mouth. I took my time, going around and around the carton and as I got further and the top surface softened scooping from there as well as the edges. The sides became diagonal as I ate away and then when I got to the bottom edge I worked in, so the block of ice cream got smaller and smaller. My two onlooker's eyes widened at how much was gone. By now my tummy was so chilled from ice cream I shivered. I got out my long sleeve top, put it on and kept eating. Soon there was just a small block left, and then I was finished! It had taken me 50 minutes.

I got to sign the special register reserved for those who dared the Challenge. Many previous hikers noted being queasy afterwards but aside from being cold I felt fine. No, I felt better than fine, I felt euphoric and laughed triumphantly! Hobbs and Flipflop kidded me about there being some mood-altering substance in the ice cream. I got a disposable camera and had Hobbes take a picture of me holding the empty carton and my trophy wooden spoon, grinning like a fiend.

Between the berries, reaching halfway and joining the Half-Gallon Club I went to bed on cloud nine. My Virginia Blues are evaporated!

-Mouse

Tuesday, June 22, 2004
Destination: Alec Kennedy Shelter
From: Pine Grove Shelter
Today's Miles: 15.5
Trip Miles: 1103.2

Hobbes generously made pancakes for all four who stayed at the hostel last night. They were enormous and filling, two were all I could eat.

On the way out of the park I stopped at the phone by the lake and found Gaiter Woman there. I had thought her well ahead of me but she had gotten sick. She was having a friend come pick her up so she can rest and get well. Hobbes arrived and the three of us chatted a bit. She asked if we have news of Slowpoke, who had gotten lost in the Nantahala wilderness. He was injured north of Erwin and Gaiter Woman had helped get him to the hospital and has not heard news of him since.

It started raining a bit as Hobbes and I headed up the Trail. He is a physician's assistant from Iowa. When we got to the Halfway Post we paused to take each other's picture. It has not been the real halfway point for several years because of route changes but the tradition endures anyway.

I stopped at the Green Mountain General Store for lunch, buying a sub and orange juice, plus a can of chili as a treat for tonight.

I keep saying the Trail is full of surprises. Today's surprise awaited me atop aptly named Rocky Ridge. It looked harmless enough on the map. But at the summit there was what looked like all the reject statues from Easter Island, or a castle crudely built by orcs. My feet were sore, but I still enjoyed following the white blazes as they led up, over, around and through the huge fantastically shaped masses of stone. Then they led into a rock alleyway ending in a vertical face reaching up as high as my chin. I couldn't manage to climb that high onto the shelf.

Weeeeee!!! Trail Riddles! I studied the problem, then backed up and started climbing the moist slippery moss-covered rock forming the left wall of the alley, intending to bypass the shelf. But it turned into a narrow tongue in between the drop into the alley and an alarmingly deep chasm between two massive stones. I backed up and tried again. The other side had an inviting stair-shaped crack up to a ledge that led to the shelf. But the ledge was on an overhanging rock face, so I would probably fall right off. Finally I took off my pack, hefted it up to the shelf, then scrambled up using what I could remember of rock climbing chimneying techniques I'd read of. The stony labyrinth went on for hundreds of yards. Later Hobbes told me he had felt like a mouse in a laboratory maze. Finally it relented into foot-friendly leaf-mold-covered smooth trail.

Not long after that the sky darkened so much it was hard to make out the blazes in the forest gloom. The wind started gusting and thunder rumbled ominously. Not wanting to get caught high up in the rocks in a thunderstorm, I started down the path as fast as I could go. The first dark cloud passed and an eerie light came through the trees. It began raining hard, but all I cared about was making it to the shelter or at least off the high ground before getting overtaken by lightning or tree-downing winds. It MIGHT not get that bad, but the severe storm at Harpers Ferry was too fresh in my mind for me to feel complacent. A fresh rumbling of thunder behind me emphasized the need to hurry.

It is funny how adrenaline works. Not long before, I had been thinking how sore my feet felt and whether I should take a rest day soon. Now I was trotting down the trail like an antelope, the pain in my feet forgotten.

As if to mock me, just after I reached the shelter, the sun came out.

-Mouse

Wednesday, June 23, 2004
Destination: Hwy.11
From: Alec Kennedy Shelter
Today's Miles: 11.9
Trip Miles: 1115.1

This morning dawned rainy and it was 7 before I got going. I broke out of the woods just as the sky cleared and found: Raspberries! Lots of them as the Trail led along the edge of a field before cutting across it towards the town of Boiling Springs.

Just before the town I found something new, what look like raspberries only longer and growing overhead in the thornless branches of a tree instead of on low thorny shrubs. I guessed, correctly it turned out, that they were mulberries. They taste sweet and watery, even more refreshing than the tart raspberries.

In the town I got a snack and bought some food to mail to myself at Port Clinton as trail guides said it was hard to buy food there. Then I went to the post office to get my bounce box. At the ATC regional headquarters I sat on the porch to go through it. I got what I needed from it and readdressed it to Delaware Water Gap. There are so many hikers sprawled about opening their mail drops that it looked like Christmas! Then back to the post office to mail off the bounce box and food shipment.

Leaving town, the Trail led down a long lane shaded by mulberry trees! I couldn't begin to make a dent in the feast of ripe berries overhead. At intervals the rest of the day there are more ripe raspberries. I practically ate my way along the trail, though I took care to leave lots for those behind me. The Cumberland Valley may be short on safe water, but it is berry heaven!

I decided to stop for the day at Highway 11 and spend the night at a nearby motel. There was a nice diner next door so I could eat up and rest.

Tomorrow I have about 18 miles to Duncannon.

-Mouse

Thursday, June 24, 2004
Destination: Duncannon
From: Hwy.11
Today's Miles: 17.7
Trip Miles: 1132.8

I asked for a 4:30am wakeup call to get an early start and was hiking by 5:30. The morning was a bit foggy but clear and by 9am it was downright warm and muggy.

There were not as many berries at the north end of the valley. Almost as if the Trail were preparing us to leave paradise and return to the rigors of the mountains. There were lots of mosquitoes and for the first time merely hiking at a good pace was not enough to keep them at bay. My hand was getting as red from squashing bloated mosquitoes as it had been the day before from picking berries! Finally I had to resort to insect repellant.

The climb over Blue Mountain and up Cove Mountain was not too hard but making my way through the rocks along the top of Cove Mountain seemed to take forever in the afternoon heat.

Finally I descended and got into Duncannon about 3. With a bit of trepidation from stories of its condition, I checked into the Doyle Hotel, Duncannon's famed hiker Mecca. Contrary to what I had heard, the mattress in my room was new and the sheets clean. The only downside was that my room was hot and there was no AC but what do you expect from a century old hotel?

The grocery provided a shuttle van from the hotel so that hikers could avoid walking on a dangerous section of road. In the van I ran into Socks, whom I had not seen in some time. JoAnn was also there, preparing to jump ahead past the rocky section to New York. She had made it clear back when she started that she was hiking ALONG the AT, not HIKING the AT. She is in her 70s so at her age it makes sense to skip the worst spots.

I had supper at a nearby pub: a thick slab of ham glazed with pineapple and a large sweet baked yam. Yum! I was stuffed when I went back to rest until bedtime.

-Mouse

Friday, June 25, 2004
Destination: Peters Mountain Shelter
From: Duncannon
Today's Miles: 11.3
Trip Miles: 1144.1

For breakfast I had two honey buns and orange juice I bought the day before. That turned out to be fortunate, for breakfast at the Doyle apparently is a slow ritual. I was away by 7 and most hikers were lucky to get away by 8:30.

I walked through the sleeping town and across the big bridge over the Susquehanna River, the next of the really big long rivers the AT crosses.

I had worried about the steep climb up Peters Mountain on the other side with me loaded down by five days of food. I needn't have worried, as the trail up was very well graded. On the other hand, once up, there WAS the way the AT went through the huge upended slabs of bedrock along the crest. Still, clambering along them was sort of fun and not as hard on the feet as walking on a rock-strewn path like yesterday. Lowering myself down a complicated series of ledges I came face to face with: RASPBERRIES! Nice big lusciously sweet ones and more than I could pick. For the rest of the day more appeared at least every ten or fifteen minutes.

I discovered a new tactic to gain a, er, moment of privacy when there are male hikers coming up behind. Just leaving several clumps of berries unpicked worked like a charm to slow them down.

The shelter is a veritable mansion complete with a balconied loft. Just as well, for an amazing number of hikers have shown up. I guess everyone decided to leave Duncannon on the same day. Then a family group of nearly twenty out for the weekend showed up and had to settle for their tents and the still existing old small shelter.

On the other hand the path to the water source reminds me of the spiral staircase leading to the underground pool deep beneath Jerusalem. I counted over 300 stone steps before I finally reached the spring!

Equally bad, there is a nice composting privy that was so badly neglected that it was heaped nearly to the level of the seat. Bleah! That sort of neglect seems inexcusable, especially with a composting privy that requires regular looking-after to function properly. If you never remove the compost, it may as well be just a regular privy.

-Mouse

Saturday, June 26, 2004
Destination: Rausch Gap Shelter
From: Peters Mountain Shelter
Today's Miles: 17.5
Trip Miles: 1161.6

I got hiking at 5:30 because of the long distance to the next shelter. It was hard to tell if the water coming down was rain or if it just getting shaken out of the foliage by the wind. The fog did not relent until after noon.

I still found raspberries but not as many as yesterday. Then the Trail cut across the valley to the next ridge to the south, called Second Mountain. That meant a thousand foot climb, but again the trail was well graded so it was not too difficult.

This ridge had no raspberries or poison ivy. Instead it had mostly laurel and some rhododendrons that were actually in bloom. I had not seen them blooming since southern Virginia.

Later I discovered more blueberries among the laurel. They were sparse so took a bit of looking. I found myself faced with a dilemma. If I walked slowly looking for berries everyone else who had stayed at the shelter last night would pass me and the next shelter was much smaller. So I could have berries or a spot in the shelter but probably not both. Oh the hard painful decisions we thruhikers have to make!

I opted for the shelter. I passed a section hiking couple on the approach trail then found Hobbes standing up ahead. "Come see the shelter mascot" he called and pointed down the bank. It was a really big rattlesnake! I had never seen one on the Trail before, only nonpoisonous black snakes. With a trailname like Mouse I knew I should watch my step; rattlesnakes like mice.

With Hobbes, Chill Out and Chasqui, the sectioning couple and I filled up the shelter. When Socks came a few minutes later she had to go set up her tarp.

The shelter was very interesting. The approach trail looked like an old road bed and there was an elaborate retaining wall with stairs leading down to the shelter. The retaining wall formed two sides of the shelter and the third was a four foot thick stone wall. Everything was so elaborate and massive I was left wondering if it had originally been built for a different building, like an inn. When I see the guidebook for this section I need to remember to look it up.

-Mouse

Sunday, June 27, 2004
Destination: 501 Shelter
From: Rausch Gap Shelter
Today's Miles: 17.4
Trip Miles: 1179.0

    Socks and I hiked most of the day together. For the first couple of hours we could hear the sputter of small arms fire from the busy ranges of Indiantown Gap Military Reservation.

    Just past I-81 we and Hobbes saw a first. A big orange sign that said "Appalachian Trail. Detour." Of course that called for some photos.

    Then came the steep rocky climb up Blue Mountain. The trail got rockier and then abandoned switchbacks and went straight up the slope.

    "This had better be worth it." I grumbled. "There had better be berries at the top!" There were. At the top we found a bush with three raspberries for each of us. I had to admit that that was as much as I asked for, berries, plural.

    "I should have specified the quantity" I commented ruefully.

    "Like a quart each" Socks replied.

    We came around a corner and were faced with bushes and bushes of raspberries, the big sweet juicy ones. We ate and ate until Socks said in a slightly berry-muffled voice "That will do me for another quarter mile." A moment later she found some more and added "As soon as I strip this bush."

    A bit later Socks made an even better discovery, a ripe mulberry tree! I pulled a branchful down into reach and happily picked several dozen. Finally the berries thinned and were guarded by thick lush beds of poison ivy. Then both were replaced by ferns that quickly became waist high.

    "This is like Jurassic Park" Socks observed.

    "Look out for Velociraptor."

    "Hopefully he is off eating raspberries and we can make our escape."

    Then we hit one of those evil spots where the trail led over an immense pile of slabs of rock. We had to pick our way carefully through them. Here and there a slab would tip alarmingly when stepped on and once we nearly lost the trail when it cut off to one side.

    Then the trail became easier for several miles but with no berries. Socks went on ahead when I stopped at a spring four miles from the shelter for water. After that the berries started up again.

The last mile was the worst. It was another of those spots where a fiendish trail planner had decided that the only way we could appreciate a giant pile of rocks was by clambering over them. Then the trail was well-strewn with rocks all the way to the shelter.

501 Shelter is one of those memorable ones. Named for the highway it is near, it is a former pottery studio. It has four walls, doors, and a huge octagonal skylight in the middle where the potter's wheel used to be. It also has running water, a solar shower, and you can order pizza via cell phone.

One hiker had been given a ride to the store by a Mennonite family and brought ice cream. The family had a relative who had thruhiked so they all came back to the shelter from the road to see what the inside looked like. We assured them that most shelters are a lot simpler than this one.

We quickly organized a feast. Well more like three feasts as new arrivals added more pizza to the menu. Yum!

-Mouse

Monday, June 28, 2004
Destination: Eagles Nest Shelter
From: 501 Shelter
Today's Miles: 15.1
Trip Miles: 1194.1

The underbrush on these ridges seems to be one of three types: poison ivy with raspberries, ferns, or laurel with blueberries.

Today was entirely a laurel and blueberry day, which is just as well, since the rash situation was starting to get a bit out of hand. A friend sent a treatment she has used for years but I beat it to Boiling Springs and had to have it forwarded to Delaware Water Gap. Until I get there it is just as well to minimize the exposure.

The pickings were more abundant than ever. They were scattered here and there, sometimes a few berries, sometimes handfuls. To be sure other famished hikers got a share I started picking only on the left side of the Trail and leaving at least half of what I found. Even so, I got a handful every fifteen or twenty minutes. Mmmmmmmmmmmmm.

The weather was perfect for hiking, cloudy and cool. At the nine mile mark there was even Trail Magic: two beers and a bag of oranges. I skipped the beer but took a big sweet juicy orange to go with my lunch. There was a road crew there with a jackhammer so I had to go up the Trail a bit to find a quiet spot to eat.

To bad they were not there to break up all the rocks on the Trail. There was more than one doozy of a boulder pile to negotiate as well as stretches of rock-clogged trail.

About a mile from the shelter it began to threaten rain so I sped up and got there before the rain started coming down. To my surprise, the shelter was deserted. I guess everyone before me decided to try to make the 20 plus miles to Port Clinton.

-Mouse

Tuesday, June 29, 2004
Destination: Port Clinton
From: Eagles Nest Shelter
Today's Miles: 9.3
Trip Miles: 1203.4

A thunderstorm rolled through at 11pm and the rain continued most of the night. Socks and I slept in a bit to let things dry out.

There were still a few blueberries and miles of rocky trail. Eventually the laurel, blueberry, poison ivy, raspberry and ferns were intermingled chaotically and ripe berries became scarce.

We made the steep descent into the Schuylkill water gap into a railroad yard with quaint old coal company signs and huge boulders of coal on display, past a memorial to war dead, over the river into Port Clinton.

We tried the bed and breakfast and found it locked shut. The little Port Clinton Hotel had no space, and the outfitter was not very helpful. I did find the clerk at the post office friendly and helpful, but we were a bit discouraged by the town in general.

Frustrated, we went down the Trail to Rt-61 and walked about two miles to a Microtel where we booked a double room for the night. On the way along the river we found our very first ripe blackberries!

Socks did laundry and took a nap while I went to the Cebalas sporting goods superstore across the street. I did find a new hat, a light blue one. Hopefully I won't loose it soon. But I did not find a new bite valve for my Platypus or even Aqua Mira water purifier. Aside from the sort of things one finds at K-Mart, the stock of camping and hiking supplies was very spotty.

We had a big dinner at a Cracker Box restaurant to round out the day. Mmmmmm, comfort food!

-Mouse

Wednesday, June 30, 2004
Destination: Eckville Shelter
From: Port Clinton
Today's Miles: 14.5
Trip Miles: 1217.9

I left before 6, skipping the motel's free continental buffet to beat the heat with an early start.

I had not heard a cicada since leaving Duncannon but this morning there they were, humming away. The berries are more scarce and I only found one or two every hour, but that was enough to continue the berry feast that has lasted my entire trip through Pennsylvania. The low shrub blueberries are nearly finished but were still the most common. The taller blueberry bushes are crowded with still-green fruit, promising feasts in the future. I found only a few raspberries but the blackberries were ripening. I even found one teaberry, which Socks had taught me about and I have been seeking out for two days.

At Windsor Shelter the register had a mixed set of reports from Port Clinton of no lodging or high prices, poor service at the hotel and outfitter and even the post office but also of very helpful Trail Angels. I guess my advice about Port Clinton is send yourself a mail drop of all the food you need as well as some goodies like canned meat to eat before departing, and be ready to fend for yourself. There may be room at the hotel and there may not. The best options seem to be camp at the pavilion, go down the road to the Microtel, or just keep going to the next shelter.

I am doing better than expected food wise. Socks got two mail drops of food in Port Clinton instead of one, leaving her with more than she could carry so she gave me some of the excess.

Near the Pinnacle overlook I met a section hiker who turned out to be a retired firefighter from Philadelphia who had once fought a fire in the apartment building I live in. Talk about a small world!

Eckville Shelter is actually a shed in a back yard of a house. It has four walls and a door, bunks for six, a solar shower and even a flush toilet. Snacks are available, paid for on the honor system. That makes it about as nice as a shelter can get! We learned from the caretaker that both it and the 501 Shelter were bought with their houses by the Trail Club and the houses rented to caretakers. By doing that, they created shelters just outside State Game Preserve land, avoiding regulations regarding shelters there.

I arrived at 2:30 and Socks made it at 3:30. She has been hiking with two older men, so yesterday I playfully dubbed them Snow White and the Seven Dwarves. There was no sign at first of the "Dwarves" at first. Then a hiker arrived who saw them at Windsor Furnace at noon, nine miles away. They finally showed up at 6:30.

By evening the shelter was full and the overflow hikers were selecting tent sites. Then we placed a mammoth order to the local pizza shop. I only ordered a cheese steak sandwich, so I can save room for the food in my pack. I need to eat it up to reduce my load for the climb out of Lehigh Gap.

-Mouse

Thursday, July 01, 2004
Destination: New Tripoli Campsite
From: Eckville Shelter
Today's Miles: 13.3
Trip Miles: 1231.2

The first nine miles were fairly awful. There was boulder pile after boulder pile. Negotiating them was a nervous business. Again and again either a foot or a pole would slip on the stone and I would have to scramble wildly to regain my footing and avoid tipping over. It would be so easy to break a leg getting through the mess. In between, much of the trail was rocky, making for slow going and sore feet.

I still managed to find some blueberries from time to time. I made sure to leave the easiest to see for Socks coming up behind. Gobbling up all the berries would be a poor way to thank her for all the food she gave me and for sending me my toilet paper. I had accidentally left it at the shelter and Socks gave it to a faster hiker to bring to me.

I had another surprise at lunch. Apparently I had left the cap loose on one of my Aqua Mira bottles, so I found it empty. Without both chemicals, it is useless for purifying water. For now I have just my filter bottle with a rather old filter element. Thank goodness I never put it in my bounce box on my pack-lightening rampages! Fortunately I asked my brother to bring more Aqua Mira when he meets me in three days at Wind Gap. If that falls through, Delaware Water Gap is just a day or two past that, with spare filters in my bounce box and an outfitter to buy more chemicals at.

I got to the campsite at 2:30. As soon as my tent was up, I went to the spring to fetch a bag of water. Then I laboriously squeezed enough through the balky filter bottle to fill my two liter Platypus to the brim. That would last the eleven miles to Lehigh Gap tomorrow.

I had considered staying tomorrow night at the Outerbridge Shelter just this side of Lehigh Gap to save time hitching or hiking the two miles from the town to the trail the next day. That would have meant skipping the famous jailhouse hostel in the Palmerton Borough Hall. But with the water problems, I think I will go into Palmerton so I can fill up with safe tap water for the climb up Lehigh Gap.

Because of a large area polluted by zinc smelting, it is ten miles past the Gap to the next water and 16 to the next shelter. So I will have a very long day two days from now. I had better relax while I can!

-Mouse

The plaque atop Springer Mountain marking the south end of the Trail

A cold evening inside Wood's Hole Shelter

Start of the snowstorm at Winding Stair Gap

The Mysterious Spaceship of Snowbird Mountain, actually a VORTAC aircraft navigation beacon

Two of the irresistable wild ponies at Mount Rogers Virginia

My empty carton and trophy spoon after finishing the Half Gallon Challange at Pine Grove Furnace

Negotiating New York's Lemon Squeezer

The only bears I saw the entire hike at the Bear Mountain Zoo

Picking berries near the Inn At The Long Trail in Vermont

Marked by rock cairns, the Trail marches eerily into the clouds on Mount Moosilauke

Crossing the Kennebec River via the canoe ferry

Finished! The sign marking the north end of the Trail on Mount Katahdin Maine

Friday, July 02, 2004
Destination: George Outerbridge Shelter
From: New Tripoli Campsite
Today's Miles: 10.9
Trip Miles: 1242.1

The big surprise for the morning came less than two miles from camp when I came to the "Knife Edge." Imagine a massive pile of foot-thick irregular stone slabs reaching above the surrounding treetops and stretching for over a quarter mile. The Trail ran right along the tip-top crest of the heap! I let my poles dangle by their straps and clambered my way on hands and feet. At one spot I had to scoot along an inclined slab like a spider for lack of anything to grab onto.

Finally it descended chaotically back to the forest floor. There it was as usual a bit of a mystery what direction the Trail exited off the pile. Rock scrambles often end up a bit of a scavenger hunt. Either they are not marked well or as in this case, the blazes painted on the rock were worn away and the ones on trees obscured by foliage.

After solving that puzzle, the Trail continued on savagely rocky ground to "Bear Rocks" where it led up into another mountainous pile of slabs. This time it went along the shoulder instead of the crest and I could walk upright and balance with my poles more than before but it was not much easier. Getting down was even harder and I found myself resorting to rock-climbing holds, using grips to force my feet sideways into a foothold because vertical hand and footholds simply did not have enough purchase to support me. Then back to stumbling through rocky Trail to Bake Oven Knoll and another scramble off that to Bake Oven Shelter.

Still, it had its rewards. Climbing up into Bear Rocks I found a clump of bushes packed with big raspberries. It was the most raspberries I had seen in days; I had thought they were all gone by now. Blueberries were also more abundant than in the last couple days, so I stayed happily fed despite being careful about leaving plenty for those behind me.

I stopped at the shelter for lunch and found a southbound young couple with an infant in a backpack carrier. She was only the second baby I had seen on the Trail, with the very cute trailname of "Beep-Beep." I warned them about the rugged trail ahead of them but they seemed confident. I bid them farewell, saying be careful and I hoped they made it safely.

Leaving the Shelter I met Goodtimes and Blueberry, a couple we had met at Eckville Shelter. The Trail now was maintained by a different hiking club and totally changed character, running along a well-graded mostly smooth logging road.

It was along there that I saw the first truly suspicious people I have seen on the Trail. I came across a man walking towards me who was not dressed like a hiker and who instead of a knapsack carried a bag slung over his shoulder, like those used for gathering plants except it was not open at the top. He avoided eye contact and was silent even after I said "hello" but as soon as he saw me turned and made arm signals as if to someone behind him.

As I passed him I could just see another man duck into the woods to the right of the trail. Something was clearly not right. I quickly freed my hands from the straps of my poles so I was unencumbered and could use them as a weapon if needed. Then I kept a wary eye in the woods just in case the man's companion was laying in wait for me. Fortunately, their goal seemed to be to avoid contact rather than confront me. I was relieved that nothing happened but still kept my pace up long enough to put them well behind me. Whatever they were doing there, they simply did not act legitimate so I wanted as far as I could get.

After a dirt road came the first signs of the area contaminated by the zinc smelting plant in Palmerton. The vegetation changed from forest to shrubbery and grass, with the decayed skeletons of long-dead trees scattered about. The openness gave a good view of Interstate-476 as it approached the Ridge of Blue Mountain from the north before plunging through a tunnel running 500 feet beneath my feet. It has to be the highest I have ever crossed above a freeway without being in an airplane!

Among the shrubbery were uncountable blueberry bushes jam-packed with ripe berries. All the starting thruhikers of the year could gorge themselves insensible and hardly make a dent in the crop. The signs of environmental damage made me too worried about residual heavy metals to really pig out, but I still grabbed an occasional handful. Others were less inhibited and later I found that I needn't have worried. Still, better safe than sorry.

At the shelter came another surprise, Trail Magic! Two local women had brought a 4th of July treat: hotdogs, chips, carrot sticks, sodas and chocolate bars. Mmmmmmmm! They even topped off my water containers with melt water from their ice chest. They were glad to have the water go to a good use so they would not have to pour it out or carry it back down the mountain. Rocket was there, whom I had helped by adjusting his Auspex Pack back in Virginia, as were Hotrock, Goodtimes and Blueberry, Palm Tree, Socks and I. The women had to leave at three and there was no sign of Boonie, Treefrog and Adam. So we had to finish off the hotdogs ourselves but saved sodas, chips, carrots and chocolate bars for them.

With an unexpected meal and no need to purify water, I wouldn't need to go into Palmerton for the night after all. That eliminated the delay or extra two miles to get back to the trail in the morning, relieving that worry. Things just have a way of working out on the Trail.

For several days I have been having trouble with heat rash on my back where the pack rubs my skin. So far I have kept it at bay by loosening the shoulder straps and load lifter straps so the pack rides away from my back, reducing the rubbing and allowing more air circulation. But on the difficult climb up Lehigh Gap I will have to keep the pack cinched tight to my back to prevent it shifting and possibly throwing me off balance at a critical moment. So I took advantage of the afternoon sun to wash my t-shirt, using a ziplock bag filled with water and a pinch of Dr Bronners Soap as a "washing machine" and hanging it out in the sun to dry. Cleaning out the accumulated sweat and dirt should reduce the irritation from my pack tomorrow.

About 7pm it started sprinkling. I hoped it would stop by morning. Climbing out of Lehigh Gap would be hard in wet conditions.

-Mouse

Saturday, July 03, 2004
Destination: Leroy Smith Shelter
From: George Outerbridge Shelter
Today's Miles: 16.7
Trip Miles: 1258.8

At 5:30am I made my way down to the Gap and across the Lehigh River Bridge. By 6 I was starting the ascent.

It began with a steep but ordinary climb through the vegetation at the base of the mountain. Then I broke out into the denuded area. All the vegetation had died years before from a century of zinc smelting in Palmerton, allowing the soil to wash away and leaving a barren rock mountainside.

At first I could walk normally but about 6:30 came to the first ledge. Looking down, I was already high enough that Socks, Adam and Tree Frog starting across the bridge looked tiny as ants. I took my pack off, put my hat safe inside, collapsed my poles and strapped them to the side of my pack. Then I put the pack back on and pulled the straps so tight it was almost a part of my body.

Once I was ready I found a handhold, then another, hoisted one foot up to a ledge, then the other, and repeated the process. The white blazes led this way and that up the steep rocks. It went from ledges eventually to slabs piled willy-nilly. I suddenly realized the hand and footholds I was trusting my life to were on stone slabs held in place only by their own weight. The thought of one shifting suddenly was unnerving because they were more than big enough to pin a hiker.

At last I reached the crest of the ridge that thrust out from the mountain into the gap. I clambered up and over, then glanced down at the town of Palmerton hundreds of feet below. As I did so, the angle I was looking made the rocks I was standing on seem very insecure and a wave of vertigo swept through me. It was not as bad as I had experienced in the past but I had to turn my head and gaze fixedly at the ridge next to me until the sensation passed. Then I gingerly moved sideways to a wider more secure ledge. The nearest hiker was on the other side of the ridge and far below me; it was just me and the mountain, matching wits.

Now I could look down and see the cars passing, ripples in the river as it flowed toward the gap and additional bare and partly bare spots on the hillsides surrounding the town.

Now the blazes led roughly parallel to the crest of the ridge and about fifty feet below it, going sideways instead of straight up. It was on a talus slope; a loose slope of 4 to 8 inch rocks that was easier to negotiate than the boulders. Soon a rough ledge was cleared through the rocks, making progress even easier.

Finally I was through the denuded area and reached scrubby trees. I sat down to eat a square of chocolate and bask in the elation of having finished the hard part of the climb. When I stood up the head of the next hiker was just popping over the ridge top far below me.

From there a much easier gravel path led through the trees. Around a bend there appeared the sign for the bypass trail used in bad weather. I was at the top! I yelled with triumph even though no one was there to hear me. It had taken just 50 minutes, the same as it had taken me to devour my half gallon of ice cream.

[The climb up from Lehigh Gap turned out to be the only time on my hike that I resorted to carrying my trekking poles strapped to my pack. In every other climb, even Mahoosuc Notch, I found it was enough to use the wrist straps. That way I could easily switch back and forth between using the poles and letting them hang from my wrists as needed.]

Looking around, the damage looked less extensive and far more recovered than I had been led to believe. The section on the tip of the mountain the trail had led up seemed to be the largest totally bare area. Most sections had at least spotty vegetation.

Out in the arid western states it would look pretty normal. Soon I even came upon healthy blueberry plants packed with big juicy sweet berries and had a couple of handfuls.

Then I broke out of the trees and stared! It did not QUITE look like another planet; there were still scattered live plants to remind me this was earth. But for as far as I could see, the north side of the mountain was nearly denuded of soil, it truly was devastated over a huge area. It looked like photos of Hiroshima, or the area devastated by WWI.

Dead trees were scattered about, along with small shrubby new trees and assorted other plants starting to re-colonize the wasteland. So at least it was more the Nearly Dead Zone rather than The Dead Zone. One of the most widespread of the colonizing plants were clumps of pink flowers on tall stems, growing from grassy-looking leaves. Scattered through the dead trees in the barren landscape, they reminded me of the famous WWI poem: "In Flanders' Fields the poppies blow, among the crosses row by row..."

The wasteland went on for several miles before the vegetation began to get more of a foothold. First more shrubs and flowers, then underbrush began to appear and grass started to sprout on the trail. Starting off, everything looked stunted and unhealthy, then it gradually improved. Blueberry bushes appeared, but too unhealthy to bear fruit.

Finally I got to lots of healthy blueberry bushes crowded with fruit. While eating, I came across a local couple there to pick berries. The woman had been there all her life. She talked about how her father had worked at the zinc plant, how far the defoliated area had been, and how her children had loved the rock climb up from the Gap when they were little.

The rest of the day was just difficult. The trail was rocky, making my feet bruised and sore. There were no good views or even blueberries. Just hiking over rough ground.

When I got to the shelter at 2:30 I was glad I had gotten such an early start. There was already a crowd there. Some moved on, but the shelter quickly filled and even tenting space was at a premium with weekend hikers coming in.

There were many reports about how friendly the town of Palmerton was and what a nice hostel they had. But as much as I regretted missing it, the extra time would have gotten me here long after all the space was taken.

The spring was a half-mile down a steep trail. I found I had over a liter of water left and decided to skip getting more. What I had would see me to Wind Gap, where I was to meet my brother tomorrow morning.

-Mouse

Sunday, July 04, 2004
Destination: Wind Gap
From: Leroy Smith Shelter
Today's Miles: 4.6
Trip Miles: 1263.4

The hike to Wind Gap was rather rocky (What else is new?) but at least there were blueberries every so often. At the highway at Wind Gap there were also raspberries. So the Pennsylvania Berry Bash keeps going unabated.

I got there at 8:30 and discovered to my consternation that the parking lot was at a side road, not the highway where I had told my brother to meet me. I sat to wait, hoping he would figure it out.

Sure enough, he and my housemate arrived by 11. We went off to the southern Poconos to spend the night at a comfy motel. After I got a shower and changed, we rested part of the afternoon and drove off to Delaware Water Gap to get a preview of the trail there before supper. Here it was a paved sidewalk past a visitors' Center, packed with families out for a holiday weekend outing. Dressed in regular clothes, I pass unnoticed. Even a fellow thruhiker did not recognize me at first. He on the other hand, was surrounded by curious tourists and asked all the usual questions.

My twin had brought two packs of Aqua Mira, a complete Platypus hydration system to replace my moldy and cracked bite valve, an interesting looking cherry flavored treat from Hawaii, a fresh pair of Capilene socks and a lightweight flashlight. That will take care of my outfitter needs for a good while. Just being able to see them was a big boost emotionally; it was the first time I had seen any family since I had started back in March.

-Mouse

Monday, July 05, 2004
Destination: Kirkbridge Shelter
From: Wind Gap
Today's Miles: 10.2
Trip Miles: 1273.6

After a nice visit my brother drove to Wind Gap a little before 10am. We all started up the hill from the parking lot, but the steep sloped quickly turned back first my housemate and then my twin brother, leaving me on my own again. The timing and spacing of everything is a bit awkward. I will end up doing only 9 miles today and six tomorrow into Delaware Water Gap since it is too late to go all the way today. Then the best spot to go in New Jersey is the Mohican Center just ten miles from the Gap. That means four short days in a row, or else try to do my mail drop, laundry and resupply and then try to get to Mohican, a very crowded day.

Today's section of trail was full of rocks and full of blueberries for the first seven miles to Wolf Rocks. That was another of those boulder-hopping overlooks where the hopping went on rather far. As my housemate's grandmother would have said, "Too much of a muchness."

Despite what some guidebooks said, aside from the overlook the rocks along the trail were not particularly awful. And after Wolf Rocks the rest of the trail was fairly smooth and forgiving. Unless something changes soon, the "Pennsylvania Rocks" seem to be much ado about nothing. My feet got sore at times but there has never been the jagged boot destroying rocks I had expected. Perhaps they really were bad but I expected even worse?

I was the first one at the shelter a little before three. As I settled for an afternoon nap Titanium Man, an 84 year old section hiker with artificial knee and hip joints, arrived with his granddaughter and her girlfriend. Then came a pair of weekender couples who headed off to tent. Then a Japanese hiker. Then sixteen 12-14 year olds and their three counselors on a summer camp outing. They laid out their sleeping bags on a huge tarp spread right behind the shelter. Then three thruhikers came, who squeezed into the shelter. They reported that yet another group of kids were on the way! When the camp teens came to the front of the shelter for supper just as I was going to bed and started singing camp songs right outside my sleeping bag I had had enough. Even though it was 7:30 at night I hastily bundled everything back into my pack and headed up the trail. About a mile away I found a quiet clearing, pitched my tent and hung my food against the bears reported to be in the area, then settled down for some rest in solitude.

-Mouse

Tuesday, July 06, 2004
Destination: Delaware Water Gap
From: Kirkbridge Shelter
Today's Miles: 5.4
Trip Miles: 1279.0

Eager to get a room before they were snapped up, I made my earliest start yet in semi-darkness at 5am. It gave me a chance to try out the flashlight my brother had given me to follow the trail in the dark on the first night-hiking of my journey.

There was just a mile or so of rocks before the Trail followed a fairly smooth roadbed along the rest of the ridge. As far as I am concerned, the infamous Pennsylvania Rocks are overrated as a trail obstacle. Sure they made for sore feet but not as sore as the steep high ups and downs had made my knees further south! And they usually alternated with long smooth stretches that gave my feet a rest before the next rough spot.

The berries started early and kept up until town. First blueberries, scattered most of the morning and one spot near a power line that had as many per foot as I had seen at Lehigh Gap. Then raspberries scattered along the rest of the hike. By now I was eager to get to town and then finish off another state, so I never stopped to truly pig out on berries. But it was nice to continue the Berry Bash.

When I came in sight of the Delaware River far below, I could not help a "Woohoo!" of delight. Another state border in sight and two weeks or so would see me all the way in Connecticut. Time sure flies when you are having fun, and I was elated. The Delaware was also the next of the Great Rivers the Trail crosses and it goes past Philadelphia where I live. So I called out "Hello Philadelphia!" Now I will be hiking away from home instead of to it but getting closer and closer to the end of the Trail.

Descending down off the mountain into the Gap I went through more Rhododendron trees with shedding flowers. In my mind they were casting their flower petals onto my path in adoration. Mouse, Hiker Empress of the Delaware! Okay, I was getting a bit silly.

In the town of Delaware Water Gap I called the Ramada Inn at 8am. Not only did they have a room at the hiker rate but I could check in as soon as I wanted. Very pleasantly surprised, I checked in, showered, and went to the post office. There I got maps and guidebook pages and other supplies from my bounce box and added my spare water bladder and spare Aqua Mira to it before sealing the box and mailing it to Salisbury CT. I told the clerk I liked the cute little twinkly handbell at the counter instead of the usual harsh sounding motel-desk-ish one. Even the pens had big flowers on the ends that were so real looking I had to sniff them. She beamed and asked "Can you tell it is an all-woman office?" sending us both into giggles.

Back at the motel I had some breakfast, then hand laundered my dirty clothes and set them on the balcony to dry. Chores done, I could relax the rest of the day.

I ran into Socks and offered to share my room with her so she could get a break from the men who were hiking with her.

-Mouse

Wednesday, July 07, 2004
Destination: Mohican Outdoor Center
From: Delaware Water Gap
Today's Miles: 10.5
Trip Miles: 1289.5

I had been tempted to make for a campsite 17 miles away. But watching the Weather Channel while sampling the buffet in the motel breakfast room changed my mind. Severe thunderstorms were predicted in the evening. Suddenly the snug cabins of the Mohican Center seemed a lot more attractive. My tent is not the most windproof and no tent stands up well against falling trees and other severe storm accompaniments.

I had to wait for Socks to vacate the room before checking out, so we ended up starting together at 7:30 and hiking the day together. A local trail alumnus drove us to the Trail and we started out across the I-80 Delaware River Bridge. I put on my best George Washington imitation, "Mouse Crossing The Delaware" but the hair on the sides of my head doesn't curl the right way and George had more gray than I do, so I did not quite pull it off.

Pennsylvania has been good to me. Between eating in towns, roadside restaurants, trail magic and all those berries I think I have gained weight. I am all fed and ready for some more states!

After bidding farewell to the Delaware, we started the climb up Kittatinny Mountain. We will stay on its ridge until we reach High Point at the northwest corner of the state, then turn east and descend. The rocks were just as bad as Pennsylvania.

At Sunfish Pond the rock situation got much worse. The Trail takes a strenuous boulder hopping route along the shore. Finally it headed uphill and I thought to myself "At least we are heading away from that rugged shoreline." No sooner had I formed the thought than we hit a double blaze with the top one offset to the right, signaling a right turn. I groaned as the trail dove cheerfully back into the rocks. Talk about too much of a muchness!

Sunfish Pond is a glacial pond too acidic for all but a few species of sunfish and perch. I joked about trekking poles, deer, and thruhikers being dissolved by the acid while Socks giggled.

The rocks continued all the way to Mohican, well-rooted and often too close to step between. Our feet and ankles got more and more sore from the uneven footing. It did not even have the long respites of smooth path I found in Pennsylvania.

In compensation, there were lots and lots of blueberries. Not only the ones we had seen earlier but a large dark variety that were REALLY sweet. A few miles past Sunfish Pond the vegetation changed; large grassy meadows topped the ridge dotted with scattered trees. It made for nice views of the river to one side and lakes to the other and was unlike any vegetation we had seen so far. Sort of like the balds but with shade trees. The sunlight made for lots of big sweet berries. We could have stopped and gorged ourselves insensible on them, but by now we were getting tired and wanting to get to Mohican. As it was, we ate our share.

At last we descended into a gap and came to the road to the Center. Because of the forecast of rain we decided to forgo the free tenting and paid the fee for bunks indoors. It was very nice; beds with soft mattresses and pillows, hot shower, even a kitchen with utensils! I showered and then hand-laundered my t-shirt and shorts. It was amazing how much gunk I washed out of them even after just one short day! I hung them outside to dry and had a nap while Socks went to swim in the lake and sooth her feet in the cold water.

I took advantage of the kitchen to heat some water and fix the dehydrated pork and beans I had gotten as Trail Magic back before Duncannon and had been carrying for a week and a half, along with some ramen. It was the first hot meal I had prepared since sending away my cooking things back in central Virginia. Socks was sharing beans and rice on tortillas, eager to reduce her pack weight, so we all ate well.

Adam came in late and was having pain in the arch of one foot. He iced it and hopefully it will be better in the morning.

The first thunderstorm rumbled through at about 5pm and the rain continued off and on into the night. I read my way through the library of books and old National Geographics. Some were so old I remembered them from my high school years!

-Mouse

Thursday, July 08, 2004
Destination: Glen Anderson Shelter
From: Mohican Outdoor Center
Today's Miles: 20.9
Trip Miles: 1310.4

Adam's foot was still sore this morning and he reluctantly decided to take a zero day. Then Socks decided she would stay too, to ruminate about thoughts she said she had been having of leaving the Trail and going home. It was an emotional scene, sort of like The Breaking of The Fellowship of the Ring. I gave her a big hug before setting off at 6am and she told me to eat lots of berries for her. Whether she stays or goes, the delay may well mean I will not see her again. I am going to miss her and could not help feeling a bit sad. She is a strong hiker and in good shape and she and her sense of humor have been a bright spot that will be missed by many.

The weather in the morning was damp and foggy, somewhat matching my mood over Sock's departure. The sun brightened the sky and my mood brightened a bit as well. Whoever was with me, Katahdin still beckoned me forward.

Much to my relief, there were not as many rocks today and there were fairly long smooth stretches. What is more, it was an excellent day for berries. Lots and lots of blueberries of all shades and sizes, some late raspberries and early ripe blackberries.

I covered the 14 miles to the sidetrail to Brink Road Shelter by 1:30. Socks had planned on everyone going a full 21 miles to Glen Anderson Shelter. My left foot was a bit sore, but I decided to stick to her plan. It would make up for the short day yesterday and open up options for tomorrow. Besides, the Brink Road

Shelter was said to have high bear activity making it an undesirable place to spend the night.

At Highway 209 I stopped in at the Worthington Bakery, a longtime thruhiker tradition. Sadly, according to a note on the door Mr. and Mrs. Worthington had passed on and the bakery was closed. Thruhikers will miss them.

Another sign directed us to Gip's Tavern nearby. Palm Tree and Sixty-five And Alive were already there eating. There was a picture window behind the bar with a great view of Kittatinny Lake right out back. Judy the bartender directed me to a cooler of sodas, got me a glass of ice, filled my Platypus and fixed me a cheeseburger with all the trimmings.

Well fed and thirst quenched, the three of us started the last three miles to the shelter. A group of girls from a summer camp got there right after us. I had to shoo them away from the snacks that trail maintainer Desperado had left in the bear box as Trail Magic. I was a bit relieved when Desperado himself arrived and took care of them, explaining that the food and supplies in the box were meant for thruhikers only. He had a good touch with teens, but told us that when they raided shelter supplies he did not hesitate to turn them over to the Park Rangers. Since this was a fairly well behaved group he rewarded them with a little treat. Nothing like positive reinforcement.

Then Desperado turned his attention to us. Besides the lemonade mix we had helped ourselves to from the box, he gave us each a soda, fruit, cupcakes and a run-through of the best places to stay all the way to Maine! He is one helpful maintainer!

-Mouse

Friday, July 09, 2004
Destination: Secret Shelter, Goldsmith Road
From: Glen Anderson Shelter
Today's Miles: 18.0
Trip Miles: 1328.4

Wow, a double Ibuprofen day!

The rocks were nasty and unrelenting. My arches were starting to pop before I reached High Point and the trail finally descended off Kittatinny Ridge. Add to that some chafing caused by yesterday's high humidity and miles that today's hiking only made worse and I was not a happy hiker. Walking quickly became painful and slow. At one of the shelters I tried the talcum powder Desperado had included in his Trail Magic first aid supplies. It kept the irritation at bay for an hour but the rest of the day was not pleasant.

On the other hand the weather was very nice, cool, dry, and breezy with lots of clouds for shade. Had I not done 21 miles yesterday and 18 today it would have been a very nice day. Of course with fewer miles I would have stayed at bear haunted shelters and still be struggling through those rocks.

I am at an unofficial shelter thruhikers call the Secret Shelter. It is a cabin just off the trail on Goldsmith Road whose owner allows thruhikers to stay in for free. It has hot and cold running water and a shower, so is very nice. The shower was just what I needed to relieve the chafing. I am too lazy to sleep in the loft, so I am making like Cinderella and sleeping on the floor under the sink on the lower level. There is just as much headroom as many shelters have. There is even a junky romance novel for me to read!

-Mouse

Saturday, July 10, 2004
Destination: Vernon, NJ
From: Goldsmith Road
Today's Miles: 13.9
Trip Miles: 1342.3

Today was not so far and much more interesting.

It began with foothills, winding through forests with old stone walls and open fields with raspberries. The trail was mostly smooth and for a stretch ran along an old rail grade where it was nice and level.

Then came the Wallkill River National Wildlife Refuge. Here the trail went around three sides of a vast marshland. The national wildlife seemed to have gobbled up all the berries, but the trail was flat, well cushioned and there were big wide benches perfect for sitting on with a backpack. The marsh itself looked almost artificial, crisscrossed by canals at right angles that made it look like rice paddies in the Mekong Delta.

Next came a 700 foot ascent up Pochuck Mountain, mostly on those steep rivers of boulders that are SO entertaining to hike upon. Bleah! I guess that after all that flatness they wanted to remind us that this is the APPALACHIAN Trail, not some easy nature walk.

The reward was that the top had vegetation like Kittatinny Ridge including: blueberries! Mmmmm...

The highlands wandered along until it reached what the map said was a recent reroute from what had been a long road-walk. Now the Trail runs along one of the most impressive examples of trail work I have seen. There is over a mile of elevated boardwalk running through a large cattail swamp. It is on sturdy foundations, elevated four to six feet above the surface of the water, firmly anchored to huge steel stakes with steel cables, and has widened sections with benches for resting or just admiring the view. Instead of going straight like something urban, it meanders in irregular curves that fit more naturally. Then there is an incredibly impressive wooden suspension footbridge over Wawayanda Creek.

Then a bit of woods with a new surprise. For weeks I had seen these plants festooned with thistly pods mixed in with the raspberry bushes. Now I passed some in a clearing and the pods had opened to reveal: BERRIES! They looked just like black raspberries only red and tasted, well, like berries. What I had thought was a mildly pesky shrub now looks like the next course on the Appalachian Trail Berry Bash! They must be red raspberries. That would solve a mystery I had pondered since childhood: how do you tell a ripe red raspberry from an unripe black raspberry, since both are red? I seem to have my answer. Unless they are something else. Maybe there is a plant called Hiker's Bane, a highly toxic false raspberry. Or maybe they are really alien space invaders like the Pod People! I've eaten some, so time will tell.

Then came another field with marsh boards. These were in need of maintenance. Some tipped toward me like seesaws when I stepped on them then tipped the other way when I reached the midpoint. Others were rotted and broken or twisted wildly. That made it a bit like an obstacle course to avoid getting dumped in the swamp.

On the far side was the road to Vernon NJ. A short distance the opposite direction is the Heavenly Hills Farm Store, a good spot for a snack and for getting a ride into town.

I spent the night at the Saint Thomas church hostel in Vernon. The church has made a mission of seeing to thruhiker needs. There is a hot shower, laundry, kitchen, phone, sleeping space and even a box of equipment on sale at cost like socks fuel etc. There were four of us there, me, Palm Tree, Treefrog and Boonie. After cleaning up, we went to the Saturday evening church service before going to supper. Then I went to the A&P for food and a drugstore for Goldbond body powder to try to keep the chafing at bay.

Finally I settled down with a good book and a quart of milk before bed.

-Mouse

Sunday, July 11, 2004
Destination: Wildcat Shelter
From: Vernon, NJ
Today's Miles: 17.3
Trip Miles: 1359.6

The day started innocently enough. I weighed myself and found I had gained five pounds since Front Royal VA and my pack was 18 pounds without food and water and about 31 with. Palm Tree and I got a ride to the Trail from an older couple the wife of whom had thruhiked in 2002.

After a few red raspberries came the thousand foot ascent to Wawayanda ridge but that seemed easier than I had expected. For the rest of the morning the trail was shady and smooth, with red raspberries starting out and lots of black ones later.

The real fun started just before the NY State line. The trail shot to the top of a long ridge high above Greenwood Lake. The spine was vertical strata of bedrock that rose and fell like saw teeth. The trail went right along the crest forcing one to clamper over the rock baking in the hot sun. It was pretty awful while it was happening yet sort of satisfying to have gotten through. The one compensation was that the sunny ridge top was packed with blueberries so I could nibble almost constantly.

The last section was the worst, with the most potential for a serious fall I have seen so far. After clambering up a series of ledges I gaped in disbelief. The blazes pointed right up a rock spine formed by the intersection of two steeply pitched rock faces. There was no avoiding it, so I looped the straps of my poles around my wrists and let them dangle to free my hands, then straddled the spine and shinnied cautiously up. Slipping off either side would have meant a high drop down one face or the other. Finally I reached the top and had some more berries, then confronted a narrow ridge with a sheer drop to either side. For the first part

I did not dare stand up, but inched along on my bottom until it widened a bit. At last the trail turned downward toward the shelter.

At the shelter were four young men hiking fast who had caught up with us. According to them, Stomach was a few days behind but Socks seemed to have gotten a ride back to near Port Clinton so it looks like she is leaving the Trail for good.

-Mouse

Monday, July 12, 2004
Destination: Fingerboard Shelter
From: Wildcat Shelter
Today's Miles: 14.3
Trip Miles: 1373.9

Have I gone back in time?

Let's see: it took me all day to do just 14 miles, it is foggy windy and raining, I came to a stone shelter with fireplaces and a leaky roof but no water or privy, and I am so chilled I had to dive right into my sleeping bag to avoid becoming hypothermic. I know, I am back in the Smokys, right? It sure feels like it! The resemblance is uncanny.

The big difficulty was rock climbing again and again and again. Up a steep ravine alongside a waterfall, then a river of boulders up to Mombasha Point, then ridge walking like yesterday. Then the rain started and wet slick rock added another factor of difficulty on steep ledges up Buchanan and Arden Mountains. A steep descent followed down into the pass to the New York Thruway. I slipped and fell once there and Palm Tree said he fell and found himself rolling down the slope like a log until he was able to stop himself. Another hiker who had joined us at Vernon fell early on and decided the trail was too much for him and got a ride off the Trail.

After a while it finally occurred to me that the New York section of the AT was planned with the goal of proving that you really have to be insane to thruhike the AT. It is so rugged that any sensible person would skip it. Naturally, since I am still here, I am insane!

Aside from the rather foggy views, the best compensation was the blueberries! They crowded every height in every sort from the bright blue tart ones to the deep blue sweet ones. I nibbled happily at the top of every rock climb.

Once across the Thruway into Harriman Park the going moderated, but only a little. The most noticeable change was that the usual forest ground cover was replaced by grass. I swear it looks like Central Park with the grass a bit long. It looked almost creepily unnatural and city park like. I can't imagine how it was done.

I caught up with Palm Tree just before the famous Lemon Squeezer. This landmark consists of two rock walls formed by those vertical strata I have come to know so well in the last two days. The passage between them is very narrow, hence the name. What makes it even more challenging is that the walls are not vertical, but are canted to one side just enough that you cannot stand up straight and there is an awkward step to climb in the middle. I made it through, then got out my camera to get a picture of Palm Tree trying it. He got stuck and had to back up, remove his pack and carry it sideway before he could get through. Then he had me put my pack on and get back in so he could get a shot of me in the Lemon Squeezer.

Right after that the white blaze path divides into two alternate routes. One went up a REALLY nasty rock climb, the other went around. It was raining again and I had gotten a wary respect for the danger of slipping on wet rock so we prudently took the alternate route.

By the time we got up the last hill before the shelter it was raining harder and the wind was kicking up. But I could not resist lingering to pick and eat handfuls of blueberries. Finally I reluctantly left the feast and headed to the shelter.

Once there it was the same routine as months ago in the cold early days: get on dry clothing and take refuge in the sleeping bag. The moment I stopped hiking my body chilled quickly until I was in the snug warmth of my sleeping bag.

The last two days have been pretty challenging but it is high time to start honing the skills needed when we get into the White Mountains in a few weeks. There with the hardest mountains of the trail and the most severe weather on the entire planet, this practice may come in handy.

-Mouse

Tuesday, July 13, 2004
Destination: Bear Mountain Inn
From: Fingerboard Shelter
Today's Miles: 13.4
Trip Miles: 1387.3

It was still windy and raining this morning. I put on my nylon jacket to stay warm and dug out what was left of my rain worthy snacks and put them into the outside pockets of my pack so I could keep my calorie level up without having to stop and remove my pack to open it. With two wet days in a row, snacks were getting a bit low, but trying to nibble gorp in rain was not going to work.

When I reached Brien Shelter I ducked inside to gobble down my last pack of Poptarts. Then I had trouble finding where the Trail went next until I discovered it went straight up the cliff behind the shelter! A bit grumpy at more wet rock, I started up. After that pitch came two more, getting me to the top of Mount whatever and a stunningly good view of empty fog. Okay, I was getting a bit jaded. At least there were lots of berries.

After that came a slippery descent to the Palisades Parkway. A bit to my surprise, there was no underpass or overpass to get across the freeway. Remember the old videogame "Frogger"? That was how I got across, waiting my chance then running as fast as my tired sore legs would carry me. First across one set of lanes, then the other. In the median there was a sign warning that there was no water at the pump atop Bear Mountain. Some wag had added "Or anywhere else in New York!," a cynical comment on the scarcity of water sources.

After that the rain slowed to a stop as I went up Western Mountain. I could begin to hear the popping of small arms and the thumps and whumps of heavier weapons from the direction of what in my ROTC days we called the Hudson Valley School For Boys, otherwise known as West Point. Coming down the other side I got my first glimpse of the Hudson River. It kept appearing and disappearing through holes in the fog, so I had to wait for a good moment before getting a picture. There were the usual blueberries on top and near the bottom a familiar spiny branch across the trail caught my attention. I followed it with my eyes to the side where I found red raspberries. But of the ones peeping out of their pods, none were ripe enough to pick. I swear they were laughing at me! It is pretty bad when the trailside fruit starts making fun of you. Hmmph.

Then I went up Bear Mountain. There were lots of blueberries up there and I gobbled my way happily across the top and down the other side, taking my time since I was nearly done for the day. At the bottom just before the playground next to Bear Mountain Inn were more red raspberries, ripe ones this time!

Mmmmmmmmm!

Back at the Secret Shelter the day before Vernon a southbounder had assured us there were no edible berries ahead. I guess he was looking for the ones that come in cartons, because the berry feast has gone uninterrupted.

I checked into the Inn, which has a certain sentimental meaning to me because of an event I attended there 12 years ago. The room was nice and cozy and I had a shower and hand laundered my hiking clothes. It looks like I will get through the entire state of New York without using a washing machine.

I had some excellent chili for lunch then tried out the recently built merry-go-round. In addition to horses, it has cute figures of local animals: bears, goose, fox, frog, raccoon, even a skunk! Next I got a present for my housemate and rested my feet until suppertime. I had a huge portion of calf's liver and onions with a mound of bacon on top. It was so big I had no room for their desserts, even though they looked tempting. Then I waddled my well-fed self off to bed.

-Mouse

Wednesday, July 14, 2004
Destination: Graymoor Friary
From: Bear Mountain Inn
Today's Miles: 7.2
Trip Miles: 1394.5

I decided that instead of a zero day I would go the short 7 miles to the Graymoor Friary. They have been hosting thruhikers for over 30 years so it seemed a pity not to stay there.

I went to the Inn's free continental breakfast at 7 and then to the post office to mail my gift. After that I was going to lie around all morning and not leave until checkout time. But the Weather Channel warned of an approaching line of thunderstorms bearing down on us, so I checked out at 9:30. I went down, ate a bit more breakfast while waiting for the Zoo to open, then headed out.

I had planned to resupply at the nearby town of Fort Montgomery on my zero day. But I had a scant day's food so decided to skip it and wait until a store 30 miles up the trail at Hwy 52. Outside the Inn was a vending machine. I got the last two packs of Poptarts in it and a couple other snacks to help stretch out my food supply.

Then my Thruhike reached a new low! Low altitude, that is. After the Inn, the Trail goes right through a zoo and it is the lowest spot on the entire Appalachian Trail at only 124 feet above sea level. There I saw my very first bears of the entire hike, lounging around in a pen. And near both the entrance and exit to the zoo were more ripe red raspberries. After the zoo and two small museums, I headed across the Bear Mountain Suspension Bridge.

Besides being short, today's hike was easier than the last few days. There was one bad moment though. Starting the second big climb, the trail went up a four inch wide ledge like a ramp formed by a split layer of a 45 degree rock face. I had hardly started when my foot slipped. I waved my arms and poles wildly trying to avoid falling off and managed to throw myself against the face instead. I was panting from fear and from the jolt of adrenalin and I sat there until my heart slowed to normal. It would only have been a four-foot fall, like falling off a tall step-stool onto rocks, but the landing might have been pretty hard. Two hikers I've been with have bashed their faces into the rocks in the past week and the results are not pretty!

At the driveway to the Friary I met another couple coming and four hikers leaving. The outgoing hikers said there was a big chocolate cake waiting for us at the pavilion near the baseball field where hikers sleep. There it was, along with Palm Tree and Boonie, who had spent the night at a motel in Fort Montgomery.

After some cake I tried the cold-water shower and rinsed out my sweaty t-shirt. Then I journaled and read until supper. Our host Brother Leo came by at 4:30 with his dog companion Buddy. He told us to come up for dinner a little after 5.

Brother Leo met us at the main building, which surprised me by its size. It was five stories and quite long, like a university classroom building. He took us up to the dining hall, where one table had a sign "Hikers" and a place set for each of us. We had hearty warm roast beef sandwiches, which Leo said was the friary's usual weekday supper, with soup and potatoes.

Over dinner Leo explained that the property had been started by the Episcopalians about 100 years ago and then became a Franciscan friary. The large building had been built as a college for educating friars. More recently when the order grew smaller it became an administrative center, and having over 250 beds it also began hosting retreats. They began feeding and sheltering hikers in 1972 when the Trail was rerouted past their hill and a thruhiker came asking to stay overnight.

After dinner Brother Leo gave us a fascinating tour. The friary was a sprawling complex built over the course of a century in different styles. One wing had been started in the 1920s and was never finished, the funds for it being used instead to help those in need during the Depression. In the original main chapel was an ornate inlaid stone altar that had been in a church in Italy on the site St. Francis was said to have received the stigmata. That church had been torn down in 1927 to be rebuilt and the altar was sent to Graymoor Friary. In a garden in the back was a memorial to the rescue workers at the World Trade Center made from I-beams and rebar taken from the wreckage.

At the top of the hill was an overlook from which one can see the Empire State Building on a clear day. But the first thunderstorm had come through just before 5 and it was too cloudy for us to see.

All in all, it was a fascinating visit. Tour completed, Brother Leo bade us goodnight and we trooped through the gardens back to our picnic shelter to go to bed. The roof had no overhang so the upwind side of the floor was wet from rain blowing in, but there was plenty of dry space left in the center and downwind side to sleep on.

-Mouse

Thursday, July 15, 2004
Destination: Shenandoah Tenting Area
From: Graymoor Friary
Today's Miles: 17.5
Trip Miles: 1412.0

Last night it rained fairly heavily but we stayed dry in the pavilion.

Today the Trail looked more like the trail had before New York, no rock climbing. But between steep upgrades, clambering over blowdown trees and puzzling over bad blazing it still took longer than usual.

Even by the first five miles my Achilles tendons were sore from the climbing. Thank goodness tomorrow will be a short day.

The most interesting spot was a stretch before Hwy 301. At first it seemed like I was walking on top of a well preserved stone. Then what had seemed a simple stone wall crossed a ravine and suddenly was twenty feet high! It was obviously a stone viaduct. After the ravine it went through a cut, then became an embankment on the side of the slope with a nicely built retaining wall that was anywhere from a foot to twenty feet high. Here and there it became a free-standing viaduct again to span ravines. It was too narrow for a wagon road and WAY too massive and well built to have been made for the Trail; not even the impressive CCC work in the Smokys and Shenandoahs was that ambitious. My best guess is that it was the bed for an old narrow gauge railway serving a mine.

The tent site was nice: a well with an old-fashioned pump, a privy, and an awning-covered picnic table. I had barely gotten my tent up and everything inside when a late afternoon downpour started.

-Mouse

Friday, July 16, 2004
Destination: Morgan Stewart Shelter
From: Shenandoah Tenting Area
Today's Miles: 10.3
Trip Miles: 1422.3

I slept in until about 7 then took my time drying the tent as much as I could. I finally got on the trail about 8:30am.

About noon I got to Hwy 52 where I headed for the deli and pizza shop .3 miles east. There I got food for the next two days and a meatball sub for lunch and a pastrami sandwich for supper. Palm Tree and Boonie were there already, having lunch.

From there it was just 4 miles to the shelter. There I relaxed and finished a copy of Michael Crichton's novel "Timeline" that I had found in the hiker box at Graymoor so I could leave it here and not have to carry it anymore. Hikers often read a book, then leave it for anyone else to take and read. Usually I just read a few chapters of a book and leave it at the shelter I found it in, but this one was interesting enough that I brought it along to finish. I am a readaholic and after just snatches of books for so many weeks it is nice to finally read an entire book.

-Mouse

Saturday, July 17, 2004
Destination: Wiley Shelter
From: Morgan Stewart Shelter
Today's Miles: 16.6
Trip Miles: 1438.9

I seem to have walked right past the biggest oak on the AT. The Dover Oak was on hwy 20 and all I could think about was finding water. I seem to have missed every famous tree on the entire trail. I wonder if having lived the past five years about an hour from a redwood grove and four hours from the giant sequoias has changed my perspective on big trees.

Anyway, if I want to see it will have to be by car. Oh well.

I DID get to admire two other New York landmarks. Nuclear Lake was the site of a nuclear fuel research site until 1972. Now it has been cleaned up and reforested and is a popular thruhiker swimming hole. I got there too early in the day to try swimming in it, too cold. Then about noon I got to see the Metro North Railway's one and only Appalachian Trail Station, complete with two thruhikers anxiously awaiting the next train to New York City. I was half tempted to ride a few stops then back again just to sit in the air conditioning!

The berries are getting a bit sparse the last couple days. I still found four different kinds today but not very many. I wonder how much longer I can keep up my berries every day streak?

Speaking of streaks, ever since my first full day in New York State it has rained at least once a day. That is one streak I would rather break. Today's installment so far has been a quick afternoon shower out of a sunny sky and a thunderstorm that rumbled through at 6:30pm. I tented to get a break from the mosquitoes so my tent got a good dousing.

Rain was not the only thing falling today. While hiking I heard a crack overhead and a dead branch fell ten feet in front of me. Next to the branch was a slightly dazed squirrel. It had stepped on the branch only to have it give way. It shook its head to clear it, fluffed up its tail and climbed a tree back upstairs as I admonished it to be more careful about where it was stepping next time.

-Mouse

Sunday, July 18, 2004
Destination: Kent, CT
From: Wiley Shelter
Today's Miles: 12.7
Trip Miles: 1451.6

Early today I crossed into Connecticut. The trail appeared better maintained, with less underbrush and no blowdown trees to clamper over and around. I found just a few red raspberries in NY and a few black ones in CT. Then the Trail climbed a mountain and swung briefly back into NY. There I found lots of nice sweet blueberries, more than I have seen in days.

After that the trail swung back into CT and entered the only Indian reservation it passes through, belonging to the Schaghticokes.

Next it started getting more difficult. It swung up down and around a string of knobs and hollows, then went steeply up Mt. Algo. I found myself running out of steam, plodding more and more slowly and finally getting hit with an "I want to just sit and not move anymore" sort of blah feeling. That was a bit disconcerting, especially after the fairly easy time I had had up to then. It was the first "fed up with thruhiking" moment I had had. I hoped it would not lead me to quit as so many others had quit before me. Even going downhill left me feeling hot and tired despite temperatures in the mid 70s.

It seemed to take forever to cover the last three miles to the road to Kent but just being there and walking on level ground for the .7 miles to town seemed to revive me a bit. Along the way I passed the driveway of a prep school where what looked like a student asked me the way to town. I was a bit incredulous that he did not know, since it was barely a quarter mile away. But we librarians are compulsively helpful, so I dug out my map and showed him the way.

Back when we parted at Harpers Ferry, The Walking Stomach and her friend Ann had invited me to come visit. So as soon as I got to Kent I gave Ann a call and she came to get me. When I told her of how tired I had gotten, she grinned and said she knew exactly the spot it had happened, having lugged a chainsaw over the same stretch on more than one muggy day clearing blowdowns. That made me feel better! So did her suggestion of spending a zero day then a day of slackpacking. It was also fun meeting their two cats, Otis and Charles. Charles looks just like Morris in those old Nine Lives commercials complete with the same indolent personality.

-Mouse

Monday, July 19, 2004
Destination: Kent, CT
From: Kent, CT
Today's Miles: 0.0
Trip Miles: 1451.6

Today was my first real zero day since Erwin TN. I napped, then drove into Kent for lunch and some shopping. At the outfitters I got a new pair of Spenco insoles for my boots because the original insoles are walked flat. I also bought socks and a spare bite valve for my Platypus. Then I got food for the next three days and more vitamins. I like Centrum Performance because they combine a multivitamin with extra B vitamins, saving weight. I also got new ziplock bags to replace the ones I had bought in Harpers Ferry, which had been too flimsy. Only freezer strength bags seem to stand up well to the rigors of the Trail. I also stopped at a bakery renowned for its cheesecake but alas, they were out. Sigh.

Back at the house, I walked to the farmers market down the road and bought some raspberries. Maybe eating them will trick me into thinking I am still on the trail instead of watching TV.

I also tried weighing myself this morning. According to their scale I am only 136 pounds, about ten less than the scale at Vernon NJ said about ten days ago. Judging by the way my watch is starting to rattle around loosely on my wrist, I suspect the lower figure might be correct. Gasp, the incredible shrinking hiker! When I started out I did not think I could get below 135 without getting a bit excessively thin but here I am at the doorstep.

-Mouse

Tuesday, July 20, 2004
Destination: Pine Knob Loop
From: Kent, CT
Today's Miles: 13.2
Trip Miles: 1464.8

Ann dropped me off at Pine Knob Loop Trail, a sidetrail leading to the AT. I would hike south back to Kent.

Within an hour I ran into Gaiter Woman coming the other direction. After a big hug we got caught up. Last I had seen her she was sick and leaving the Trail at Pine Grove Furnace. She had not only gotten well but had caught up and passed me. She will never admit it, but Gaiter Woman is one strong hiker despite her sixty-some years.

Next was a lovely five mile walk along the Housatonic River, then there was a steep climb up St. Johns Ledges, with some rock scrambling but not as bad as in New York. Going up I passed two rock climbing classes from local summer camps on the adjacent cliffs. From there it was a fairly level hike along the ridge south to the road to Kent.

I found a ripe black raspberry almost as soon as I started hiking and blueberries up on the heights. Not enough to totally gorge on but enough to keep up my berry streak.

While I was hiking I had a chore to do. Ann and The Walking Stomach maintain the section from the Ledges south and Ann had asked me to count the blowdown trees that needed clearing. Weeheee, I get to be a Junior Deputy Trail Maintainer for the day!

Back in town I bought a whole cheesecake, then carried it back to the house. I was just about to take a shower when I heard voices outside. It was Little Tree and The Walking Stomach! They had hitched in from HWY 55 in New York to start slack-packing from Stomach's house.

After hugs of greeting Stomach had a very touching reunion with her purse and car; those indispensable symbols of life off the Trail. After Little Tree and I finished giggling, we headed to the store to find enough food for 3 hungry hikers.

-Mouse

Wednesday, July 21, 2004
Destination: Falls Village, CT
From: Pine Knob Loop
Today's Miles: 12.6
Trip Miles: 1477.4

After I had a filling but slightly unorthodox breakfast of leftover cheesecake, The Walking Stomach drove me back to Pine Knob Loop Trail and I climbed back up to the AT but headed north this time.

I met and re-met Bluebell, Castro and Little Bit, two men and a woman who had been about a day ahead of me for weeks. It was interesting to finally meet them. When thruhiking, people are always speeding up and slowing down or taking breaks so you end up meeting hikers who were once far ahead of or behind you. News and gossip spreads that way too, disseminating up and down the trail like lightning sometimes. They say nothing is easier to carry than gossip!

The blueberries are continuing up on the heights, but lower berries seem supplanted by other plants here. Oh well, Ann promised me that the really big blueberries are ripe just a bit north. Mmmmmmm.... I reached Falls Village by 3 and crossed the river. Right next to the Trail is the home of an Aunt and Uncle of my housemate's where I stopped in to visit. As well as two cats, they have three very cute dogs and I found myself with the pleasant role of the menagerie's babysitter for the evening while the aunt and uncle were out at a modern dance performance.

-Mouse

Thursday, July 22, 2004
Destination: Riga Lean-To
From: Falls Village, CT
Today's Miles: 11.0
Trip Miles: 1488.4

I did not get on the Trail until 9am because, well gee whiz, I hadn't visited them in 8 years; the least I could do was wait until they were awake, eat breakfast, pet the cats, sign the guest book, take pictures, say good morning to the dogs. Oops, I forgot to give them our new address. Oh, well.

I was nearly to Salisbury CT without seeing a single berry and was reconciling myself to the end of my berry streak when two tiny black raspberries came to my rescue, leaping heroically into my mouth to keep the streak going.

In town, I started with the post office. My bounce-box was there but a tube of poison ivy medication a friend has been trying to get to me ever since Boiling Springs PA was not. From my box I got maps and companion pages through to Hanover NH. I decided to get the entire rest of the Data Book as well instead of just ripping out the pages to Hanover. That will let me start planning all the way to the end. I also got my fleece top and my big clothing stuff sack as well as my stove and pot, which I had been doing without ever since Pearisburg VA. That will make me a bit better prepared for the colder temperatures as the mountains start getting higher. To compensate a bit for the weight, I left my pack towel, a bandanna, and my small clothing stuff sack in the bounce box. Still, I think I have added nearly 2 pounds to my load.

Then I got two days worth of food including a packet of tortellini in honor of having a stove again, as well as a quart of milk which I drank down outside the store. Finally I went to the White Hart Inn for a slice of quiche served with a really nice salad. Then to a water tap in the cemetery at the edge of town to fill my Platypus, trying not to step on anyone buried there. I wonder, do they mind, lying beneath the grass? Someone drives a lawn mower over them all the time. Hmmmmm.

Anyway, back on the Trail I found my load noticeably heavier. It will get heavier still by the time I get to the White Mountains. I trudged uphill to Lion's Head Overlook. There, inspired by the selflessness of those two raspberries, a few handfuls of blueberries brought themselves to my attention and politely asked if they could be eaten too. Needless to say, I was happy to accommodate them.

I decided to stop at Riga Lean-to instead of going on to the next one just over a mile away. It was hot and late and I was tired. It was the first night I had camped in Connecticut, having stayed four nights in homes, and will be the last as tomorrow I will be in Massachusetts.

I decided to tent both for the mosquitoes and because Connecticut shelters have an awkward design with a log placed in front of the sleeping platform. I'd probably break my neck clambering over it in the dark if I stayed in the shelter and had to get up in the night. Once my tent was up I cooked my first hot meal in I don't know when, then ate it hastily before the mosquitoes could devour me. Then I hung my bear-bag from a tree for the first time since New Jersey because Stomach, my relatives and trail notices all warned of recent bear sightings in the area. After that I took refuge in my tent from the swarms of mosquitoes.

-Mouse

Danie Martin

Friday, July 23, 2004
Destination: Hemlocks Lean-To
From: Riga Lean-To
Today's Miles: 10.0
Trip Miles: 1498.4

Yesterday was hazy like an inversion. Today dawned overcast, threatening rain.

I found two blueberries right off. Then the Trail headed up Bear Mountain. It was one of those never-ending climbs, logically enough since it is the highest peak in Connecticut. At last I reached a huge ramp-shaped edifice of dry masonry whose plaque declared it a monument built around 1885 commemorating the state's highest point. Actually the highest point is actually somewhere else on the shoulder of a peak whose summit lies in Massachusetts but the builder still gets an A for effort. And there were lots of blueberries, so who cares if someplace else is higher?

After that the Trail turned to the right and plunged down a steep ravine. Again and again I had to sit down and slide my way down rock faces too steep to walk. I was thankful it was not raining and the rock was dry! Finally it leveled off and I crossed the border into Massachusetts.

I was greeted with true exuberance; one peak after another the like of which I had not seen since Virginia, all topped with lots of blueberries!

Mount Race would have had a spectacular view on a clear day, with an almost sheer drop for hundreds of feet off the right side of the Trail. As it was I could still dimly make out the valley floor far below through the haze. It was an odd mix of the rocky spine of my first day in New York and the high foggy ridges of the Smokys.

Again the Trail turned right and went downwards and again I was thankful not to have to do it in the rain. Across a ravine the Trail started up Mount Everett. On my way up I heard an ominous rumble behind me. I paused to listen hoping it was just a passing jet airliner but no, it was thunder.

The last thing I wanted was to get caught on an exposed rocky peak in lightning. I did a swift check of how far it seemed and whether to retreat to the campsite back in the ravine or make for the two shelters beyond the summit. I decided to go on, hurrying up the steep slope as fast as my legs would carry me, gasping for breath, racing the storm to the summit. The slope leveled, going along lightly sloped rock outcrops weaving through scrub pine but the summit seemed to take forever to get to. I had neglected to check the height; it was 2600 feet up, higher than any mountain I had seen since Virginia. As the sound of thunder started to drift ahead of me and the first drops of rain fell I came upon the foundations of the recently removed fire tower. I was at the top!

Frantic with haste, I searched madly for the way down. I found a yellow blazed path marked "this way to car" in spray paint that led downwards but had no white blazes. Certain it was not the Trail but reassured that I knew a quick way downwards if the storm broke, I backtracked to the foundation and looked around again. There it was; a white blaze. I dashed down the trail. For a while it looked almost like the path I had taken up, threading down rock outcrops, and I paused. But the trees were too tall and anyway even if I was turned around it would still get me off the peak to a campsite.

The Trail led to an exposed rocky overlook that I knew I had not passed before. I WAS on the right track but it was leading me over as much of a lightning magnet as the summit had been. I redoubled my pace to get free of the exposed area, heedless of the wet rock and bad footing. At last it went over a shoulder to fairly low ground and I could start to relax again.

That storm cell seemed to have passed in front of me. But one cell can spawn another. Twice before I had thought I had been bypassed only to find another cell right on top of me and lightning unnervingly close. So I kept going, making for the shelters, stopping only to hastily put the rain cover onto my pack, then heading on. I stepped on a slab of rock and had my feet go right out from under me and I fell, wrenching one shoulder when the pole stayed firmly planted and jerked my arm up. I picked myself up, gave the shoulder a cautious shrug to check for injury, and kept going.

Soon I reached the first shelter, Hemlocks Lean-to. It was luxurious, with a covered porch with picnic table, four big sleeping shelves arranged like bunks and a loft above the porch. I stopped to make a note in the register and check the previous entries. Gator Woman had been by as well as Sanguine, who I had last seen at Grayson Highlands, but no sign of more recent companions.

The next shelter was only .1 miles away and was said to have a better water source so I went on. It turned out to be much smaller and damper. There I found two male hikers who had already taken the choice spots by the side walls, and made no move to make room for me at the center. It seemed almost claustrophobic so I made a quick note in the register and went back to the more cozy Hemlocks.

I got settled and set out my filter bottle and big Platypus water bag to catch rain dripping off the roof for water. It was only a little after 1pm and I had gone only ten miles. But thunder was still rumbling and there were eight miles and three more peaks before Highway 7, where I could hitch a ride to Great Barrington. I had had enough dodging lightning in high places and the last time I had tried hitching a ride in a pouring rain I had failed miserably. So I decided to stay for the night.

As if to endorse my decision, the rain came down harder than ever. In just an hour my filter bottle was overflowing and the bag had two liters. So I did not have to worry about water.

I spent the afternoon journaling, purifying water and napping. When suppertime came I really did not feel like getting up to cook. So I lay in my sleeping bag and crunched the rest of my tortellini right out of the package. I found it chews nicely even uncooked and is a nice change of flavor and texture from eating uncooked ramen noodles. Then I munched down a 3oz block of cream cheese that had been in my pack for days and then had two breakfast squares for dessert. Yum, hiker high cuisine!

Supper over, I hung my food bag and curled up with the flashlight my brother had given me and (gasp) a copy of Joyce's "Portrait of the artist as a young man" I found lying around the shelter.

-Mouse

Saturday, July 24, 2004
Destination: Tom Leonard Lean-To
From: Hemlocks Lean-To
Today's Miles: 14.4
Trip Miles: 1512.8

I ended up having the shelter to myself for the night. The rain ended by dawn but it was overcast, dark and gloomy. I got going by 6am but soon realized I had left my pack cover hanging in the shelter and had to go back.

The Trail went up a steep channel that must have been flowing with water in the rain, then wove back and forth between laurel groves and rock outcrops overlooking the valley. Blueberries started appearing as if to apologize for the inhospitable weather.

I made my way cautiously over the wet rock and went even more carefully when it started slanting down into the valley. Even so I fell badly once, bashing my left elbow on a rock and bruising it.

Next came several miles of marshy ground swarming with mosquitoes that seemed unimpressed by repellant. I swatted away at them and considered going to Great Barrington when I reached Hwy 7 and finding a nice dry cheery motel room, eating away and maybe even seeing a movie. I was already gloomy from the weather and yet another delay made me fret about taking longer than I expected to get to Katahdin. But I had hit my limit and yearned for a break.

Still, there were compensations. I passed a memorial at the site of the last battle of Shay's Rebellion. Then I found two blackberries, then discovered a new kind of red raspberry; without the pods and more tart, like store-bought ones. The larger ones were extra juicy from the rain. That helped a bit.

I found handfuls of them just before Hwy 7. At the road I looked for the fruit stand in the guidebook but only found a greenhouse and antique shop. I was considering whether to go into town here or to go in by a road 8 miles further to get in a more full day when a man made up my mind by offering me a ride.

He dropped me off at the grocery store. I got more tortellini, instant pudding, cocoa mix to use instead of milk, granola to go with that for breakfasts, fig bars for lunches and a quart of chocolate whole milk. Downing the milk with its 1000 calories did wonders for my mood, as did a thinning of the overcast. At a gas station I got a sub for lunch, filled up on water, checked my email with my Pocketmail at the pay phone. With all my needs seen to and brimming with energy from the chocolate milk, thoughts of rest were forgotten and I decided to skip the motel and hitched a ride back to the Trail. I'd get in an honest 14 miles, salvaging the day.

I grazed on the new red raspberries on the way to the last Trail crossing of the Housatonic River, then crossed the bridge and ate my sub in the shade on the other side. Then up to the ridge top, now dried out from the sunshine and cooled by breezes, nibbling blueberries all the way to the shelter.

I ran into my second southbound thruhiker. The first had been before the rain with the name Fort Wayne for his hometown.

There were weekenders at the tentsites and lots of mosquitoes. But the lower bed platforms were big enough to pitch my tent on one, making a bug refuge inside the shelter. The two hikers from yesterday found nowhere to tent and too many bugs so they headed on.

I fixed tortellini with tuna and a bit of tomato paste, then pistachio pudding made with hot cocoa mix. The shelter started filling up, with two weekenders, a pair of male section hikers and a female section hiker who had tented near me two nights ago. She had been caught by yesterday's thunderstorm on Mount Race and ended up at the campsite I had considered going back to. There was even a ridgerunner by the name of Fred tarped in front of the shelter.

-Mouse

Sunday, July 25, 2004
Destination: Upper Goose Pond Cabin
From: Tom Leonard Lean-To
Today's Miles: 21.1
Trip Miles: 1533.9

The day started normally enough, except that my hat seemed to have vanished. Maybe a porcupine saw it as a salty treat and carried it off? That is my third lost hat. I am starting to feel like Peter Rabbit the way I lose clothing!

The Trail went up several steep climbs then settled into rolling terrain and a soft pine needle surface. In some open spaces I found more new red raspberries and up on the heights some blueberries.

All that was forgotten at lunch when the mad idea hit me to hike the full 21 miles to Upper Goose Pond Cabin. Even though it is a famous trail stop, I had reconciled myself to skipping it because staying there would mean two more short days and I had had all too many short days lately. Then it occurred to me to do a very long one instead and make up the time lost by the rain as well as getting to stay at Upper Goose Pond. Galvanized by the decision I strode as fast as my legs could go, hoping to arrive well before dark. I found myself actually passing the two male hikers I'd crossed paths with the past several days, named Myst and Bones, as well as Loon and Little' Bit and her twosome, all of whom had started closer to the Cabin than I had!

Despite the fact the last miles turned rocky I somehow got there at 6pm. It is a cabin maintained by the AMC with a caretaker and kitchen rather like the Mohican Center. It has a legendary pancake breakfast, so my effort should be well rewarded. I also found Palm Tree. He said he had left Kent with Boonie and Tree Frog, then had taken a zero day in Great Barrington while they had gone ahead. He expects to rejoin them at Dalton.

-Mouse

Monday, July 26, 2004
Destination: Kay Woods Shelter
From: Upper Goose Pond Cabin
Today's Miles: 17.6
Trip Miles: 1551.5

Since the pancakes would not be ready until 6:30 I had the luxury of sleeping in until 6am this morning. I had five (seven?) pancakes plus two mugs of nice strong coffee.

I had meant to go a nice conservative 12 miles and camp, but Palm Tree said he heard a weather prediction of heavy rain and flooding tonight. So I decided AGAIN to go long and make for the Kay Woods shelter eighteen miles away where I would be under cover.

I headed up the hill, over the Massachusetts Turnpike, and across Hwy 20 just five miles from Lee, Mass, home of the Tanglewood Music Festival. Then up a REALLY big hill and then off over more or less rolling ground.

A little after halfway, I came to the home of "The Cookie Lady." Her name is Marilyn Wiley and she lives on a blueberry farm and is famous for the home-baked cookies she has given to thruhikers for years. I think the farm has sucked in all the berry Karma for miles around because I did not see a single blueberry until a mile away, red raspberries started appearing closer but the farm itself had blueberries the size of grapes! They were the biggest I had ever seen. Her husband Roy greeted us, explaining she was off in Indianapolis. He showed us where to fill our water bottles and invited us to go pick blueberries. I gathered a pint of huge berries for just a dollar. Then he brought us a basket with a soda for each of us and six yummy cookies! Yum....

Then we started the last six miles. When Palm Tree said there was a flashflood watch in less than an hour I shifted into high gear and sped to the shelter lest I get drenched. I was first there so I was able to get one of the lower shelves where I could set up my tent for the bugs.

-Mouse

Tuesday, July 27, 2004
Destination: Dalton, MA
From: Kay Woods Shelter
Today's Miles: 3.0
Trip Miles: 1554.5

It was only 3 miles to Dalton but none of the other towns just down the Trail had reasonable motel rates and the heavy rain had not arrived yet and still threatened, so I decided to stop there. With the short hike, my only berries were Cookie Lady blueberries with my granola for breakfast. Oh well.

While there I ran into Sanguine, whom I had last seen in southern Virginia. To my surprise, I also saw Little Tree, who was taking a break with a friend from home. Adam was here too, returning to the trail after waiting three weeks for his damaged arch to heal. He will do the section he skipped later.

There was another reunion too. Little' Bit's friend Bluebell asked if I had left a hat at a shelter, then pulled my missing hat out of his pack! Someone had hung it up and with all the gear in the shelter I had not been able to see it. Gee was I glad to see it! The weather is getting rainy and its broad brim keeps the water out of my face and glasses.

Carefree, who is hiking with her friend Freedom, noticed what she thought was a spider bite. Today it got blistery and she went to see a doctor here. She found out it was really the onset of shingles, probably brought on by exhaustion and stress. She is on an antiviral medication for a week and they had already decided to take the next day off and relax, so she ought to be all right.

An email from my father suggested I go visit the Crane Paper Company's museum of papermaking. So I went through the rain to see it and found it rather interesting. They specialize in fine cotton based paper and have made the paper used for all US currency for over a century!

I had the misfortune of having a room near the motel's pub. For most of the evening there was loud music hammering the walls of my room, so I ended up watching TV until 1am when it was finally quiet enough to sleep.

-Mouse

Wednesday, July 28, 2004
Destination: Mark Noepel Shelter
From: Dalton, MA
Today's Miles: 13.7
Trip Miles: 1568.2

I got going a bit sleepily from the late night. The forecast called for late afternoon thunderstorms so rather than waste time having breakfast at the excellent diner I had been to the previous morning I went to the convenience store on the way to the Trail. I got two pre-made egg-muffin things, zapped them in the microwave and wolfed them down.

There was light rain and the woods were dark as the evil woods in a Disney cartoon. Here and there was a less dense spot where light shined through, reminding me of the cover illustration of the old paperbacked edition of "The Light in the forest" I had read in grade school. The ground was drenched from the recent rain, streams ran high with water cascading noisily and the stepping stones were often awash which made crossing tricky.

I found two red raspberries, then on the hill called The Cobble I found blueberries, those frosty friends of mine. I had a handful, then left the rest for other berry addicts.

It was nine miles to the town of Cheshire. I ran into a whole string of southbounders who spoke glowingly of the hostel at the Catholic Church. I was inclined to stop there, since there were five more miles before the next shelter high up the flanks of Mount Greylock.

In Cheshire I stopped at Diane's Twist, an ice cream and sandwich shop right by the trail just inside town. I had a nice roast beef wrap with a coffee shake. On top of that, she let me fill up on water, use the restroom behind the counter, and for good measure she wrapped up a couple of the ends of roast beef left over after slicing to give me for free, saying they should get me up the mountain. Well after that generosity how could I slink off to a hostel? Invigorated, I headed up the mountain.

I could see the top disappeared into the base of the low clouds. Soon I was up there, swallowed up in the cloud as well. It was not raining but was quite foggy and the ground was even more saturated. I had to pick my way through large boggy areas.

The shelter was over 2800 feet up, the highest I have slept since Shenandoah Park in Virginia. I am back in the serious mountains and they will get higher and more rugged as the days go on.

-Mouse

Thursday, July 29, 2004
Destination: Sherman Brook Campsite
From: Mark Noepel Shelter
Today's Miles: 11.4
Trip Miles: 1579.6

Today started even more inside-a-cloud-ish than yesterday ended, very foggy and everything drenched. I made my way up to the summit of Mount Greylock, stepping carefully through the boggy spots trying to find firm stones to step on. Every now and then my boots went into the deep mud, but by some miracle the waterproofing and Gore-Tex lining kept my socks dry.

At 3491 feet Mount Greylock is the highest mountain in Massachusetts and the highest I have been up since Virginia. Right next to the summit is Bascom Lodge, an inn rather like LeConte Lodge in the Smokys except it is a single stone building built in the 30s by the CCC and the food is brought up by truck instead of helicopter and llama. In theory you need a reservation even for meals. Breakfast is "family style" at 8am and I arrived outside about 8:20. Perhaps I looked forlorn because when I went past the dining hall and a worker saw me he went around and let me in. When I asked if the snack bar was open he got me a plate for breakfast, which was still going on even though I had no reservation. I lucked out, my timing was perfect and there was enough food for one more person so I sat down to my second breakfast of the morning! I had mushroom omelet, bacon, a delectable and filing mixture of fried onions, potatoes and cheese, plus cantaloupe, toast, orange juice and coffee. Mmmmmmmm. He was a very good cook so everything was delicious and I thanked him profusely as only a satiated thru-hiker can.

Then I went outside and refilled my water bladder from the tap and started groping through the dense fog for the northward Trail off the summit. Just as I found it I noticed a faint shadow through the gloom off to my right and suddenly realized it was the huge memorial to Massachusetts's WW1 dead, almost invisible in the murk. Going closer I managed to get a picture of the lower part, then went in the door at the base. I found myself in a round room with an arched arcade around the perimeter. Around the top were passages from "In Flanders' Fields," the same WW1 poem I had quoted back at Lehigh Gap, including the end part about keeping faith "Or the dead shall not sleep, though poppies grow, in Flanders' Fields" A staircase wound upwards invitingly, but since all I would see from the top was more fog I decided against climbing up.

Outside I ran into more red raspberries, the only berries I found all day. The sun finally started to break through and start drying things out, but not fast enough. On the slippery descent off the mountain I slipped, fell, and bent the same lower Leki pole section that had been replaced in Damascus after I bent the original near Roan Mountain.

Down in the town of North Adams at the foot of the mountain I went to the supermarket and bought food, including a pint of whole chocolate milk for today and a pound of liverwurst for tomorrow. Then I checked my email and went to the Friendly's restaurant next door, where I had a double chocolate shake, a chicken breast sandwich and a free sundae! Of course I picked black raspberry ice cream in keeping with the berry theme of this part of my hike.

Then across the Hoosic River. It drains into the Hudson, so for the last couple days I have gone from the Housatonic basin back into the Hudson basin. I wonder if any of the Trail drains into the St. Lawrence? Then the last two miles up Sherman Brook to the campsite.

It was the first time I had to put my tent on a wooden tent platform, which becomes quite common in New England. To my delight, my Nomad tent went up without needing any extension ropes or even hooks or nails. I could slip each rope or cord between the ends of the boards and slip a stake through the loop to hold it in place. By careful siting, everything fit nicely! The tent is so long I had to put it up diagonally, hogging the entire platform. I had hoped it would leave room for another tent for sites where there is a shortage of platforms, but no such luck. I guess you can't have everything!

Today I put my third filter cartridge in my filter bottle. The last replacement was somewhere before Damascus and by now I could barely get water through the old cartridge. I have one spare left, which ought to last the rest of the hike.

With two big meals in me today, several others recently, and a resupply I am ready for the four day trek through Vermont's Green Mountains to Manchester Center.

-Mouse

Danie Martin

Friday, July 30, 2004
Destination: Congdon Shelter
From: Sherman Brook Campsite
Today's Miles: 12.3
Trip Miles: 1591.9

I SAW MY FIRST MOOSE!!! Two of them! Or is that Mooses? Meese? About 1pm I came to a beaver pond and there they were, out in the water grazing. I slipped out my camera, advanced the film and crept closer. I got one shot and went closer still, where the Trail went along the edge of the pond right past them. One turned and looked at me, then went back to grazing. I got a couple more closer pictures before they decided they had had enough. They splashed out of the pond, crossed the Trail and disappeared in the underbrush.

I went on cautiously, clacking my poles together every few seconds so they knew where I was. I did not want find out what they do when surprised at close quarters!. In a few moments I saw them splash into another pond below the beaver dam. I went over some large stepping stones across the fast-running outflow from the dam, went up a hill, and my first moose adventure was over.

Gee, a few days ago I saw a porcupine. Now all I need is to be snowed on and then I will have had all the Northern AT experiences and can go home, right? Guess not. Well, on to Katahdin.

Earlier at around 9am I had crossed the border into Vermont. That point is the south end of Vermont's Long Trail, which shares the next 100 or so miles with the Appalachian Trail, then runs 165 more to the Canadian Border. The Long Trail was completed in 1930 and helped inspire the idea of building the Appalachian Trail.

A southbounder I ran into has dubbed the state "Vermud." It has probably dried out a little but was still quite muddy. It made for a slow day, picking the driest way through. Several times I sank a boot nearly up to the top into soft mud. They managed to keep out the water, that is until I slipped crossing a stream and plunged my right foot into the cold water and scrapped my left leg in the bargain.

I managed to find blueberries on both sides of the border, mostly on the high peaks, along with two red raspberries.

Early in the day I found the lining of my left boot was starting to fray at the heel, exposing the hard edge of the plastic heel cup. I cushioned it with a square of moleskin and added a large piece of duct tape over that to hold it in place. Hopefully I can keep it repaired until I can replace them, probably at Manchester Center.

The shelter tonight is odd, almost like being in a garage with its narrow front opening and three glassed-in windows on the other walls. It has two double-bunk things that seem to be meant to hold two people each. That looks a bit optimistic, so I hope I get a shelf to myself.

Ponderer arrived with one hand swathed in gauze. He had fallen and slashed the palm near the border and had to hike back down to the road and spend a zero day getting it stitched.

-Mouse

Saturday, July 31, 2004
Destination: Kidd Gore Shelter
From: Congdon Shelter
Today's Miles: 18.7
Trip Miles: 1610.6

If I walked an even 14-15 miles each day until Manchester Center then tomorrow I would have to camp in the woods away from a shelter or campsite. This was allowed in Vermont but was discouraged, and the muddy and bouldery landscape promised little in the way of a flat dry tentsite. To stay at a shelter meant doing one long day. So I got on the Trail at 5:30am to get an early start and kept as fast a pace as the terrain would allow. The weather was blustery with gusts all day that threatened rain yet stayed dry.

The hike started with the discovery that the water we had drank last night came straight from a beaver pond; not the cleanest source. To emphasize the point, the trail followed a line of marsh boards, most of which were submerged beneath the pond leaving my feet drenched.

From there it went uphill to a height that had the first real view since entering Vermont as well as a good handful of raspberries. Next it plunged down a deep gorge to the road to Bennington, doing so via a fearfully steep flight of rude stone steps for hundreds of feet down. I slipped and fell once. I was unhurt but more than a little unnerved falling on such a dizzy slope. I suddenly felt really tired of falling and for a moment wondered for the first time if the whole thruhike was really worth it. By a miracle there was a cooler of Trail Magic at the bottom and I got a bottle of Gatorade which helped restore my composure and forget thoughts of quitting. Across the road the trail went over a river then up again, fortunately less steep without so many steps.

The shelter I might have stayed at was high up the side of Glastenbury Mountain, which loomed over 3700 feet high. At the top I climbed the fire tower, hanging on against the strong wind. It was the first fire tower I had seen still standing since Virginia or before. Most have been taken down as eyesores or safety hazards.

Four miles later I reached the shelter and the long-threatened rain showers finally started. I cooked two days worth of supper, using up the spare food I had brought in case I was delayed and followed it up with hot chocolate. Ponderer arrived as well as a man named Snowman who was hiking the Long Trail but everyone else who was with me seemed to have stopped at the last shelter.

-Mouse

Sunday, August 01, 2004
Destination: Stratton Pond Shelter
From: Kidd Gore Shelter
Today's Miles: 15.1
Trip Miles: 1625.7

It rained heavily during the night with some lightning. The trees were still dripping when I started hiking and within twenty minutes it was pouring again.

I was starting to get a bit tired of the wet, when the sun broke through for a moment. That got me singing "You are my sunshine, my only sunshine..." which got me in a silly mood again and I sang it over and over as the sun came and went.

It looked like it was going to be my first berry-less day when at the parking area before Stratton Mountain I found a nice patch of raspberries. Saved!

It was a 1700 foot climb from the parking lot to the top of the mountain. About 3/4 of the way up my right heel started to hurt. I stopped and found it had been too many miles in the damp and the skin was turning tender. I put on a patch of moleskin, which helped enough to let me limp to the top.

There at the base of the fire-tower I took off my pack and threw myself on the ground in front of a tour group from Europe. While the caretaker chatted about how my hike was going and explained to the tourists what thruhiking is, I took off my shoes and tried to let my socks dry a little. I put a whole half sheet of moleskin on my heel, doused my foot and the inside of my shoe with powder and put my shoes back on. Then I climbed the tower for a look around, signed the register and started down.

Up at the top the vegetation was very different than lower down. Sort of dwarf evergreens and small seedlings, moss, lichen and shamrock-looking things so it looked like Christmas Tree Town. As I descended the pines got taller, the undergrowth changed to more normal. Then rather abruptly broadleaf trees replaced the pines.

I walked extra carefully, avoiding the mud as much as possible to try to let my shoes start drying out. Hopefully that would get them dry enough to avoid more foot trouble tomorrow.

My feet took a beating yesterday and were sore all night. I feel like my physical and emotional reserves are starting to wear a bit thin and I need to start conserving them, avoiding high mileage days unless conditions are quite good and possibly taking more zero days than in the past. Several times in the last two days I have found myself getting really really tired of falling down, of the wet and soreness and of everything. I had to remind myself that I have felt worse in the past months and conditions have been harder. Like when I was coming down from Clingmans Dome with my boots full of Icewater. I was REALLY grouchy then until my encounter with Louisiana Lou's Trail Magic and the Easter bunnies.

Someone has said that by this point it is a head game, that anyone who gets this far can get the whole way as long as they keep the will to continue. That is all it takes, the refusal to stop until the very end. The trick is to keep that will. Quitting is easy, as Socks found, but going the whole way is an accomplishment worth working for. It is just like running a marathon which I have done dozens of times except that when you hit the wall you have to hang on for six or seven weeks instead of six or seven miles.

The Shelter was one of the busy ones where a $6 fee is charged to reduce usage and maintain things. For that, the water supply was very far away.

Ponderer arrived a bit after me, having taken the gondola lift down to the foot of the mountain for a meal. Then Palm Tree, Boonie, and Tree Frog arrived too. They had given up their idea of camping in the woods and hiked over 19 miles to get to the shelter. Adam was having more foot trouble and decided to leave the Trail again, probably for good.

-Mouse

Monday, August 02, 2004
Destination: Manchester Center, VT
From: Stratton Pond Shelter
Today's Miles: 10.6
Trip Miles: 1636.3

Today the sun was finally out for real. We learned this has been Vermont's wettest July ever, with 3 times the normal rainfall. Hence all the mud, which is like that of springtime here when hiking the Trail is discouraged. It is finally starting to dry out. But we have also been assured that today's section is muddy ALL of the time so our mud fest will continue.

The first half was indeed muddy. To make it more fun part of it ran through a wilderness area where the undergrowth is allowed to encroach on the footpath, meaning more scraped legs from squeezing past the underbrush to get past bogs.

Finally I got to a drier section and on a sunny hillside eight miles in I found two ripe blackberries. By such a thin thread is my berry eating streak sustained. Later I also found some raspberries but left them for anyone else who is hiking for berries.

Just after that while crossing a stream I slipped on a stepping stone and fell. The fall should earn extra "Technical Merit" points because I ended up sitting in the water with my legs tangled in an awkward knot and one pole underneath me, pinning my right hand to the ground by the wrist strap. I managed to shift my weight enough to free the pole, then got it through the brush until it was in front of me, then levered myself back to my feet. No harm done that time.

Shortly after, the Trail led along the brink of a 3 foot waterfall with hard rock below and one pole slipped just as I put my weight on it. A yelp of sheer panic ripped from me as I frantically scrambled to avoid toppling over. Once I had my balance again I had to just stand there and take several deep breaths to regain my nerves. I would surely have survived the fall, but bashing my head on the rock from that height would have been nasty. When meeting a family of dayhikers I could tell my face was drawn and haggard instead of bright and smiley. I found myself wondering about taking tomorrow off to rest in town, but it was equally tempting to press northward instead.

I got a ride at noon to within a mile of Manchester Center and walked the rest of the way then found "Sutton's Place," where I hoped to stay. It turned out to be a hostel in the owner's house, with the nice decor and furnishings worthy of a good bed and breakfast. I took my pack up to my room, then tripped and nearly fell down the staircase! I hope I get over this falling-down thing, it seems to be following me everywhere.

I started off at a Scandinavian deli where I had a delicious pickled herring platter and a root beer float. At the local outfitter I got my bent pole section replaced, again for free. At the EMS store I got a new pair of the same model as the worn out shoes I have been wearing and a bottle of Nikwax to waterproof them with. Then I did laundry and bought food, including a supply of textured vegetable protein as a lighter alternative to meat.

I spent the rest of the afternoon resting and applying coats of waterproofing on my new shoes, went out for pizza, then continued the process until bedtime. I could not hog the bathroom to do this like I could in a regular motel room. So I would wet the shoes in the sink, then take them into my room to coat them and let them dry, then repeat the process. I was a bit nervous about doing it in a room with such nice carpet, but managed to keep it over plastic bags and confined the mess that way. Hopefully it will work out as well as if I could concentrate on doing a good job instead of avoiding damage to the rug or bathroom.

-Mouse

Tuesday, August 03, 2004
Destination: Lost Pond Shelter
From: Manchester Center, VT
Today's Miles: 14.8
Trip Miles: 1651.1

It is surprising what a shower, three big meals and a night in a comfy bed can do. I was all smiley, bright-eyed and bushytailed this morning, my zero day yearning evaporated, and I hit the Trail.

I had hardly left the road when I found a nice patch of raspberries, enough to graze properly and still leave plenty for others. It was nice and sunny and the mud was much better, largely dried and only a few boggy spots.

I spent much of the day high up in that Christmas Tree looking landscape, very cheery and a deeper more alive looking green than the broadleaf forest lower down. At Baker Peak the Trail went up a rock spine straight up the side of the mountain. It was steep enough to be exhilarating but not steep enough to be unnerving. It was long enough to make you work for it but not too long. The view was incredible. And at the top, the trail dove back into cool Christmas Tree terrain again. One of those perfect experiences that one discovers along the Trail!

At the shelter there was Ponderer, who had preceded me, and a pair of southbounders. Also there was Hobbit, a woman I had last seen at Partnership Shelter in Virginia! I got there just in time to avoid a light thundershower, just enough to cool things off for a good night's sleep.

There are good days on the Trail as well as hard ones, and today was a good one.

-Mouse

Wednesday, August 04, 2004
Destination: Minerva Hinchey Shelter
From: Lost Pond Shelter
Today's Miles: 14.9
Trip Miles: 1666.0

Today was nice hiking, with long stretches of smooth level footpath.

The highpoint was a spot called White Rocks. Here hikers over the years have gathered rocks of all sizes and stacked them into dozens of fantastic sculptures. Just before there I found empty blueberry bushes and just when I had nearly given up hope, I found one bush with a handful of berries. They were the first blueberries I had seen since the first day in Vermont! I found a scattering of more blueberries on the next mountain. Perhaps there is hope for this state.

At Minerva Shelter I could not decide whether to stop at a sensible 15 miles, do 14 tomorrow and then just five the next day to the Inn At The Long Trail, or go 4 more miles to the next shelter and reach the inn tomorrow evening. The second choice would put me a day ahead, but a 19 mile day would take a lot out of me. I couldn't decide and couldn't decide. Suddenly it started sprinkling, making my decision for me!

There were lots of mosquitoes, so I hung my tent from the rafters as a mosquito bar with my mattress inside.

-Mouse

Thursday, August 05, 2004
Destination: Cooper Lodge Shelter
From: Minerva Hinchey Shelter
Today's Miles: 13.8
Trip Miles: 1679.8

Today was another great day.

It started by going to the Whistletop restaurant in Clarendon a half mile off the trail. I ordered two eggs with ham and pancakes. It was all yummy and the pancakes were the size of a large dinner plate! At the nearby general store I called and reserved a room at the Inn on the Long Trail, then got a pint of milk to gulp down and a day's food. That way I won't need to get a shuttle from the inn to buy food in Rutland, so aside from laundry I can spend my stay just resting.

This morning I found more berries than all the rest of Vermont put together! Blackberries, red raspberries and lots of blueberries. Yum yum yum.

A trail angel had sodas waiting for us in a stream. Trail Magic is one thing Vermont has excelled in; I have had some every day and it really boosts the spirits.

I stopped for lunch at the Governor Clements Shelter. It is odd, being the only one I know of that hikers are advised in the guidebooks NOT to stay in overnight because of locals coming to drink, party and harass hikers. A Long Trail hiker had warned us a few days earlier, saying a woman had stayed there alone recently and they had come at 11pm in four wheel drive trucks driving in circles right around the shelter. Sure enough I could see tire tracks circling the shelter so I suspect the story is true.

The afternoon I spent ascending to the top of Killington Peak, Vermont's second highest mountain at over 4000 feet. I am spending the night at Cooper Lodge just a few hundred feet from the top. The Trail goes to the top of nearby Little Killington, then along a ridge to the main peak. The path there was level and easy to walk despite being so high up and the sky was that deep blue it just never is down at sea level. I found myself singing "I'm on the top of the world" out of utter silly happiness.

I had not planned on doing the steep climb from the shelter to the summit, just as I had not planned on doing the Half Gallon Ice Cream Challenge. But seeing how flat the trail was gave me the idea of trying to get to the snack bar at the summit before it closed at 4pm. I ran along the trail as fast as my legs would carry me. At the shelter I threw down my pack and grabbed my wallet then charged up the steep path to the top. Two male northbounders stormed past me yelling "They've got Ben and Jerry's up there!" Just short of the top I saw them coming back empty-handed looking dejected, reporting that the snack bar had just closed.

Being a resourceful Mouse, I dashed to the Gondola Lift and asked how long it was still open. Just enough time and I could go down for free, so I hopped into a gondola and made the ten minute ride to the shops at the bottom of the mountain. At the bottom I prudently asked first about a return ticket and how much time I had. The worker there told me the return was free for thruhikers and I had fifteen minutes. Running inside, I found all the food places were closed, but the sports shop was still open and it had pre-made subs and other snacks. I got a sub, some chips and a Ben and Jerry's ice cream bar, gulped down the ice cream then dashed back to the lift with minutes to spare. Then back to the top with my loot!

Woohoo, Success!!!

The view at the top was the best all around view I have yet seen on the Trail. I could see the valleys far below and mountains marching off in every direction as far as the eye could see. Being just below 4000 feet, it was getting quite chilly well before dark. For weeks I have slept lying directly on my air mattress and using my sleeping bag just as a cover to keep from getting too hot. I am sure this will be the coldest night I have seen in months and I will have my bag zipped right up to stay warm.

-Mouse

Friday, August 06, 2004
Destination: Inn At The Long Trail
From: Cooper Lodge Shelter
Today's Miles: 8.2
Trip Miles: 1688.0

This morning was chilly as I had expected and I took my time about leaving my nice warm sleeping bag since there was only a short distance to hike. I nearly gave up hope on berries, but a nice patch of raspberries near the Inn saved the day.

I was sitting reading in the lounge waiting for my room to be cleaned when the manager called my name. I gaped in astonishment. My friend Libby was standing by the desk. She had driven all the way from her home in Missouri to visit me and had not only guessed where I would be but she had arrived within an hour of me! An amazing feat considering all the emails and coordination that had been involved in all my previous Trail rendezvous.

We spent the rest of the day together getting caught up and watching vintage "Rocky and Bullwinkle" cartoons on DVD with her laptop computer. That brought back a lot of fond childhood memories. We ate in the Inn's pub. Libbie was unfamiliar with thruhiker appetites so she was a bit astounded by my capacity for food.

-Mouse

Saturday, August 07, 2004
Destination: Chateauguay Road
From: Inn At The Long Trail
Today's Miles: 12.8
Trip Miles: 1700.8

After a night in beds so soft and comfortable they should be outlawed anywhere within 50 miles of the Trail, Libbie and I went down to our complementary breakfast. To my delight, it was not one of those pale thin continental things, but serious food from a menu. Libbie had French toast and I had a big omelet with sausage, toast and potatoes. Mmmmmmmmmm!

At the table next to us we discovered Palm Tree, his wife, Boonie and Tree Frog. Palm Tree had been slack packing and spending evenings with his grandchildren. The other two had hiked in last evening and tented across the road.

Then we packed, for me a bit more work since Libbie had been like Santa Claus. She brought me poison ivy cream she had tried to mail to me way back at Boiling Springs, sunscreen and best of all, a half dozen packets of instant Thai iced tea mix. We checked out, then Libbie took more photos and we said farewell. I had my day's raspberries and went the half mile up the side trail to the AT.

It was a wet day, raining off and on much of the afternoon. It was also surprisingly chilly, never getting above 60 degrees. At Stony Brook Shelter I met Pilot and Polar with whom I had hiked the Shenandoahs. The three of us hiked together the last 5 miles to the road. Just as we got there it started raining again and there was a rush to get our tents up and things inside. Like at Big Meadows we were three women with three Nomad tents.

It let up long enough to cook and eat. Palm Tree, Boonie and Tree Frog showed up and tented with us.

My tent seems to be leaking a bit on one side, probably from the seam. If I get a chance I will try to seal that section again in Hanover.

-Mouse

Sunday, August 08, 2004
Destination: Thistle Hill Shelter
From: Chateauguay Road
Today's Miles: 17.8
Trip Miles: 1717.6

The morning was chilly but clear.

Instead of haunting the road crossings, the raspberries grew up on the heights where I am used to finding blueberries. As we had a lot of heights, I had a lot of raspberries. A few miles from the shelter I hit the mother lode, a huge thicket packed with ripe berries. I ate them by the handful and still there were plenty left for those behind.

I stopped at the first road to spread out my tent and try to dry it in the sun. I got the worst of the moisture dried before the sun hid behind clouds. It showed no sign of reappearing so I packed up my tent and moved on. Naturally then the sun came back out to laugh at me.

I had been told that the southern section of Vermont was easier because it ran along a ridge while this section went across the grain of the ridges. There WERE a lot of ups and downs, but the going seemed no worse than the Long Trail section with its steep deep gaps and high peaks.

I got to the shelter just in time as a rain shower started right after I arrived. Pilot and Polar got in about an hour later and Palm Tree after them. Of course the sun came out to laugh at us again right after the rain. Don't you hate it when the sun starts teasing?

I burned my supper trying to simmer it and then of all things, the handle broke off of my Lexan spoon! I thought they were supposed to be indestructible. I had to eat by holding the bowl of the spoon with my fingers. At least my timing is good. Tomorrow I get into Hanover and can get the spare spoon from my bounce box.

Everyone else straggled into the shelter after me and they all thought this section of Vermont was brutal, far worse than the early section and that I was nuts to think it was just the same. Hmmmmmm, maybe my brain is getting soft. Oh well.

-Mouse

Monday, August 09, 2004
Destination: Hanover NH
From: Thistle Hill Shelter
Today's Miles: 14.6
Trip Miles: 1732.2

Everyone started stirring around 5am. I waited as long as I could, then started to get up. I guess having my breakfast Poptarts in a ziplock next to my bed saved too much time; I found myself on the Trail at 5:45 and noted wryly that I could have stayed in bed another 15 minutes!

Still, it was good watching the world wake up. The trees were very tall with no underbrush and there were frequent meadows so were actually views for a change, unlike most days when the forest cut off sun and sky. I saw the first sliver of sunlight pop above the mountains to the east, casting long patches of light on the leafy forest floor like shadows in reverse. Out in the meadows the low sun brought out the rounded texture of the treetops and the sky was blue. Puffy white rivers of fog filled the low valleys in sharp contrast to the clearness above. The forest floor and leaves were dry but the grass and tall milkweed of the meadows were wet with dew so my boots alternately dampened and dried as I went. I found my first blackberry at 6:05, a new record! Then two more and several handfuls of raspberries. As I got lower into the first valley I expected to plunge into a cloud but all I noticed was a damp chill, a slight decease in visibility and wisps of white cloud overhead where there had been none.

The breakfast counter at the deli in West Hartford seemed busy and I did not see any milk in the grocery refriderator, so I bought two Klondike ice cream bars instead and ate them on the bench out front.

At the Elm Street trailhead in Norwich a Trail Angel had left a cooler of snacks and sodas as a Trail Magic farewell to Vermont. I drank my soda with one hand and carried my poles in the other as I walked along the road to the Connecticut River Bridge. Right in the middle there was a vertical line on the bridge parapet with the letters "Vt" and "N.H." on either side. Playfully I did the same game I had once played at the Prime Meridian line at London's Greenwich Observatory, standing with one foot one either side of the line and standing alternately on either foot. Vermont; New Hampshire, Vermont; New Hampshire. I giggled at jumping from state to state and started up the hill to Hanover, getting to Main Street at 130.

The Dartmouth Outing Club was closed until 2 so there was no lodging information there. I decided to go to the post office and see to my bounce box and winter clothing. I found my housemate had sent the wrong box with just two air mattresses and a bivy sack, no clothes except a too-heavy fleece jacket. I kept the bivy sack in case I got nothing better and turned to my bounce box.

To save weight over the Whites I took every nonessential from my pack to go into the box. The spreader bars and pole sack for my Nomad Tent, the bottle of body powder after putting a small supply in a ziplock, my new flashlight, the anti-itch cream and poison ivy lotion, the old water filter element I had saved to see what happens when you filter Coca Cola and any other odds and ends I could do without for two weeks. Then I got New Hampshire maps and guidebook pages, my light balaclava hood, and vitamins from the bulk jar in the box. I sealed up the two boxes and sent the bounce box to Gorham NH, beyond the Whites, and sent the other box back home.

Knowing I needed to call my housemate and not knowing when she would be home, I splurged and got a room at the pricey Hanover Inn where I would have a phone and a good central location. I was lucky, she was home! So over the phone I went item by item over the things I needed as she gathered them together, then asked her to take them straight to the post office and mail them to Glencliff NH by priority mail. What a relief to know my winter things would get to me after all with no delay!

Next I went to the Hanover Food Co-Op. It really is hiker heaven! For the first time since Hot Springs NC I found Bear Valley Pemmican bars. They are light and have over 400 calories, making a good hiking lunch that really keeps me going. I took all they had, then got a 12-pack of Cliff bars on sale, dried pea and lentil soup mix, tortellini, Poptarts and odds and ends. I would mail food shipments to Glencliff NH and North Woodstock ME, then mail the extras ahead to Gorham NH to feed me in Maine, where lightweight high nutrition food would come in handy.

Finally I could relax and eat the rest of the evening. The Hanover Inn was comfortable, but I had been in nicer hotels for the price. But the cheaper motels were too far away and the Dartmouth fraternities no longer put up hikers so I had had little choice.

-Mouse

Tuesday, August 10, 2004
Destination: Moose Mountain Shelter
From: Hanover NH
Today's Miles: 11.0
Trip Miles: 1743.2

I had breakfast then split the food I had bought up and mailed it to Glencliff, North Woodstock and Gorham.

After that I needed to go to the EMS outdoor store in West Lebanon. To save time I ended up taking a taxi. It took half an hour to get there from the inn, so rather than get another one at the store after I was done I had him wait for me. That meant shopping in a rush. So I only got a new fuel canister and a pair of lightweight Teva flip-flops to wear when fording rivers in Maine. The whole trip took less than an hour, less than the bus ride one way.

In between forays out of my room on those errands I put three more coats of waterproofing on my boots, being careful to wet them thoroughly with water before each coat. Hopefully that will fix the leaking I noticed after I did them in Manchester Center.

I had time for one last shower before packing up and checking out at 11:30. On the way to the Trail I stopped off at the Co-Op for one last food buying spree. They had not restocked the Bear Valley bars so I settled for more Cliff bars. I got more iron pills and also some bananas, Fritos and chocolate milk for lunch, which I ate at the picnic tables outside the store.

I got back onto the Trail at 12:30 and had ten miles to the shelter. My pack weight was heavier yet the hike went a bit faster than I expected. Up Velvet Rocks I found my first New Hampshire blueberry and there were raspberries scattered along. Up Moose Mountain there was a patch thick enough to pick by the handful.

I went to the old Moose Mountain Shelter, which guidebooks say was to be torn down last fall. There is a new shelter but it is farther away from the water source and seemed more crowded judging by how many people came from it past the old one to get water.

-Mouse

Wednesday, August 11, 2004
Destination: Hexacuba Shelter
From: Moose Mountain Shelter
Today's Miles: 17.7
Trip Miles: 1760.9

It started raining around 3am and was still drizzling at 5:30. Since yesterday's hiking went so fast I hoped to get to the Hexacuba Shelter, which was known for it's unique shape and accompanying Pentaprivy. So I made an early start rather than letting things dry out.

There were raspberries then blueberries higher up then raspberries again. Enough for both by the handful with plenty left for others. Yummy!

Much of the hiking was good but much was hard too. There were two mountains to go over. The second one had a steep climb then a ridgewalk over exposed outcrops like back in Massachusetts then an even steeper climb near the top. I was so worn out by the time I reached the top I nearly decided to stop at the shelter on the summit after just 12 miles. But it was full of noisy boy scouts and it was only 2pm. So I decided to press on and hope Hexacuba was quieter.

The Trail followed a ridgeline down in a two hour descent. Warned that the water source at Hexacuba was not the best, I stopped at the stream at the bottom to refill with water before going on to the shelter. As I finished and started eating a Balance Bar, Two Cents caught up. Just then I heard the rumble of thunder in the distance.

The shelter was only 1.3 miles away and I was off the high ground so I was not too worried. And the first part was a fairly steep 500 foot climb so it was hard to hurry. Up at the top I could see the sky darkening and the wind coming straight from there toward me. There were some plump blueberries too and it was hard not to get a nice helping but the rumble was getting closer so I curtailed my berry eating and headed on.

A little later the first drops fell and long before the shelter the downpour began. I got a good drenching and for good measure the lightning was getting closer. My glasses were covered with water and between that and the dark of the storm it was hard to find my way. Finally I sloshed my way up to the shelter. It was the first solid drenching I had had in well over a month.

To my surprise there was no one there yet. I got out dry clothes and took advantage of the privacy to strip and dry off. Naturally Two Cents appeared right then but fortunately his glasses were as rain-blurred as mine had been. Otherwise he would have seen more than I wanted!

Over the next hours four southbounders appeared along with Crash and William Wallace, with whom I had talked back in Damascus. They were not the only visitors. Another thunderstorm arrived at 6 and yet another came around 7pm.

I was surprised by the shelter design. From the name Hexacuba I expected some exotic complex shape. But the "cuba" part seems to refer to Mount Cube whose flank the shelter is on. The shelter is just a nicely made six-sided log structure reminding me of pictures of old frontier blockhouses but with two sides open to make a porch overhang. It was a dry and cozy retreat from the bad weather.

I expect this will my last high mileage day for a long time. It is 15 miles to Glencliff and then I will be in the White Mountains with the rugged part of Maine after that.

-Mouse

Thursday, August 12, 2004
Destination: Glencliff, NH
From: Hexacuba Shelter
Today's Miles: 14.7
Trip Miles: 1775.6

The morning was foggy and damp. I got my clothes from the line no drier than when I had hung them last night and put on the wet shorts. I could not bear to put on the cold clammy t-short, so left that ordeal for later and kept on my long-sleeved Capilene top instead. Then I cautiously made my way up the slippery rock slabs and slopes to the summit of Mount Cube. Blueberries were everywhere and I nibbled contentedly. What does a hard climb matter as long as there are lots of blueberries at the top! Near the top the wind picked up and the trail was marked along the slabs with rock cairns. The summit was a high barren slab.

The way down looked worse on the profile but was dirt slope and much easier to negotiate than the slick rock that I had ascended. At the bottom I folded my wet t-shirt into a narrow band, put it across my tummy and buckled the pack waist belt over it to hold it in place. That warmed it up so I only had to put on a warm wet shirt instead of a cold wet one. Along the way the blueberries switched to raspberries and I snatched them to eat as I went.

It started raining again before noon and kept up all the way to Glencliff. By then I was getting raw spots on the tops of my right toes from hiking so far in wet boots and socks. It was also boggy from all the rain and there were lots of aggressive bloodsucking bugs of different sorts.

I checked into the Hikers Welcome Hostel across from the Post Office. There I learned a tropical storm was moving up the coast. No wonder it was so wet! There was another tropical storm on the way and the wet weather might keep up into next week. Well, I will take at least tomorrow off to dry out, do laundry, let my foot heal and sift through my gear to decide what not to carry over the White Mountains.

My cold weather gear had arrived from home and I sorted through it and mailed the summer sleeping bag and the bivy sack back home. Any other items I don't need in the Whites I will mail to Gorham. Then a load of us went by van to nearby Warren NH to order take-out supper at the restaurant and stop at the grocery store. Back at the hostel again, I ate my way through a half pound cheeseburger, large salad and a half gallon of milk while we watched the movie "Hidalgo" on DVD before going upstairs to sleep on mattresses laid out on the floor.

-Mouse

Friday, August 13, 2004
Destination: Glencliff, NH
From: Glencliff, NH
Today's Miles: 0.0
Trip Miles: 1775.6

There was lightning in the sky when I went to bed and it poured around midnight. The forecast is for heavy rain and flooding today and tonight because of the remains of Hurricane Bonnie but only partly cloudy tomorrow. If it clears I might be back on the Trail then.

Pilot and Polar arrived in the afternoon and so did Pilot and Vaportrail. So the two women named Pilot finally got to meet!

The real rain started around four and let up around suppertime. Okie had his pickup here and took a load of us in to Warren to eat at the town's other restaurant. There we ran into Boonie, Tree Frog and Palm Tree, whose wife had picked them up one road short of Glencliff to go to a motel last night.

Several of us are planning to slackpack from Kinsman Notch tomorrow. That will let us climb the difficult north face of Mt Mooselauke with a light load instead of descending it with a heavy load and also gives the option of staying here Sunday when Hurricane Charles is expected.

-Mouse

[The White Mountains brought a renewed concern for hypothermia, a potentially lethal drop in body temperature caused by cold wet conditions. It was something I had not had to think about since North Carolina. That not only meant carrying warm clothing. It also meant keeping a close watch on the weather as well as making and remaking my plans in order to avoid potentially dangerous conditions. It had another effect as well. One hypothermia experience I had read about occurred right here on Kinsman Mountain when a woman arrived at Eliza Brook Shelter late in the afternoon and got talked into going over the mountain instead of stopping for the night. She got caught on the summit at nightfall in a cold rain and barely managed to get down. Learning from her experience, I vowed never to give in to the temptation to get in "one more peak" before dark. That cautious mindset meant repeatedly stopping for the day in mid afternoon and getting left behind several times by friends who pushed on, but it did get me safely through the Whites without ever having to face truly hazardous weather. Since I was hiking mostly alone, avoiding risk was important to me as I could not count on having help if I got into trouble.]

Saturday, August 14, 2004
Destination: Kinsman Notch
From: Glencliff
Today's Miles: 9.5
Trip Miles: 1785.1

Today the weather looked promising, though the next hurricane is due Sunday.

Pilot and Polar hiked out. Three more slacked north to Kinsman Notch, where they would pick up their packs and continue north. Okie, Lonesome Dove and I would go in the van with their packs and slack south from Kinsman Notch back to the hostel.

The climb up from the notch was not what I had expected. I had a mental image of the trail snaking precariously up a sheer face. Actually it runs up a ravine near a picturesque brook cascading down. It was certainly steep and slippery but there were no dizzy heights or really serious drops. There were rock slabs at a 45 degree or so angle with wooden steps bolted to them where there were no footholds and with rebar handrails to pull oneself up the taller steps and ledges. It takes some care but was not too difficult. The weather was sunny with scattered clouds, nice and dry climbing.

The terrain gradually got that high altitude Christmas Tree look like on the peaks in Vermont. Then the trees got even shorter, scattered with old dead trees, indicating that I was nearing the tree line. I got one good view to the south from an overlook before I found myself ascending through the base of a cloud.

Up a rise and the trees abruptly ended. Before me was the North Peak of Mooselauke blanketed with grass and other low ground cover. A line of tall rock cairns marched spookily up into the mist with the rock-covered Trail following them. A chill wind blew the mist across the ground with a whispering sound and the air turned damp and cold, making me put on my nylon windbreaker. I saw what at first looked rather like Stonehenge in a thick fog. Coming closer, it was people gathered at the summit. Here and there were makeshift windbreaks, circular walls of piled rocks. In one I found Palm Tree, Boonie, Tree Frog and several other hikers I knew including Lonesome Dove. I joined them and had Poptarts for lunch while we talked. The thick drifting mist gave a closed-in feeling, like we were in a Hollywood soundstage set with fog machines instead of an open mountain peak. Sort of like scenes of heaven in movies, where everyone walks about in fog.

Now and then a patch of blue sky would become visible. A moment later there would be a momentary view of the landscape downwind before the mist closed in again. I tried to get a picture but it would turn foggy before I got in a good spot for a shot.

Finally we started down, the three men heading north and Lonesome Dove and I going south to the hostel. She and I talked for half an hour or so before I dropped behind and hiked the rest of the way alone.

The trees reappeared. At first a carpet of tiny ground-hugging ones, then dwarves and Christmas Tree sized and then finally tall pine forest. Before we parted we saw beautiful views of the valley to the northwest. Alone, I reached broadleaf forest and the Trail evolved from mountain path to regular looking trail. It grew warm and sunny again so I removed my jacket and put it away.

I began to despair of finding any berries today but finally where the Trail skirted the edge of fields at the foot of the mountain I found a thicket of big ripe sweet juicy raspberries. I had two large handfuls. Yummy!

Jeffers Brook just before the road was twenty feet wide with no bridge. Fortunately the water had gone down just enough that I got across on stepping stones without having to ford the cold water. The first time I tried, the path of partly submerged rocks led to a gap too wide to get over. I turned back but found another line of stones just downstream that got me across.

Back at the hostel, Lonesome Dove's sister came to visit her and they drove off for dinner. Okie got back and drove me and two southbounders to Warren at the same place as before. The five of us were the only ones staying at the hostel tonight, a surprise since yesterday it had been packed. We spent the evening watching "The Fellowship of The Ring" and then "Spaceballs."

I checked the forecast from time to time. As the evening went on the predictions of the possible effects of Tropical Storm Charley on our area grew less and less severe. I might be able to hike out tomorrow!

-Mouse

Sunday, August 15, 2004
Destination: Eliza Brook Shelter
From: Kinsman Notch
Today's Miles: 7.5
Trip Miles: 1792.6

Hurricane Charley went elsewhere and this morning's forecast was for a good day with some showers and clearing. So I decided to head out. I was the only one going to Kinsman Notch today so I would have to pay the whole $25 shuttle fee but still it would cost less than another night at the hostel and going with Lonesome Dove the next day.

Before leaving I made a final trimming of my pack, putting items in an envelope to mail ahead to Gorham. I sent off one pair of socks, my water filter bottle, Teva flip-flops, nylon windbreaker and heavy balaclava. I kept three pairs of socks, lightweight Capilene top and bottom, midweight Capilene top, Polartec top, Gortex rain suit, thin gloves and thin balaclava. I also kept my Platypus hydration bladder. I will use a new pack of Aqua Mira for purification and will keep what is left of the old pack as a reserve in case something happens to the new pack. My reasoning is that that will be lighter than the filter bottle, pure water is available at the huts and I don't expect as much freezing weather as I saw early in the hike, when the filter bottle was easier to protect from freezing.

Kinsman Notch marks the beginning of the section managed by the AMC, the Appalachian Mountain Club. It includes the White Mountains and extends to Grafton Notch Maine. The Whites have special rules, rather like those in the National Parks. Above treeline, Hikers may only stay at designated campsites and shelters, or at a chain of "huts." Most of the shelters and campsites charge a fee of $8. The huts cost $82 for a bunk and two meals with a reservation, but a very limited number of thruhikers can stay overnight on a work-for-stay basis. Some of these restrictions are because of heavy use of the area, others are due to the frequent dangerous weather conditions the Whites are known for.

I got to the Trail at 10am and got my raspberries first thing, then started up and over Wolf Mountain. The trail had a lot of slanted rock slabs, ledges and even boggy spots with and without stepping stones or marsh boards. I can understand marsh in low spots, but marsh high up a tall mountain strikes me as a bit unfair! Between the bad ground and steepness it took longer than usual to cover the eight miles to the shelter.

Then there was the Wolf Mountain Mosquito Air Force, valiantly giving their lives to attack intruding thruhikers like me. They must have tiny little oxygen masks to operate up at high altitude! Between their biting and my slapping there was blood spilled on both sides, most of it mine. I found myself longing for cold weather to put them out of action.

In the shelter I found a group of six women out for a three day backpacking trip along with Polar and Pilot in their tents. I set up my tent too, for the mosquitoes.

It was the largest all-woman group we had seen on the Trail. The nine of us talked for hours. The six women were a circle of roommates and former roommates who got together every year for a backpacking trip in the White Mountains. They were full of questions for the three of us about the experience of women thruhiking. But we also talked about everything under the sun, like whether to use a regression formula or a factorial formula to determine the potential number of unique cabbage patch dolls possible assuming a given set of variables! Ahh, nothing like a nice big dose of "girl-talk."

-Mouse

Monday, August 16, 2004
Destination: Franconia Notch
From: Eliza Brook Shelter
Today's Miles: 8.8
Trip Miles: 1801.4

It started raining around 4am and kept up past 6. I took my time getting going in hopes it would either stop or at least warm up. By 7am I had completed the metamorphosis from warm and cozy in sleeping bag to hiking in the rain in just shorts and t-shirt. I had just crossed the brook that ran past the shelter when one of the six other women called me back. She held out a bandana and asked if it was mine. It was not, but by the dog theme on it I guessed it was Polar's and took it to give to her in the evening.

The path to the top of Kinsman Mountain led mostly up a rock jumble straight up the side of the mountain for hundreds of feet, interrupted by smooth slabs and steep ledges. I took my time, placing my feet carefully to avoid slipping on the wet stone.

The rain stopped but I went up into a cloud. Near the top the trees shrank to dwarf size and there was an eerie quiet. Beyond the treetops was nothing but white. At the summit was a small treeless zone covered with moss, lichen, succulents and other dwarfed plants. Once my head was above the trees the silence was replaced by the rustle of wind past my ears. The fog gave a profound sense of aloneness.

Making my way down from the south peak a jab of pain in my right knee warned me and I took my weight off it before the cartilage shifted enough to dislocate the joint like it had back in Virginia. Holding that foot off the ground I flexed the knee cautiously to check for damage then carefully started off again. The rough going made me very worried about wrecking my knee high up the mountain and being unable to get down and no way to summon help. Hiking alone in remote wilderness could be a nerve-wracking business but there was nothing to do but keep going as carefully as possible.

I found a grouse in a small clearing right next to the Trail. Rather than running away it simply gazed at me. Something in the way it looked at me reminded me of my very affectionate pet cockatiel back home and I found myself missing her. Out of the blue I burst into tears. That bit of homesickness was enough to make the mix of strain, fatigue and isolation boil over. I laughed briefly at my reaction then went back to crying again. The grouse impassively watched me blubbering. After a bit I pulled myself together and headed along the boggy saddle to the north peak.

The descent from north Kinsman was not as rocky or steep as the ascent had been but going down was trickier than climbing. My knee nearly went again, this time with a lingering soreness warning me that the joint capsule had been hurt and to be even more careful to avoid a more serious occurrence.

Finally I arrived at Lonesome Lake Hut, the first of the chain of huts the AMC maintains in the White Mountains. It has a hexagonal kitchen/dining area and what must be a sleeping wing. Inside, I got a bottomless bowl of nice hot mushroom soup. It is amazing how a good meal makes everything right in the world! Just past the lake I ran into blueberries, the first I had seen in the Whites. Savoring them finished putting me back in a good mood.

After the hut the Trail was a bit less rugged and I made faster progress to the Road at Franconia Notch. I was hesitant about hitching a ride on the Interstate so I hiked another mile along a side trail to Hwy 3 at the Flume Visitor Center. Car after car went past me and I feared I'd have to walk the whole 5 miles to North Woodstock. It occurred to me that I was at least as vulnerable walking along the road as trying to hitch a ride, but there was no way around it. There are some spots along the trail where supplies are miles away from the trail and this was one of them. I got about a mile down the road before a pickup pulled over to give me a ride. I put my pack and poles in the bed and got into the front seat with relief.

I got to the post office just in time to get my food shipment that I had sent from Hanover. Nearby was a motel where I got a room. I put my pack in the room then went straight to the Woodstock Inn with the lost bandana. Sure enough, it belonged to Polar and she was glad to have it back. I was happy to do a bit of the same Trail Magic that got my hat back when I lost it a few weeks ago.

I had supper, bought a sandwich and pint of Ben and Jerry's ice cream and a quart of chocolate milk for later then did a load of laundry.

The weather forecast says tomorrow will be sunny, so it will be time to head back up into the next stretch of the White Mountains.

-Mouse

Tuesday, August 17, 2004
Destination: Garfield Ridge Campsite
From: Franconia Notch
Today's Miles: 10.3
Trip Miles: 1811.7

Today I got to see what the Whites are all about!

I had trouble getting a ride. Then a police car parked pointedly near me so I started walking rather than tempt fate by defying a possible law against hitchhiking. I got nearly 2 miles before a nice older woman who on her way to work at a local motel stopped and picked me up. I did not get to the Trail until nearly 10am. I nearly stopped for the day at Liberty Tentsite, fearing it was too late in the day to make it to Garfield. But with a perfect forecast and an assurance from the Liberty caretaker that it should only take five hours I decided not to waste a day of clear weather.

Climbing up through the tree to timberline, I was surprised that the weight of my pack did not bother me. I found that I could climb even steep slopes at a steady pace without getting out of breath! I guess that by adding my winter gear gradually, then going over the mountains leading up to the Whites I had built the stamina to carry my winter gear and six days of food with no trouble. Lucky me, I had dreaded the weight increase.

I was glad I went ahead. Except for some haze and high clouds the visibility above the treeline was great. Words could not capture the incredible view and even photographs can't do justice to the panorama I found spread before me. You almost have to be there to really grasp the scope of it. The view of the Trail snaking along Franconia Ridge like the Great Wall of China, the line of cairns marking it, the valleys nearly a mile in altitude below, the cliff below where the NH state emblem, a rock formation called The Old Man Of The Mountain, used to be until it fell last year and smashed to rubble, Mount Washington off in the distance. It was stupendous! I even found what seemed to be blueberries on tiny dwarfed bushes, getting my daily berry fix.

Up above treeline, going up Little Haystack and across to Mount Lincoln and Mount Lafayette the Trail was well made. But coming down in the trees it seemed rugged to the point of recklessness, several places were just accidents waiting to happen. Then going up and over steep Mount Garfield was even worse, the trail little more than a rockslide marked with white blazes. Yikes!

It took six and a half hours to get to camp instead of four or five. It was nearly 7pm when I paid the $8 fee and got a spot in the shelter. But it was worth it! It might be the clearest day I see in the Whites so I was glad to be on the high ridge to enjoy it.

At the shelter I ran into Palm Tree, Boonie and Tree Frog. They had caught up with me by making a grueling slack pack from Kinsman Notch to Franconia Notch in one day. Ponderer was there as well but Pilot and Polar stayed back in North Woodstock to take a zero day.

-Mouse

Wednesday, August 18, 2004
Destination: Zealand Falls Hut
From: Garfield Ridge Campsite
Today's Miles: 9.7
Trip Miles: 1821.4

It was chilly but clear last night with brilliant stars. I got going a bit before 7. The first order of business was getting down the rest of Mount Garfield. It was as steep and tricky as yesterday's part had been.

Kinsman Mountain and Mount Garfield in particular seemed to border on what can only be called gratuitous ruggedness. I have seen other stretches where there was ruggedness for the sake of ruggedness but the AMC takes the cake. I found myself getting angry; aren't the Whites dangerous enough already without making the trail surface dangerous too? I really question whether avoiding safety improvements enhances the hiking experience. Sections like the Beaver Brook ravine on Mount Moosilauke prove that a better job of trail construction is feasible. So there seems little excuse but sheer bravado. If the AMC wants trails worthy of Eco-Challenge, fine, but does it really belong on the Appalachian Trail? If my thruhike were ended because of an injury sustained on a bad trail section after five months of effort I'd be resentful as all get out!

At Galehead Hut I stopped for three bowls of beef-barley soup. Then I made the half mile, 900 foot ascent of South Twin Mountain. It was better trail than Garfield but still took me an hour to get to the top. The view showed what a difference a day makes. Mount Lafayette was obscured with haze, not nearly the visibility of the day before.

Then came a chain of successively lower peaks. On Mount Guyot I found Tree Frog, who had passed me hours before. He was worried about whether he had made a wrong turn. I reassured him that we were on the right path and we hiked together for a while until he stopped for lunch.

At the Zealand Cliff Trail Junction I hit blueberry pay dirt! I had found a couple before but here there were bushes and bushes full of ripe berries. Not only that but some were the largest wild blueberries I had seen on the Trail, nearly a quarter inch in diameter. I could have eaten for hours but knew that afternoon thunderstorms were forecast and I really ought to keep moving. I hardly tore myself away from one patch before I would run into another and start picking and eating again. Finally I reached a downslope where the berries gave way to other plants.

At the bottom I found another potentially confusing trail junction and another one right after that, neither with white blazes to show the correct way. I worried about Tree Frog getting lost. So I went back and left little AT symbols made with dead twigs to show the way. Then before going on, I listened on the chance he might be close behind me. Sure enough, I heard the "click, click" of trekking poles and then saw his head bobbing through the tree. I waited for him to be sure he did not get lost, and we hiked together to Zealand Falls Hut where he hiked on to Ethan Pond to join his two companions.

At the hut I asked if there were any open bunks. Miracle of miracles, there was one left! For the somewhat stiff price of $82 I could get a dry bed and two good meals. Just what the doctor ordered! Ponderer was there as well, having reserved a space in advance by phone.

I could have done the "work for stay" option for free. But then I would only get whatever leftovers there were and a bit of floor to sleep on and would have to work 2 or 3 hours in the morning, making for a late start. Sounds like Cinderella. This way I'd get an earlier start as well as getting to experience the non-thruhiker hut experience, getting fed and doing no work.

Had there been no space at all, I would have had to either find somewhere to camp in the woods or hike another 3 miles to Ethan Pond Campsite and risk getting drenched if the predicted thunderstorms arrived. But my friend Aloha Ann had warned me by email to slow down and that she would be checking up on me. If she got wind of me hiking 13 miles in one day here in the Whites, I think she might come up here and dismember me! So just as well I stopped here. I hate getting dismembered!

Supper was wonderful: minestrone soup, salad, steamed vegetables, lasagna and chocolate pudding cake with coffee. Burrrrrrp! After that I took a walk and found a blueberry bush so I can get tomorrow's berry quota out of the way first thing in the morning.

Tomorrow I hike down to Crawford Notch and stay at the hostel of camp. Then if the weather holds, I hope to climb to Lakes of the Clouds Hut the next day and go over Mount Washington the next morning.

-Mouse

Thursday, August 19, 2004
Destination: Crawford Notch
From: Zealand Falls Hut
Today's Miles: 7.7
Trip Miles: 1829.1

Every morning in the huts starts with the hut workers, or "croo" as they are known as, coming into the bunkroom at 630 and singing to wake everyone up. This morning they sang a cute rendition of "You are my Sunshine." I loved it, having memories of when I sang the same song that rainy day in Vermont when the sun finally came out.

Breakfast was plentiful: hot oatmeal with peaches raisins and brown sugar, scrambled eggs, sausage and pancakes. I even had a dozen blueberries I'd just picked from outside to go with my pancakes. After breakfast comes a skit. The plot varies from hut to hut, but the themes are always the same: fold your blankets properly, pick up your trash and don't forget the Croo Tip Jar.

The moment I started down the steps from the Hut I noticed that my knees were showing the effects of the past several days. Although the pain eased a bit once I got going, I decided to stop at Crawford Notch rather than trying to push on to Mizpah Hut where everyone I knew seemed to be going. My knees would benefit from a short day and the morning forecast predicted bad weather coming after tomorrow so I'd be taking my time getting over Mount Washington in any case.

"Zealand" seems to be another word for blueberry. As soon as Zealand entered the place names, the trail became packed with blueberries. Or maybe blueberries just have an affinity for disaster; the area I hiked today was clear-cut in the 1880s and then burned to the ground. The only place I have seen more blueberries at was the polluted zone at Lehigh Gap. With the short day, I took my time and nibbled constantly.

When I reached the highway in Crawford Notch I leaned my pack on a signpost and sat against it to decide between a campground to the south or the AMC hostel to the north. I had just settled on the hostel when a couple arrived. Their names were Rick and Sue and they were the maintainers for this section. They were here to retrieve a Trail Magic cooler. After plying me with a coke and fudge brownie they gave me a ride to the hostel and were even nice enough to wait until they were sure there was a bunk for me. What nice people! Without so many nice folks along the Trail, thruhiking would be much more difficult, perhaps impossible. My thanks to all of them!

After a shower and lunch I spent the afternoon journaling and relaxing. The day was overcast and from time to time dark clouds drifted overhead, the wind gusted and sprinkles fell, making me just as happy to be down here under a roof rather than up there on the Trail. Looking up I could see that the heights were shrouded with cloud and probably getting even more rain than down in the notch.

Tomorrow I plan to head up to Mizpah Hut/Nauman Campsite and wait out the rainy day up there. Then as soon as it clears enough, Lakes of the Clouds Hut and then the dash over the summit of Mount Washington. If I took a zero day here tomorrow to wait for good weather, it might be two days before I could hike up to the high country. Going to Mizpah will give a bit of a head start.

The trick will be to get a good day on which to summit Mount Washington. It is notorious for dangerous weather conditions year-round and hikers are warned to turn back if the weather turns bad. It is a full ten miles from Lakes of the Clouds to the next regular campsite so a full day of reliably good weather would be best. There are nearer campsites where one could shelter if a storm comes up but they are a mile off the Trail and about 1500 feet down on steep side trails so I'd prefer not having to use them.

-Mouse

Friday, August 20, 2004
Destination: Lakes of the Clouds Hut
From: Crawford Notch
Today's Miles: 11.2
Trip Miles: 1840.3

Two men joined me at breakfast. When he learned I was thruhiking north, one offered me a bunk at Lakes of The Clouds Hut this evening. He had reserved for two and ended up coming alone so he said it would just be wasted otherwise. I happily accepted. That would put me as close as one can get to Mount Washington. If I sat out the bad weather day up there I would be perfectly placed to head over Washington when the sky cleared. I could save a full day compared to my original plan to stop at Mizpah Hut/Nauman Campsite.

The other man said he was hiking to Pinkham Notch today. He left me worried about his safety, since he was going to hike in jeans and a cotton sweatshirt and the trail he was taking went above 5000 feet! That was incredibly dangerous as cotton clothing is notorious for chilling the body in wet weather, causing hypothermia. I admonished him to read the safety information posted on the walls and to keep a very open mind to turning back if the weather turned bad but that was as much as I could do. He clearly did not want to take advice from me.

After breakfast I packed carefully. I made sure that warm layers, gloves, balaclava, space blanket and heat packs were in the small waterproof stuff sack right at the top of my pack where I could get to it quickly if needed. My Gore-Tex rain jacket went on the bungee cord on the back of the pack and my tent strapped to one side so it was right at hand if I needed to set it up in a storm. A supply of snacks to keep my energy level up went on the other side with the water bladder.

I went out to the road to hitch a ride and did not have to wait long. The second car to come by stopped to give me a lift to the Trail. It turned out to be the superintendent of the Crawford Notch State Park. By 7:30 I was on the Trail and making my way to the top of Webster Cliffs. The trail was steep and many sections had serious rock climbing, hauling oneself up hand over hand. There was no lack of good hand and footholds so it was safe but it was definitely hard work. Some spots I had to stop and gaze at, like a jigsaw puzzle, until I could see the secret of how to get up. Then I would reach for the first handhold, hang on and start working through it. At the top of the obstacles I would often pause with relief at getting past in one piece.

At the top were excellent views of Crawford Notch, the road 2000 vertical feet below with cars and trucks passing like toys, the mountain opposite looming high above, and clouds drifting in and out of the scene. There were also excellent blueberries. With the long distance to Lakes of The Clouds and no idea how long the weather would hold, I had no time to gorge, but did nibble constantly and grabbed a whole handful when I passed a particularly plentiful bush.

Next came more rock climbing up to the top of Mount Webster. It was just like how we imagined mountain climbing as kids; hand over hand up a steep rocky slope. Once up, the trail swung away from the Notch and took a more level (And boggy!) course along ridges and peaks to Mizpah Hut.

I stopped in and started asking questions of the hutmaster: Was the weather holding? What was the trail ahead like? If I needed 5 hours to get there from Crawford Notch, was it still reasonable to try for Lakes of The Clouds Hut?

I needed to decide whether to hold to my new plan or stop short and stay at Mizpah. He seemed to think it was fine, no storms were expected until after midnight and it should take me 4 hours.

Naturally as soon as I had gotten over the next peak it started pouring down rain! I stopped to put on my rain cover and Gore-Tex coat, then was in a quandary. Should I turn back? Here I was, venturing above tree line by myself. Pushing on through bad weather sounded like a very iffy proposition. Still, it was just rain, the temperature was not dropping, there had been a rising barometer when I left Crawford hostel. Was it such a surprise for there to be rain? After all clouds ARE made of water. Every hiker I ran into coming the other way I interrogated about time from Lakes of The Clouds, trail conditions etc. Then I found two more hikers behind me were continuing on and decided to go on as well. I figured I would trust my wet weather gear unless the temperature started to plummet. But I shuddered to think of that man I'd met at breakfast hiking up here in soaked jeans and sweatshirt!

I stopped in the lee of Mount Eisenhower to take shelter from the wet wind so I could add my Capilene top under the Gore-Tex coat. That left me nice and warm for when I started up the higher peaks. By Mount Franklin it had stopped raining but the world was wreathed in fog. All I could see was the cairns in either direction for a few hundred yards. Then it began to break and the landscape would come in and out of view as clouds drifted through. This was more like it; "summits in and out of cloud" just as the forecast had predicted. Instead of being on edge about the weather, I began to relax and enjoy the ghostly landscape. Off through the fog I heard the whistle of the cog-railway engine as it chugged up to the top of Mount Washington. I am glad to have seen so many moods of the Whites, in both good and bad weather.

At last I topped a final ridge past Mount Monroe and the Lakes of The Clouds Hut came into view. I had arrived! I was as good as over the most worrisome part of the Whites, all I need is one day of good weather.

Inside, I met the man who had offered me a bunk that morning and he checked me in. In the meantime they had reassigned the bunk to someone else but since it was already paid for I still had my two meals and a spot on a table to sleep on at night so I was happy. I offered to repay the man for the cost but he would not hear of it. Talk about Trail Magic! It was like the hot meal I had at the LeConte Lodge back in the Smokys.

I also found Lonesome Dove, who was doing work for stay.

Every now and then for the rest of the afternoon a clear patch would drift overhead and the sun would come out, like a gift. The opening would inch across until Mount Washington came into view. Then the clouds would drift across like the curtain closing in a theater after the play.

-Mouse

Saturday, August 21, 2004
Destination: Lakes of the Clouds Hut
From: Lakes of the Clouds Hut
Today's Miles: 0.0
Trip Miles: 1840.3

This morning at breakfast the Croo read the weather forecast. Rain was predicted and they advised anyone planning on hiking today to consult them about safer routes. But Lonesome Dove held to her plan to hike over Mount Washington all the way to Pinkham Notch, where she was to meet someone in the evening. No one else seemed too deterred by the bad weather either, and within two hours the hut was nearly deserted.

Then around noon soaking-wet hikers started drifting in, trying to dry off as best they could and warming up with hot chocolate or soup. Polar and Pilot came, as did Andrew, now trailnamed Megabyte, whom I had not seen in months. By evening the place was packed again.

This was despite the fact it was raining with dense fog and according to the digital weather instrument readout by late afternoon the wind was around 25mph in the sheltered hollow the hut was nestled in. Hikers related that up on the heights the gusts were strong enough to blow them right off their feet. It seemed odd to have so many hikers out when this seemed just the sort of weather that guidebooks warned about.

This was an unusual evening, as the Hurricane Ridge Hiking Club had booked the entire hut and had brought in a band for a party. Because of the bad weather I managed to get a cancelled bunk for the night, a real bunk this time instead of a table. This was fortunate, since the party would run to midnight and no one sleeping on tables could go to bed until after it was over.

The best moment of the day came during supper when the sun peeked through the murk for the first time all day. The whole dining room burst into applause and cheered!

-Mouse

Sunday, August 22, 2004
Destination: Osgood Tentsite
From: Lakes of the Clouds Hut
Today's Miles: 10.0
Trip Miles: 1850.3

What a strange day.

It started out well, with clear cloudless skies and perfect weather.

It started to go bad when I discovered that the ziplock bag I used for a wallet was missing with all my money, ATM card, telephone calling card, credit card and ID. Everything. I searched my sleeping bag in case it had fallen out of my pocket while I was asleep but it was not there either. By now I was frantic. I turned out my pack and stuff sacks, retraced my steps through the hut. Nothing.

I worried my way through breakfast with a rising sense of concern, then asked the information volunteer if it had been turned in. Nope. I rechecked everywhere again and again. Where could it be? I had had it just last night, the hikers were not the sort of people who would run off with it, and the hut only had so many places where a wallet could hide.

When I told the volunteer I had gotten up in the night he asked me if there was any chance my wallet had fallen into the toilet. I replied that sounded pretty far-fetched. But after looking everywhere else all over again, for lack of alternatives I checked the toilets. Sure enough, one had a suspicious clump of tissue in the bowl. When I probed it with a stick, there was my wallet! I think it had gotten tired of thruhiking and had tried to drown itself.

A thorough rinsing and it was good as new. Weak with relief, I thanked the volunteer profusely for his lucky guess. It had been equally fortunate I had lost it here, where the hut had rather anemic flush toilets. All the other huts had composting toilets that would have swallowed my wallet without a trace. I stuffed an extra $20 bill into the tip box in gratitude, grabbed my pack and headed for the Trail.

That turned the day good again as I started up Mount Washington swaddled in nylon pants, Gore-Tex coat and balaclava against the cold wind. I got to the summit without trouble and got a picture of the locomotives and cars of the 140 year old cog railway, sent some emails to let everyone know I had reached the summit safely, and refilled my water. The essentials done, I went on rather than going to the snack bar and exhibits as I had gotten a late start and needed to get below treeline by dark. The day turned even better when I crossed the railroad tracks and started along the chain of peaks in the Presidentials. The view was incredible and the weather warmed nicely.

The day got a bit worse again when the trail, or lack of one, began to wear me down. Many places were nothing more than a line of cairns to mark the route through the boulders. I was amazed that Lonesome Dove had braved it in yesterday's bad weather and hoped she was all right. Finding my way was hard enough in good weather! Then I ran into her slackpacking southbound! She told me she had gotten as far as the summit before wisely heeding the advice of the rangers not to go further. She had gone down by road and taken shelter for the night in Gorham.

I started stumbling and reached the state where common sense indicated it would be wise to stop at Madison Hut for the day. But the hut-master, all smiles, said in a silky voice that it was suuuuch a nice day that they were encouraging everyone on to Osgood Tentsite. Even after I told her how much longer than expected it had taken me to get to Madison, she assured me it was only three miles and I could easily make it in 2.5 or 3 hours.

That was when the day turned really sour and all the good feeling I had built up towards the AMC evaporated into hot anger. The "trail" led steeply up and over Mount Madison and down a long ridgeline over large boulders. The inevitable happened and I tipped over backwards and crashed hard onto the rocks. I passed a sign and to my disgust I found it had taken two hours to go just one mile. Not even blueberries were enough to put me back into a good mood.

It was nearly dark when I finally got to the tentsite nearly 11 hours after leaving Lakes of The Clouds. Other hikers were stumbling in long after dark.

-Mouse

Monday, August 23, 2004
Destination: Pinkham Notch
From: Osgood Tentsite
Today's Miles: 4.8
Trip Miles: 1855.1

My knees were not happy this morning when I started the descent into Pinkham Notch. Everyone who had stayed at Osgood passed me by the time I got to the Notch. On the good side, I did find some nice raspberries.

I decided to rest the rest of the day and go over Wildcat Ridge tomorrow. Especially after we read the AMC guidebook in the gift shop and it gave a rather grim description of the trail to Carter Gap. I got a bunk, then joined everyone else at the AYCE lunch. Megabyte kidded me, asking how I liked my BED and saying I should eat at another table because I was a traitor to thruhikerdom.

After lunch we sat around until nearly 2pm before everyone started drifting up the Trail to Carter Notch. I went and got the key to my room and rested the rest of the day, reading things I found in the Lodge's library. (We librarians love libraries!)

-Mouse

Tuesday, August 24, 2004
Destination: Carter Notch Hut
From: Pinkham Notch
Today's Miles: 5.9
Trip Miles: 1861.0

I am very glad I did not try to go on to Carter Notch yesterday.

Yesterday the heights had clouded over by three and even in the notch it was pouring rain by 6:30. Today it took me nearly 7 hours and that would have gotten me drenched and arriving very late.

What is more, I ran into my nightmare image of the north face of Mount Moosilauke, only for real! Life and death rock-climbing on narrow ledges zigzagging up a steep rock face with a yawning void behind me. Yikes! Not something to face when tired and sore.

The trail went past some nice raspberries then headed steeply upwards. Jumbles of boulders alternated with steps and steep faces and curved masses, all hair raisingly steep. It was the kind of climbing that called for all my attention, senses wired, watching every move, sometimes having to make heart-stopping moves to get to a handhold just out of reach. Some of it with just open space behind me or with treetops close in and well below as a blunt reminder of how far below the ground was if I slipped.

That frayed my nerves and I found myself getting what you could call climbing fatigue, wishing desperately to be somewhere other than high up a rock face with no choice but to keep going, fighting to keep my composure and stay focused. It got so each time I found myself confronted by another pitch the fear was palpable and I would have to force myself upward. At least I had a dry sunny day. And here and there bushes offered me blueberries in mute apology for the climb.

At one point ascending a face brought me to a rounded surface where the rock curved from vertical to horizontal in a smooth surface. The one crack forming a foothold was too high to step up to and there was nothing to grab onto to pull myself up except smooth rock. I had to reach up and trust to friction to hold my hands in place while I dragged myself over the curve until I could get a foothold. But then I had to go sideways several feet before getting to the safe flat surface above and the foothold was not enough. I had to turn and seat myself on the sloping rock to maximize the surface area contacting the rock, then inch cautiously across, held by nothing and with nothing to grab if I slipped, until I was far enough over to clamper to safety. When I was on the top I was afraid I'd vomit from horror at the risk I had had to take to get up. In the evening another hiker said that was exactly what he had done. That I managed to hold onto both my nerves and my breakfast was reassuring in a strange way and I felt a little better getting to the top of the steep section.

Up there was a flat rock outcrop with a spectacular view of the Notch and Presidentials, but I had been so occupied with trying to survive that it was hard to enjoy it.

After that the trail led away from the cliffs on a less steep course up a ridge to the first of a chain of five peaks along the ridge. There was more rock climbing but not as bad. But by then my nerves were so jangled that anything needing my hands to pull myself up was enough to set me on edge.

I felt REALLY tired of rock climbing especially the dangerous kind. But there is more ahead and I didn't know what to do about it except try not to do too much in a day and hope I get desensitized to it. Or just hope the next bad climb didn't come until I was ready for more. Army officer training had taught me to confront and master fear of heights with everything from walking logs 20 feet up to rappelling to riding helicopters with my feet out the open door but it never made the fear go away.

At last I got over the first peak, Wildcat E, to where a gondola lift offered visitors a safe easy way up. I had meant to stop and eat there, but the knots of relaxed tourists were such a totally different reality from the one I had just been through that I just kept going.

At Wildcat D I stopped at a wooden observation platform and had my snack there. An older woman came up who turned out to be a southbound thruhiker named Birch. She encouraged me, saying I could make it, one careful step at a time.

Then came C, B and finally A before descending into Carter Notch. It was nearly 3 and I decided to stay at the hut there rather than making another steep climb out of the notch and stealth camping on a mountaintop. I had had enough for today even if it was only six miles.

I did a work for stay along with two other thruhikers, my first and only work for stay in the hut system. Since there were only six guests all we had to do was wash a modest stack of dishes. Carter Notch Hut is unusual in that the bunkhouses are separate buildings up the hill from the main hut, reminding me of the NOC.

-Mouse

Wednesday, August 25, 2004
Destination: Gorham, NH
From: Carter Notch Hut
Today's Miles: 15.2
Trip Miles: 1876.2

Another berry great day!

It was nice and sunny all day. I got one raspberry early on then blueberries almost all day, more than I could possibly spare time to eat, especially since I hoped to get to Gorham.

The ascent out of the notch was steep but mostly on stone steps. Allegheny, one of the other two thruhikers, caught up with me there and we climbed and talked until I stopped for a break at the top of Carter Dome. The hiking was fairly reasonable after that and the views from the heights were great. The valleys were blanketed in fog like a fluffy river. I got a shot towards Gorham with the town under a billowing blanket with a few pillars of clouds rising from warm spots, perhaps paper mill chimneys. Doesn't Speak, the other thruhiker, caught up with me at the descent to Iris Campsite. It had some moderately intense rock-climbing but nothing like yesterday. Still, he slipped once and bent one pole so badly it was unusable and he had to strap the remains to his pack and use just one pole. He got ahead of me lower down and I did not see him again until the turn-off to Iris.

It had taken me six hours to go about 7.5 miles. But it was already 1pm and I worried about making the remaining 8 miles to the road before dark. I went to the caretaker's tent hoping to find what the estimated hiking time was, but found neither a caretaker nor information. So I went on to the shelter thinking to do the conservative choice and stop for the night. I was thinking that if I did not get to the road then two medium size days were better than a long one and a very short one. The next shelter was less than 2 miles short of the road. At the shelter Allegheny was finishing his lunch. He made it clear he planned to make Gorham.

I found myself really wanting to get out of the AMC domain with its fees and restrictions. That galvanized me into action, along with knowing I had kept pace with the men all morning and they were heading for Gorham. I purified a liter and a half of water in my Platypus, put on my pack and tore the wrapper off a Bear Valley bar for lunch. I did not even stop long enough to eat, instead nibbling it as I hiked.

It is amazing what a difference less steep trail made. I had fretted at the low miles of the last few days but now the miles piled up as I covered the last of the heights and started the descent to the road. The lower I got, the flatter and smoother the trail was. Soon I was loping along furiously.

I got to Rattle River Shelter by 5, early enough that there was no question of stopping. Now the Trail was practically smooth dirt road. A Mouse unchained, I found myself trotting and jogging along at an idiotic rate for a backpacker. Just as I heard the first truck go by I saw Allegheny up ahead and we got to the road together.

I was ecstatic! I had made the whole 15 miles and had finished the Whites! Whoohoo, Mouse has her groove back!!!

Just before the road we had met a 2002 thruhiker trailnamed Mahoosuc who suggested a good motel to stay at. After days of crowded bunkrooms, that sounded better than a hostel. A group who had just finished a section hike from the north offered us a ride to Gorham. They even drove us to the grocery for supplies before dropping us at the motel.

My room was the oddest motel room I had been in. It had one door to a shady second floor balcony with chairs and nice view and a second interior door that led to a bathroom down the hall past a stairway leading to BEHIND the motel desk. It must have originally been living quarters for the motel keeper. The key did not work on the inside door so I promptly found myself in the hallway locked out of my room. I had to go downstairs, around the desk out the front door and back up to the balcony to let myself in again. Then we had to track down the TV remote, which was missing. But it was a cute room with a very comfy bed so I did not mind.

-Mouse

Thursday, August 26, 2004
Destination: Gorham, NH
From: Gorham, NH
Today's Miles: 0.0
Trip Miles: 1876.2

I spent the day doing laundry and going between store and post office.

I got my bounce box and the food and excess gear that I had mailed to here. I got everything from the bounce box that I might need: maps, guidebook pages, topped up my toothpaste and hand sanitizer and counted out a month's supply of vitamins, iron and calcium. Next I put in the gear I won't need: filter bottle, windbreaker, extra socks and t-shirt and so on. The bounce box will go home.

Then I prepared shipments forward. I am taking 4 days food with me on the next leg to the town of Andover in Maine. I am sending a few Bear Valley bars and leftover food odds and ends to Andover for the next leg. I sent enough Bear Valley and Cliff bars for the first 70 miles of the 100 Mile Wilderness to Monson. I also sent 3 days food, a disposable camera, my Gore-Tex pants and midweight top to White House Landing to get me through the last third of the Wilderness and to keep me warm on Katahdin if the weather turns cold.

Today was spent mostly on such chores. Tomorrow I will take one more zero day mostly just relaxing as sort of a reward for getting past the Whites and to get over the wear and tear I experienced there. Then I should be more ready to tackle the Mahoosuc Mountains coming up.

-Mouse

Friday, August 27, 2004
Destination: Gorham, NH
From: Gorham, NH
Today's Miles: 0.0
Trip Miles: 1876.2

Today that devoted helper, my bounce box, got its reward. It is going home. Battered and worn, with a thick bulge of address labels taped one over another, it has preceded me in big jumps up the Trail to bring me maps, guidebook pages and anything else I did not want to carry. Why, it even had my stove and cooking things for more miles than I did. Now its job is finished. This morning I bade it farewell at the post office. It showed little response, but I am sure it was as moved as I was.

The weather here in Gorham is rather hot and uncomfortable. I can't wait to get back to the cool mountain forest. I spent most of the day watching television in the air conditioning of my room.

-Mouse

Saturday, August 28, 2004
Destination: Gentian Pond Shelter
From: Gorham, NH
Today's Miles 11.8
Trip Miles: 1888.0

Today the Trail was more normal Trail-like. It had its ups and downs but not nearly as steep as the Whites. I made about 45 minutes to the mile, average for rough terrain, and got to the shelter well before 4pm.

It was a nice day for berries as well. The higher places had lots of blueberries and the low spots had big ripe honey-sweet blackberries, the best I have seen. So I nibbled my way along and could have gorged on them had I known the trail was so easy that there turned out to be plenty of time to reach the shelter before evening. Still, I was just as glad to leave plenty of berries for everyone else.

It was hot and sticky much of the day except high up where finally the clouds drifted over and blocked out the sun. I was drenched in sweat climbing up from the road even though it was before 8am! I hope the rain that is forecast cools things down.

Checking the register I found Palm Tree, Pilot and all their assorted hangers-on were here two nights ago. Over half a dozen twenty-something NOBO thru-hikers caught up with me at the shelter, then hurried on to get in the five miles or so to Maine today. I was sore despite two zero days and was happy to stop, especially since tonight will be rainy. I expect to stop at Full Goose Shelter next, then a 5 mile day through Mahoosuc Notch and up Mahoosuc Arm to Speck Pond Shelter. If it is pouring tomorrow morning I might either spend all day here or do a short day to Carlo Col Shelter just beyond the border. That would let the weather dry a bit before I hit the Notch and Arm.

Cooking supper, I discovered my hat makes a good pot-cozy. I have usually wrapped a bandana around the pot and laid its stuff sack on top to hold the heat in and let pasta finish cooking without having use fuel to simmer it. But adding the hat over that arrangement seemed to work even better and my tortellini was nice and tender tonight instead of half-cooked as usual. I used a handful of TVP but only a third of a pack each of tortellini and pea soup instead of half, adding extra water to make it seem more filling in order to stretch my food an extra day.

-Mouse

Sunday, August 29, 2004
Destination: Carlo Col Shelter
From: Gentian Pond Shelter
Today's Miles: 5.2
Trip Miles: 1893.2

There was a little sprinkle around 4am but the predicted thunderstorms did not materialize. It was just colder and foggy with gusty winds. I lay in bed trying to decide what the weather would do. I finally decided to at least try to make it to Carlo Col before the real rain arrived. Of course I had just stepped out of the shelter at 7am when it started pouring!

So I went back in the shelter, got unpacked for a zero day and got into my sleeping bag. Naturally, then it stopped raining. I could hear the sky laughing at its little joke.

I restlessly decided to go on regardless of the weather and by 8:15 was packed up again. I had a raspberry and a couple blackberries for luck, then hit the trail.

Other than being steep and having a fair number of boulder scrambles the trail was not too bad as I climbed the interestingly named Mount Success. Near the top, ABOVE tree line, were long stretches of bog bridges made of boards or well-decomposed logs. It got even windier and the fog was so thick it was hard to make out the cairns marking the trail. I would take a guess and if I got to another bog bridge I knew I was still on the Trail. At last I reached a signpost saying 2.2 miles to Carlo Col and knew I was on the summit.

Those 2.2 miles took forever. First I started running into sloped rock slabs and moderate rock scrambles. Not TOO hard but enough to eventually try my patience despite lots of blueberries. I ran into a couple who were doing trail maintenance, clipping back the vegetation with pruning shears. Trying to decide whether to try for 9 miles, I asked them if there were many rock scrambles between Carlo Col and Full Goose Shelters. The man got an odd look on his face and replied no, that section was all right but there WERE some scrambles before Carlo Col.

I was a bit puzzled by his expression but thought it could not be much since I was nearly to the shelter. Was I ever wrong! I came around a corner and found myself confronted with a lulu! Descending in front of me was a near vertical cascade of gigantic blocks piled willy-nilly. It was like the top of the ridge at Lehigh Gap only instead of being two or three feet high each, the blocks were more like ten feet! Now I understood why the man had a strange expression when he said there was some rock-climbing.

I got down one block then went back and forth on the top of the next, gazing and gazing for a way down. I was stymied and had some choice words for the maniac who had routed the trail through this mess. Finally I took my pack off, lowered it as far as I could, and let it drop. Then I went back up to the first block, down to a different one, and found a route I could just manage without the encumbrance of the pack. Next I had to slide the pack down another block and then slide after it before I could manage the rest with my pack on. Yikes! I think whoever it was who decided that the Appalachian Trail needed some nearly impassable spots to feel like true wilderness has rocks for brains! Had anyone offered me a magic way home just then, I would have accepted it in a heartbeat.

Eventually I reached the saddle at the bottom of the hill. The sun shined dramatically through a hole in the clouds (honest!) and there before me was a sign that declared "Maine: the way life should be"! I had finally reached the 14th and last State of the Appalachian Trail.

In the half mile to the sidetrail to Carlo Col Shelter I found two more blueberries, extending my berry streak to yet another state. When I found that patch of berries at the Mason-Dixon Line I had no idea it would last so long!

It was only 1pm and I considered my options. It was tempting to try to make the 4.4 miles to Full Goose Shelter. Then if the weather was good I could tackle Mahoosuc Notch the next day. But I was worn out by the rock climbs and was not sure if my water would last or if the rain would hold off that long. So a bit reluctantly I took the .3 mile sidetrail down to Carlo Col Shelter. I figured by the time I got to the shelter and purified water it would be too late to climb back to the AT and on to Full Goose.

Despite ominously gusting winds and thickening fog it still had not rained by 6pm when a NOBO thruhiking couple from Austin TX named Up and Down arrived. They had come from Trident Col Tentsite a few miles south of Gentian Pond.

-Mouse

Monday, August 30, 2004
Destination: East End of Mahoosuc Notch, Stealth Camp
From: Carlo Col Shelter
Today's Miles: 7.0
Trip Miles: 1900.2

Whoohoo, I am through the Notch!

Last night thunder started rumbling in the distance at 8pm and about 10 the storm reached the shelter with lots of lightning and a heavy downpour. At 4am the rain had stopped and the full moon glowed brightly through a hole in the clouds into the open front of the shelter.

By the time I got on the Trail at 6:30 it had clouded up again. Atop Carlo Mountain and Goose Eye Mountain it was damp, foggy and chill with a brisk wind. There were long stretches above treeline, much of it on bog bridges. There were also a lot of dwarfed-down alpine blueberries. Some were packed with extra big berries and all were sweeter and tastier than normal blueberries. They were my reward for all the rock climbing. Despite what the maintainer had said, there were several pretty challenging sections. I know the AT is supposed to be a wilderness trail but there seems too much emphasis here on the word "wilderness" and not enough on the word "trail"!

Not for the first time I found myself wondering if the risk was really worth it. It is a good thing those tough spots are far from a road or the temptation to give up would be hard to resist. As it is, by the time I get to a road I will have gotten some of the hardest going on the trail behind me so it will make less sense to give up. That and the reassurance of seeing all those bright-eyed smiling southbounders who obviously got through here and lived to tell about it.

Up and Down caught up with me on the middle peak of Goose Eye and we kept pace the rest of the way to Full Goose Shelter. Down was faster than me going up but she was slower going down. Descending the middle peak of Goose eye we found something new. There was a long string of inclined bog bridges with cleats nailed across the planks (or sometimes across a single plank) to provide footing so you don't slide down the incline and fall. Intermingled with the bridges were flights of log steps so that much of the descent was on wood. Too bad the rock-climbs have not gotten that kind of tender loving care. Oh, well.

About 11am we heard voices and at the top of a ladder we found ourselves at Full Goose Shelter. In it were the ten or so students from Tufts University I had seen at Gentian Pond. They had spent the night here and were thinking about taking the day off. They were on a freshman orientation trip, one of about 24 groups from Tufts scattered along the Trail. Most were backpacking for the first time. Watching them struggle to prepare freeze-dried hash browns in a wok and pancakes in a skillet was the best entertainment we had had in weeks!

We were torn between staying as I had planned or pushing on through Mahoosuc Notch while the weather was still good. Up and Down decided to go on but I still was not sure. The sky seemed to be darkening and while the extra day would stretch my food thin, staying with the Tufts students promised lots of leftovers. I nibbled gorp and drank hot chocolate mix in cold water while deliberating.

Finally I tore myself away from the prospect of rest, company, fun and extra food. I purified a liter of water, put on my pack and started off just after noon. I had just started up the next peak when I realized I had forgotten my hat. I dumped my pack and poles and went back to recover it. The sky darkened even more and just one drop of rain would have made me change my mind, but no such luck and I regained my pack and poles and headed on. Finally I made my way over the top of Fulling Mill Mountain. The fog had begun to thin when I had been back on Goose Eye but now it was thick and damp as ever. Going down toward the Notch, far too late to turn back, the rain came. Fortunately it lasted only a few minutes, just long enough to make me stop and put the rain cover onto my pack.

I reached the Notch at 1:45. Here again I had the choice of stopping but decided to press ahead. Now I was committed to finishing the Notch no matter how long it took!

Mahoosuc Notch is a mile-long ravine between two high steep cliffs. What makes it famous as the hardest mile of the AT is that the bottom is filled with boulders ranging up to the size of a house! The trail wanders over around and even under them in a sort of boulder funhouse or crazy maze.

The first thing I noticed was a blast of cold air. Ice from the winter accumulates deep in the crevices between the rocks and lasts far into the summer. It cools the air near the crevice exits. I went over some boulders then the trail went over normal ground for a short distance. Here the cold air was replaced by what in comparison felt like sweltering hot humid air. Talk about microclimates! The air temperature switched back and forth between hot and cold for the rest of the Notch.

Now the climbing got more and more challenging. Here and there it plunged deep through a crevice or under a giant boulder. Sometimes I had to squeeze through the passages flat on my belly, barely getting through with my pack on. Two men thruhiking north caught up with me, one by the name of Hawk. He took some pictures of me emerging from a passageway, then they pulled ahead of me.

Above ground it was not easy either. Once the only way to get up a rock was to place my recently scraped shin onto it, grinding the wound into the rock. Ouch! I found myself using all the rock-climbing techniques I could remember and some I thought up on the spot, even chimneying down a crevice once.

It really was kind of fun, but it seemed to last forever. I was tiring and with all the scrambling around the waist belt of my pack was rubbing me raw. Finally the Trail got to flat normal stream bank and I thought I was done. Nope, false alarm, more rocks. A long stretch of normal sized rocks raised my hopes again only to have the Trail plunge beneath another gigantic boulder the size of an apartment building.

At last the rocks dwindled away and the Trail started climbing the left bank. I came to a turnoff that led to a cozy secluded campsite, complete with a path down to the stream running out of the Notch for water and a perfect bear bag hanging tree. Here I made camp for the night. The mile of the Notch had taken me two and a half hours!

-Mouse

Tuesday, August 31, 2004
Destination: Speck Pond Shelter
From: East End of Mahoosuc Notch, Stealth Camp
Today's Miles: 2.5
Trip Miles: 1902.7

Last night a thunderstorm came through with heavy rain at about 8pm. The ground spatter reached high up the mesh on the open side of my tent, sending a fine mist of droplets inside. I spread my Gore-Tex jacket over that side of me to try to keep off the worst of the wet. Another storm came at midnight with still more heavy rain. I managed to keep most of the damp off my sleeping bag and also found my tent really did not have a leak. The puddle I had experienced in Vermont was from water splashing through the mesh sides.

In the morning the weather seemed better at first with no fog, although the ground was drenched with puddles everywhere except on the sloped spot my tent was on. About 7 I brought in my food bag and awaited developments. From the increase in water dripping from the trees onto the tent it seemed certain that it was raining at least intermittently and a gusty wind picked up. Not the best weather to ascend Mahoosuc Arm!

I was glad I had done the Notch yesterday. It had been dry and the extra distance gives me more options. I can afford to wait long into the day for better weather and spend tonight at Speck Pond Shelter. Or assuming it never clears, tomorrow if I make the 9 miles to Baldpate Brow Shelter my food will still last to Andover. Had I stayed at Full Goose I would have had fewer choices. Of course if I had pushed on up the Arm yesterday and spent the night at Speck Pond I would be drier and in even better position but that is water under the bridge, or under the Notch as it were. If all else fails, I can hitch from Grafton Notch just seven miles from here to a campground with a store where I can resupply.

So I decided to wait until the weather improves or until I am too restless to stay. I know; "No rain, no pain, no Maine." But I am in Maine now and have six weeks before Katahdin closes and I have read that Mahoosuc Arm is not a safe ascent in wet conditions.

Another hiker passing at 11 stirred me into action. The rain had stopped but there were still hard gusts and ominous clouds. But if he can make it, couldn't I? Funny how knowing another hiker is out there can make one willing to try it. By noon I was on my way.

I made my way up slowly and carefully. Some has dried but there is still a lot of running water. The path up the Arm was not too bad. All steep, some sections reminiscent of the Notch and others like a steep granite sliding board or waterslide.

Much of the Trail since Hanover has had those granite sliding boards. It seems the soil is only a few inches thick and under it is all solid granite so the path gets reduced to that smooth stone slope. Where it is too steep and smooth to climb, which is most of the time, hikers end up going up the edges using tree roots and trunks for footholds and handholds. The result is that the bare stone slope gets worn wider and wider. I know making stone steps is sort of an anathema here, but setting wood steps or cutting toeholds in the rock might be better in the long run than leaving it as it is. Maybe someone really clever could turn it into a pork-barrel project with Americorps or troubled teens or whomever paid to do the work.

At the top the first gust of wind threw me sideways. It has turned into a windy but fine day with scattered clouds and lots of sunshine. The top was rather broad with many bog bridges. I think how it works is that any undrained hollow in the stone turns into a peat bog. From here to Speck Pond the blueberries were excellent and with such a short hike there was plenty of time to pick and eat all I want. Mmmmmmm.

The whole two miles took three hours. I hope the going gets easier sometime! I spent the rest of the afternoon spreading things out to dry. Also, there was free food in the bear box, left by earlier groups. From it I had some dried prunes and a big pot of instant mashed potatoes, making up for stretching my food out an extra day. Mmmmmm, foooooood.

There was a weather forecast posted, one of the good things about the shelters where the AMC charges $8 to stay. It said rain until midday today, just as it happened, then several days of nice sunny weather. YIPPEE, SUNSHINE!!!!

A college group from Bates arrived and then the shelter filled up with four section hikers. It got cold and I added layer after layer, even sleeping for the first time since spring in my balaclava hood for warmth.

-Mouse

Wednesday, September 01, 2004
Destination: Frye Notch Lean-to
From: Speck Pond Shelter
Today's Miles: 10.4
Trip Miles: 1913.1

261 Miles to go!

Today was more like Maine ought to be, though still a bit slow. I actually made 10 miles in less than nine hours.

It was only 50 degrees this morning and I'd start by going to nearly 4000 feet. So I kept on my long pants, Capilene top and balaclava and cinched my hat down on top of it all. I hiked up Old Speck Mountain in dense fog with a strong wind, needing every bit of clothing I had on. And only found three stunted blueberries! I needn't have worried.

Going down, the blue sky broke through the fog and I stopped to remove layers. Right there in front of me were BLUEBERRIES! Nice big sweet ones. Somehow the best alpine blueberries grow on the east side of the summits, sweeter and juicier than anywhere else. Yummmmmmm! The blueberries continued most of the way down to the road at Grafton Notch and the going was much better than before. I nibbled the whole way down.

Then at the road was a blackberry and then a not too bad climb up to Baldpate Lean-to where I stopped at noon for lunch and to get water. The bushes looked suspiciously like berries and I scanned them until I found a few nice red raspberries.

Then came a steep but not dangerous climb up West Baldpate. It was just as windy but finally there was a view! I whooped with excitement getting to the top. You could see for miles, with big fluffy clouds scattered through blue sky. Here and there were the dwarfed-down variety of alpine blueberries, with a hint of tomato flavor. Going down into the saddle leading to East Baldpate came the big juicy sweet ones. I LOVE alpine blueberries and the only way to get them is to go climb a mountain!

Going up East Baldpate was a climb up the surface of an enormous bare granite dome, guided by a line of cairns and lashed by a ferocious wind. It was euphorically exciting, like being on the ceiling of the world. I felt awash with happiness at being there to experience it all, on such a perfect day way up where relatively few people ever venture.

Going down were more berries and then several wooden ladders over the steep spots down to another granite dome, Little Baldpate. Here I was going into the wind and had to move slowly and carefully so as not to fall going down the curved surface of the dome. I heard a load roar that could only be a fighter jet heading low and fast through one of the passes in front of me but try as I might I was unable to spot it. Fissures in the granite appeared at the treeline, one three feet wide that I had to step across. Then came a zone of sheets of granite that had spalled off and slid down the mountain, making the way more difficult. Here I found something new, ladders made of angle iron bolted together to get past the steepest spots. I liked the effort by trail maintainers to make the way passable.

Then down into the notch to Frye Notch Lean-to. It was the first Maine-pattern shelter I had actually stayed at. They have an awkward waist high log wall several feet in front of the sleeping platform. The idea seems a bit idiotic, as it forces one to clamper over the wall to get in or out. I found shelters like this in the Smokys and Connecticut but avoided them like the plague. But it was 3:30pm and with 4.5 more miles to the road to Andover I doubted I would make it before dark, so I decided to stop here. Tomorrow I will get to the road in the morning and hopefully get an early ride to Andover.

There is yet another college freshman orientation group tenting above the shelter, this one from Colby. I chatted a bit before supper. It seems the idea is for the new freshmen to bond with a group so they have a set of ready-made friends when classes start and they won't feel so alone.

10pm: I am awakened by the bright full moon shining into the shelter. I suppose the really appropriate thing to do would be to turn into a werewolf, go up the hill, and gobble up all the college freshmen. Isn't that how it works in the movies? Or more likely, since I am a thruhiker, turn into a werewolf and gobble up all of their food! Instead, I just lay there and watch it climb up through the trees, then go back to sleep. Not even a howl. How disappointing. Oh, well.

-Mouse

Thursday, September 02, 2004
Destination: East B Hill Road
From: Frye Notch Lean-to
Today's Miles: 4.5
Trip Miles: 1917.6

I had been warm in shorts and long-sleeved top when I went to bed but by 3am it was so cold I added long pants and balaclava and burrowed into my sleeping bag to stay warm. In the morning it was in the upper 40s. I guess those warm nights are a thing of the past.

After a steep 500 foot flight of steps up Surplus Mountain the rest of the way was easy downhill. NOW the trail gets good, when I have to get off for supplies so can't get in a long day of hiking. Oh well.

Going down, I saw the first blueberry bushes and started looking for berries. I found two small ones, then a bigger juicy one. I savored it slowly with a contented "Mmmmmm, blueberry....." Before I found more I had gone from the blueberry zone into raspberry territory. I picked one and ate it, this time with a slow contented "Mmmmmm, raspberry...."

Because it was only 4.5 miles to the road I took the time to go on a sidetrail and see the waterfalls in Dunn Notch. Just after that was the road, where I was lucky and got picked up by the second car.

In Andover I got the food I had mailed to myself, bought more at the General Store as well as a pint of Ben and Jerry's, and called the Cabin hostel run by Margary and Earle Towne, also known as Honey and Bear. Bear picked me up and by 11am I was comfortably ensconced.

Up and Down were there already and before the day was out a few men and five more women had arrived, including the Hobbit Twins, whom I had not seen since Damascus. What is more, they told me Crash Bang was still on the Trail and he was staying at the Andover Guest House nearby.

In addition to the usual nondescript loaner clothing to wear while washing all one's clothes, the Cabin had a whole closet of dresses. All the women had fun picking out our choice to wear that evening. I got a solid green ankle-length long-sleeved one in thick cotton, frumpy enough for a librarian. Our outfits made for lots of fun and picture-taking that evening.

The Cabin is a great place to stay. Bear and Honey kept us stuffed to the gills with home cooked food with three AYCE meals a day.

256 Miles to go!

-Mouse

Friday, September 03, 2004
Destination: South Arm Road
From: East B Hill Road
Today's Miles: 10.1
Trip Miles: 1927.7

Having the bunkroom packed with women made for a peaceful, nearly snore-free night. Most of the men were exiled to a teepee outside.

This morning Up and Down got back on the Trail and headed north. We other six women slacked the ten mile stretch from South Branch Road back south to East B Road but with a twist: We all wore our dresses from the night before! We were accompanied by Neon in a florescent violet fright wig.

The basic plan was based on the fact that going south put most of the ups and downs early on while the day was still cool, followed by a long gentle descent. We kept a very fast pace and I was huffing up the first mountain and had a sore hamstring by the end of the day. Still I managed to grab some raspberries on the run.

Every time we encountered other hikers they stared at our dresses with disbelief. A college orientation group did not know what to make of us. Northbound thruhikers laughed and got out their cameras. We lined up again and again for pictures and I bet we were the most photographed sight of the Trail today. It was the silliest and most fun thing I've done the whole hike.

My dress was nice and warm in the chilly morning but I don't recommend flannel for hiking in warm weather. I ended up very sweaty but it was worth it for the fun we were having. Another woman had the best outfit, a frilly polyester party dress that was nice and cool.

At the road a car stopped and a couple got out. They were Mama Finch and Finch, who had thruhiked in 2003, there to set out Trail Magic. At first they did not think we were thruhikers, then Finch guessed. He asked "Are you with Bear?" Apparently this is not the first time Bear had sent oddly dressed hikers out from the Cabin. We lined up yet again for pictures before riding back to Andover and the Cabin. Tonight the cast started changing with new arrivals. Crispy Critter and his wife came, who I last had seen just before they went to Trail Days.

246 Miles to go!

-Mouse

Saturday, September 04, 2004
Destination: Hwy. 17
From: South Arm Road
Today's Miles: 13.3
Trip Miles: 1941.0

The Hobbit sisters and I decided to slack south from Hwy 17 to South Branch Rd, this time more appropriately attired for hiking. A new couple, Scarecrow and I-need-a-hug, went along planning to hike the full 23 miles back to East B Hill Rd.

Beginning on a height with a nice view of the rather oddly named Lake Mooselookmeguntic, we had a short somewhat steep descent from the road which left me far behind. Then came what according to the guidebook was a stream fording, but it was shallow enough to get across on stepping stones. Then across a dirt road and up Bemis Mountain with its four widely spaced peaks.

By the first peaks I was running into blueberries. Did I remember to mention how much I love alpine blueberries? Mmmmmmm..... With thirteen miles and the need to make a 4:30 pickup time there was not enough time to really gorge, but I could not resist grabbing a handful whenever I could.

Despite delays for berries I found myself passing the others when they stopped for a break. We leapfrogged for the rest of the day because I was slow but took fewer breaks. Scarecrow and I-need-a-hug rather wisely decided to give up on their 23 mile idea and stop at 13 miles like the rest of us.

At Bemis Shelter I ran into the Twins and we stopped for lunch. I was in a silly mood and wrote in the register new words to "We Three Kings"

"We three twins a' slacking are,

With light packs to travel so far,

Bemis, Elephant, Old Blue Mountain,

Hiking south to the car..."

There were some good views and overlooks and nice weather. Elephant Mountain was not too hard and there was a long level spot after that with lengths of bog bridging. But Old Blue was steep and so was the descent, forcing me to slow down because my right hamstring was extremely sore from the fast pace of the past two days. It had been injured two years ago when I had been hit by a car at a stop sign while training for the New York City Marathon but it had not bothered me on the Trail up to now. I was the last one out to the road. Along the way were several wooden ladders including the first I had seen on the Trail made of a single log with foot notches cut in it. It was a bit tricky to negotiate and I have been told there will be more ladders like it further north.

Back at the Cabin, after my shower I snagged the polyester dress, freshly laundered after Party Girl had gone hiking in it. I love how un-thruhiker it makes me look, a fun break from the Trail.

I decided to take tomorrow off. It has been more than a week since my last break in Gorham and I had better let my bad hamstring rest. The last thing I want is to have an injury force me off the Trail after getting this far.

233 Miles left!

-Mouse

Sunday, September 05, 2004
Destination: Cabin Hostel, East Andover
From: Hwy. 17
Today's Miles: 0.0
Trip Miles: 1941.0

With a higher portion of men, the bunkroom snore volume was higher last night. I finally gave up trying to go back to sleep about 4:30am and got up to read.

At breakfast I found myself appointed Empress of the Cabin. That is sort of like Staff Duty Officer in the Army, except you don't get to carry a loaded .45 pistol. I spent the day minding the phone, picking up after breakfast, emptying the dishwasher, cooking the evening desert and delegating pre-supper tasks. Not QUITE the lazy day of napping I had planned, but that is how things are. Besides, it was a lot of fun helping out.

-Mouse

Monday, September 06, 2004
Destination: Rangeley, ME
From: Cabin Hostel, East Andover
Today's Miles: 13.1
Trip Miles: 1954.1

Seven of us left the Cabin and set out from Hwy 17 today but due to other shuttles before us we did not get to the trail until 10:30am.

The going was much much easier than past days and I made as good time with a full pack as I had made slackpacking. The ground was fairly level with just a few hills and some mud. There were a fair number of blueberries, scattered raspberries and even a blackberry. Some of the blueberries are getting a bit shriveled and past their prime as they turn overripe and then dry in the sun. I suspect the first frost will finish them altogether.

I had planned to go straight through to Stratton. But with the remains of Hurricane Francis looming and heavy rain predicted on the day I'd be crossing a river I decided to go into Rangeley. That would allow me to get the morning weather forecast and would let me start this leg with an extra day of food in case I have to wait next to a river for the water to go down enough to ford safely.

At the road a couple who had finished a backpacking trip from the north generously gave five of us a ride to town. We ate at a pub called Sarge's and then found a motel for the night.

Tomorrow back into the mountains for what could end as a wet leg to Stratton.

220 Miles to go!

-Mouse

Tuesday, September 07, 2004
Destination: Poplar Ridge Lean-To
From: Rangeley, ME
Today's Miles: 10.7
Trip Miles: 1964.8

I was lucky this morning as when walking to the center of town where I meant to hitch a ride I was offered one by a young man in an SUV. He had sectioned north from here, had just summited Katahdin yesterday and was on his way home.

The weather was good with a cobalt blue sky with only the distant edges marred by cloud. From the top of Saddleback Mountain one is supposed to be able to see both Mt Washington and Mt Katahdin. I was not sure which peaks on the horizon were them, but took pictures in the appropriate directions for posterity.

On the way down my hamstring was aching more emphatically. Either the Ibuprofen I had dosed myself with had worn off or my hip was starting to bother me more. The first tiny dwarf alpine blueberries had appeared going up, some so ripe they burst when I picked them. Now on the sheltered east face they were big and sweet and irresistible. Several times I sat next to a patch to rest my sore hip and picked all within reach. Berries are my cure-all for any problems of spirit or body; they are so good they make any difficulty seem more manageable.

Next came The Horn and Little Saddleback. Going up the latter I ran into and passed an orientation group from Harvard and pulled ahead steadily despite my hip.

At the Lean-to I decided to stop as I had planned. Had I been fit I would have went on several miles, then tomorrow press on to ford the South Branch Carrabassett River before the rain hits. But my hamstring has been bothering me for several days and it seems unwise to push too hard, especially with the Bigelow Mountains coming up right after Stratton. So I will stick to an easy pace and take a rain day if needed.

I had settled into reading a mystery novel when first the freshmen arrived then a thruhiker who announced six more are behind him. So much for my solitude! On the upside, the other Pilot and Vaportrail are coming, so there are familiar women.

209 Miles left!

-Mouse

Wednesday, September 08, 2004
Destination: Spaulding Mountain Lean-To
From: Poplar Ridge Lean-To
Today's Miles: 8.0
Trip Miles: 1972.8

The rain started during the night, moderately heavy then stopped by morning. But sprinkles started as soon as I put my pack on and there were showers off and on through the morning. Rather sillily I brought along a thick heavy mystery novel I had started and could not put down.

I went up and over Poplar Ridge and on the reverse slope the blueberries started. Lower down at a logging road I found some nice late raspberries as well. But on the way I slipped and fell on a mud slope, bending a pole. Bleah! I am not sure I can get a new section out here. It is usable but crooked and I would not trust my full weight on it anymore.

Aside from that I made good time and my hamstring was not bothering me too much when I reached the shelter at noon. I dosed myself with Ibuprofen and used my water bladder as a cold pack on my hamstring in hopes of soothing away the damage. Then I spent the afternoon cocooned in my sleeping bag reading the novel. It rained within an hour and went on and off all afternoon becoming steadier into the evening, so I was just as happy to be under a roof.

The others from the last shelter filtered through. They hoped to reach Crocker Cirque Tentsite or even Stratton today. As soon as they left a bold red squirrel came right up on the sleeping platform five feet from me to gobble up the crumbs.

I was joined by two other thruhikers who chose to tent outside as well as the group from Harvard who set up their usual tarps in an open spot behind the shelter. It took just until 10pm before the freshmen had had enough of the rain. They forsook the inadequate shelter of their crowded tarps and as many as would fit packed into the shelter.

201 Miles left!

-Mouse

Thursday, September 09, 2004
Destination: Spaulding Mountain Lean-To (Day 2)
From: Spaulding Mountain Lean-To
Today's Miles: 0.0
Trip Miles: 1972.8

The next day the two thruhikers were gone by 7 and by 9 the freshmen had gotten packed and left as well. Outside it looked remarkably like the remnants of a hurricane passing through with lots of rain and strong gusty winds. I guess that was not too strange, since what was left of Frances WAS forecast to hit today. I stayed snug in my sleeping bag with a copy of Jules Verne's "Journey to the center of the Earth" which I had found in the shelter.

Strangely, I did not feel hungry at all until around 1pm when I had just one small packet of Cheese Combos. That was particularly odd since at the Cabin on my last zero day I had felt the stirrings of hunger not long after my huge breakfast and had been ravenous by noon. I was just as glad to save some food in case I had to wait for the river to fall.

About then drenched thruhikers began arriving from Poplar Ridge. About four passed through, including HeatMiser whom I had not seen in months and Bluebell who had found my hat for me in Massachusetts. They each stopped for a quick lunch under shelter and then went back into the rain towards the summit of Sugarloaf Mountain 3.5 miles away. It is .6 miles off the Trail and up a steep climb but apparently there is an enclosed cabin there where they planned to spend the night.

Around 4 Sweaty Pig arrived and decided to stay here instead of pushing on to the cabin. By then there were occasional lulls in the rain, broken by renewed pouring. The gusts almost never stopped.

I hope this blows over tonight. I could stay another day before food became a problem but would prefer to get moving. Particularly since I have run out of new books to read.

STILL 201 miles.

-Mouse

Friday, September 10, 2004
Destination: Crocker Cirque Tent Site
From: Spaulding Mountain Lean-To (Day 2)
Today's Miles: 6.2
Trip Miles: 1979.0

The rain kept up until nearly dawn. I took my time getting up to let things drain a bit and to let the South Fork have a chance to subside a bit before I forded it, so it was 915 before I was hiking.

The rain had completely stopped but gusts of wind would come roaring through the trees like an approaching airplane then recede; small pockets of fast-moving air. It reminded me of the wind on my wild first night backpacking alone up in the High Sierras in California, above Sonora Pass two years ago. As I ascended Spaulding Mountain I plunged into the cloud ceiling and the world turned to fog. The ferns were mostly wilted and the leaves were turning flame-red on the broadleaf trees scattered among the pines; portents that summer here is rushing to a close. The going was pretty good and I found a raspberry going up and scattered blueberries the rest of the day. I bet readers are sick and tired of hearing what berries I found, but a thousand-plus mile berry streak is worth documenting. Besides, looking for berries keeps me occupied and out of trouble. Who knows what mischief I might get into?

The terrain changed abruptly when I reached the steep canyon of the South Branch Carrabassett River. The walls were steep and rocky and I had gotten below the clouds. So there were splendid views down into the canyon. The Trail plunged down a string of rock climbs. They required care in the wet, but were not too complicated or hazardous.

Finally I reached the ford. To my relief, a plank crossed the widest part and was a full foot above the fast-rushing water. It was so high that the tops of several of the boulders used for stepping stones to approach the plank were several inches below the water so I ended up dunking both hiking boots. But nothing worse than that. The water was moving fast enough I would not have liked trying to ford it.

The moment I got to the other bank the clouds divided, blue sky appeared and the sun shined for the first time in days. Isn't it odd how those dramatic Hollywood touches happen just at the right moment? (Looking nervously over shoulder to see if I really am just in a movie)

Next came Caribou Valley Road. It turned out to be just a dirt road, not too promising for getting a ride. But the perfect place for Trail Magic, so I kept my eyes peeled. Sure enough, lying in a cold stream just across the road were eight cans of beer from a Trail Angel named Recon. Too bad I don't like beer! Oh well.

I reached Crocker Cirque Tentsite at 1:30. It was seven miles and two 4000 foot mountains before the road to Stratton so I doubted I could get to the road before dark. Besides, my hamstring seemed better and I did not want to jinx it by rushing into a high mileage day. So I stopped at the tentsite for the night, as I had originally planned.

The site had privy, water source and three tent platforms. The boards of the platforms did not project past the edge and were too close together to stick a tent stake between them but I still managed to put up my Nomad tent with the help of a convenient tree to tie the front awning guy rope to. Within half an hour I had camp made, water purified and was snug in my sleeping bag. Ahhhhhhh..... Gee, me and my sleeping bag are getting quite attached to each other lately!

The gusts here are pretty impressive. They get funneled through the canyon, then since cirques are bowl shaped they hit from any direction. Despite the cover of surrounding trees, the tent shudders or the awning inflates like a parachute. A dead tree is dropping small branches on me. I'd move but the other platforms are even more exposed. Could be an interesting night.

195 miles to the end.

-Mouse

Saturday, September 11, 2004
Destination: Stratton, ME
From: Crocker Cirque Tent Site
Today's Miles: 7.3
Trip Miles: 1986.3

It was a chilly 45 degrees when I woke up. With the mornings getting colder I have been getting up later to let the sun warm things up a bit, so it was 7 when I got on the Trail.

It was a crystal clear perfect day. Too bad I was here going up Crocker Mountain, which only has limited views, instead of Sugarloaf with its panoramic vista. At the same time, I was miles of rough terrain ahead of where Sugarloaf was. You can't have everything. At least there were blueberries! What is more, the five miles from the top down to the road to town was an easy gentle descent.

The second car to go by picked me up and dropped me off at the White Wolf Inn in Stratton. During lunch I discovered Little Bit, whom I had last seen worrying about Lyme Disease in Dalton Mass. She had gone the whole 3 week course of antibiotics but was waiting until she finished to get tested. She advised me to get tested as well, just in case I had a case that skipped the initial symptoms. Speaking of symptoms, she also told me about Freedom, who had been diagnosed with shingles when we were at Dalton. Well, three weeks later her shingles developed a ring and SHE was treated for Lyme disease! Little Bit, who is a nurse, guessed that Freedom had both shingles and Lyme disease.

For lunch I put away a half-pound cheeseburger, sweet-potato fries, a Maine delicacy of fried ferns called fiddleheads, topped off with peanut butter pie. It was the biggest meal I had had in ages.

Next I bought food and did laundry, then went off to my room to relax.

Just 15 more miles of the Bigelow Mountains before things flatten out until Monson. Woohoo! Maybe I can finally start speeding up.

187 Miles to go!

-Mouse

Sunday, September 12, 2004
Destination: Safford Notch Tent Site
From: Stratton, ME
Today's Miles: 10.4
Trip Miles: 1996.7

When I finished hiking yesterday I felt all right but by evening my entire right hip and left knee were hurting like crazy. I fed myself Ibuprofen every 4 hours and by morning they felt better. I also noticed a very small leak near the mouth of my Platypus, so I switched it for the one my twin had brought me at Wind Gap PA. Since the leak is so small I kept it as a spare. I also went and forgot to try to have a new Leki pole section sent to Monson so I will probably have to use the bent one for the rest of my hike.

After breakfast at the Mainely Yours Diner I left my room and hitched a ride to the Trail. An older couple who were trying to climb all 100 or so peaks in New England above 4000 feet picked me up. Odd since a couple on a similar quest had taken me to the Trail at Rangeley!

I was hiking by 9am and started the long ascent to Horns Pond. At the tentsite there I fell into a conversation with a group of caretakers when I stopped to purify water. They had made a bet between themselves whether I was a thruhiker or section hiker. The losers gave me some Oreos and while I ate I complemented them on how much nicer the Trail layout and maintenance was since I went from AMC land to MATC land. That made them all beam with pride and they wished me well on the rest of my hike.

Next I climbed up West Peak and Avery Peak of Bigelow Mountain. Much was above timberline and the view was splendid. Using my compass I oriented my map and picked out what might be Mount Katahdin off on the horizon between two nearer peaks. It was hard to be sure without knowing what its silhouette should be at that angle. The real Katahdin might have still been hidden by haze.

Going down I enjoyed those yummy alpine blueberries for what might be the last time of the hike. I think the Bigelows are the last 4000 foot peaks until Katahdin and I will probably get there too late for blueberries. So I bid them a sentimental farewell, saying "Goodbye, Alpine Blueberries." It was an emotional parting, but I managed to avoid tears.

Then came a seemingly endless string of switchbacks winding down the very steep east face of Avery Peak into Stafford Notch, dodging in and out of house-sized boulders that had tumbled off the peak over the centuries. It seemed to go on forever. Even when I reached the sidetrail it even went UNDER one of those huge boulders through a sort of cave before I finally got to the tentsite at 5:30. It was alive with mosquitoes, the first I had been bothered by since Vermont, so I hastily set up my tent on a platform, got water, cooked supper and put it under my hat to set, hung my food bag and took refuge inside the tent.

To save weight I am having ramen noodles with peanut butter for protein instead of meat. All the store had was canned meat and fish, which seemed too heavy. So I will have sort of fake Thai food for now.

177 Miles to go!

-Mouse

Monday, September 13, 2004
Destination: West Carry Pond Lean-to
From: Safford Notch Tent Site
Today's Miles: 12.2
Trip Miles: 2008.9

I am a very happy hiker! Today I passed the 2000 mile mark, finished the western Maine mountains and ran into some awesome Trail Magic.

At 7am I started up Little Bigelow Mountain. It is a string of peaks with dips between very like the ridge walks on the AT south of New Hampshire. In each dip were blueberries and not knowing how many more I would see, I was constantly grabbing a handful. More and more are shriveled and some bushes have even shed all their leaves leaving just the bare twigs hung with berries. There is no doubt that autumn was rushing towards us.

A little past the middle of the ridge I came to a big "2000" made of pine twigs placed along the Trail. I had come 2000 miles! Woohoo! As soon as I came to a blueberry I held it up, said "To 2000 miles" and ate it as a toast to the event.

The descent down to Little Bigelow Lean-to was long and moderately steep with many ledges to step down, so it required some care. I stopped there for lunch and water. According to the profile the rest of the way down was just as steep but to my delight it actually was a smooth almost level path. The last time I saw one of those was coming into Gorham. Now I was in a REALLY good mood.

Coming to East Flagstaff Road I decided it was just the sort of place Trail Magic appears; remote enough to be left alone by non-thruhikers but easy enough for Trail Angels to get to. So I kept my eyes open. At the parking area across the road were big cloth signs with the words "Hikers, come see what we have. Incredible Trail Magic." I went in and was amazed! There was a cluster of plastic chairs and a long table under a row of canopies on and around which was almost everything a thruhiker could possibly dream of! I have seen whole Trail Towns with less to offer.

The founder of the feast was 2000 thruhiker Walkin Home. He showed me around and asked if I wanted one cheeseburger or two. I settled into a chair. It seems he has done this every year since 1998 except the year the thruhiked and every year it gets better. Talk about Trail Angels!

A large cup of coffee, two tasty cheeseburgers, a plate of nice pasta salad, some carrot sticks, a slice of cake and a pint of orange juice later I made my very grateful thanks. I waddled back to the Trail stuffed to the gills as Walkin Home wished me a Class 1 day at Katahdin. If I had been happy before, now I was positively euphoric! It is amazing how getting stuffed with food makes every problem disappear and leaves one ready to conquer the world.

Now there were just two foothills and six miles left to West Carry Pond Lean-to. The birds were pretty quiet now but the squirrels more than made up for it. They chatter furiously, chase each other about and I could swear they were throwing pinecones at me from the treetops.

There was a brisk wind blowing in off the lake with waves coming in like ocean surf. Filling my water bag without getting totally drenched was an interesting challenge. I finally found a small pool cut off from the rest of the lake by a line of rocks. Standing on a large rock above the spray, I held my bag between two rocks and let the surge of water each time a wave came in fill it up.

Papa Bear and Badger were there as well but they tented, leaving me the whole shelter to myself. I fixed my usual ramen with peanut butter for supper. After two cheeseburgers, protein was not a worry!

I am thrilled to be here. The dangerous climb up out of Pinkham Notch up to Wildcat Ridge had been quite a shock and for days I had wondered if staying on the Trail was worth the risk. I had been SOOOO tempted to give it up and go home. But now I am through the mean mountains of western Maine and have just one easy day of hiking ON LEVEL GROUND before the canoe ferry ride across the Kennebec River. There were days when I did not think I would EVER get this far and now here I am. Nothing lies between me and Mount Katahdin that can hold a candle to what I have already been through, so I am excited to see it through to the end. I am REALLY one happy hiker.

165 Miles left to go!

-Mouse

Tuesday, September 14, 2004
Destination: Stealth Camp. N. of Caratunk
From: West Carry Pond
Today's Miles: 14.0
Trip Miles: 2022.9

The loons on the pond made their haunting call through the night and into the morning, which was a cold 45 degrees. Knowing the ferry shuts down at 4pm, I got going by 6:30 despite the chill. The big juicy blueberry I had spotted the previous day at the turnoff to the shelter was still there so I broke my berry fast first thing. There was a scattering of blueberries the rest of the day, mostly along the ponds and streams.

I needn't have worried about time. All the way to Pierce Pond Lean-to most of the Trail was soft, smooth and flat. Just the sort of easy hiking I have missed all these weeks! There were great shoreline views of the large ponds, really lakes, which I passed. Along the way a section of the Trail followed the route Benedict Arnold had marched 1100 troops north to join in the historic storming of Quebec on Dec 31, 1775. I was at Pierce Pond by 1:30.

The rest of the way down the Pierce Pond Stream canyon was a bit more rugged but I did not mind. It had some nice rapids and waterfalls to look at and I still got to the Kennebec ten minutes before the ferry would open for the afternoon at 2pm. Two men arrived soon after and one of them kindly took my camera to take a picture of me when I set off on my canoe trip.

Soon a man dragged a canoe out of the woods on the opposite shore and paddled across. He introduced himself as a stand-in for Steve "The Ferryman" Longley, who had the day off. He had me sign a liability waiver and handed me a lifejacket to put on while he set my pack in the canoe. Then he adjusted my vest and had me get in. The hiker took my picture and handed my camera back to me, along with his pack to go across with me to lighten the next load, and shoved us off. There was an extra paddle, so I even got to paddle instead of just sitting. The current was fairly fast, sweeping us downstream so we had to paddle back upstream on the other side to get near the landing. He helped me out, unloaded the packs, then went back for the two men and the remaining pack.

I put on my pack, hiked to the road and turned towards Caratunk. I saw a man in front of one house and was about to ask directions when he offered me a soda and snacks from a big cooler and introduced himself as One Braid, owner of Caratunk House. Or former owner. It seems someone had reported him for serving food to hikers and forced him to close! That was an unpleasant surprise as I had planned on staying there.

Fortunately One Braid was still selling off his stock of hiker supplies. I bought enough food to get me through to Monson, including a 5 oz pack of tuna to make up for the cheeseburger I had been hoping for. Then I gave him my thanks and headed back for the Trail.

I went high enough above the road that the noise of passing lumber trucks would not disturb my sleep, then started looking for a campsite. At what looked like a very overgrown abandoned dirt road I pushed through some low trees to a level spot out of sight of the Trail. There I set up my tent and hung my bear rope ready for my food bag after supper. There were so many mosquitoes that I ducked into my tent.

I had less than a liter of water and the next water was another 2-3 miles ahead. Between that and the mosquitoes I decided not to cook but instead to go back to the cold food routine I had followed in the middle of my hike. Just as well, as I suddenly realized I had only bought food for the next two nights. Having planned on eating tonight's supper at the hostel, I had not bought food for supper! Digging around, I got out my last bar of Halvah I had saved from the Hanover Food Co-Op. It had even more calories than a pack of ramen so with the extra big pack of tuna it would feed me for supper. I had gotten an extra pack of Poptarts so breakfast was taken care of, and I had peanut butter and Ramen for the next two nights. Saved!

This was the first night I had simply camped by myself alongside the Trail in a long time. I think the last time was when I fled the singing summer campers back before Delaware Water Gap. It worked out for the best, because I got a bit nearer to the next stop and avoided the late start usual with towns and hostels.

Now just 151 miles left!

-Mouse

Wednesday, September 15, 2004
Destination: Bald Mountain Brook Lean-To
From: Stealth Camp. N. of Caratunk
Today's Miles: 14.7
Trip Miles: 2037.6

A long but satisfying day.

I started with a very gently climbing six mile hike to Pleasant Pond Lean-to. It was full of new and not totally welcome sounds: lumber trucks, power saw or wood chipper, and the loud barking and baying of a pack of large dogs that passed the trail in front of me uncomfortably close. I remembered it was bear season and hoped that whoever was with them was careful when shooting. Crossing a logging road I got a surprise, 3 ripe raspberries. I was amazed that there were any left with September half over.

At the lean-to I purified water and had some Cheese Combos for an early lunch to fortify me for the thousand foot climb up Pleasant Pond Mountain. While there I discovered a large cooler with sodas left by a Trail Angel named VanGogh. Woohoo, calories and caffeine! Talk about fortifying. I surged up the slope, which was not too steep and with only a few spots that needed handholds.

At the top were fairly good views between the trees and nice clear weather. It was hard to know if any of the distant mountains to the northeast were Katahdin. I guess I have to get closer to be sure.

Going down always takes more time and care than going up, even though the slope was shallower. It was turning into a hot afternoon as well. So it felt more like a hiking day months ago and far to the south rather than up here in Maine. I saw lots and lots of blueberry bushes but only a scattering of berries. Proof that the season was later than it felt.

Finally I crossed over a beaver dam and came to Moxie Pond at the bottom of the slope. Then came what was supposed to be a wide ford of Baker Stream. I was lucky, it was just low enough to pick my way across dry shod over large boulders, the water rushing through the gaps in between. That is the second ford I have escaped actually having to ford.

The day ended with a gentle 2.5 mile climb up to Bald Mountain Lean-to. Long before then I was starting to get high mileage sore spots to add to my steep slope sore spots, but both were within reason. My hip has trouble but not as bad as a few days ago.

There was a section hiking couple tenting but no one in the shelter. Because of the mosquitoes I experimented again with hanging my tent from the ceiling and putting my air mattress inside it. Naturally the mosquitoes vanished so I decided to put my tent away. Still it gave me a chance to let it dry off from last night. And I found five slugs on it that had sneaked a ride with me this morning, a new record! Usually there is just one and I find it before packing the tent in the morning. Caratunk must have a lot of slugs!

There was one more chore. I took out my bear bag rope and cut off two pieces long enough to use as extra laces for my sandals, then burned the ends so they won't fray. My sandals just have regular flip-flop straps with a toe eyelet. Passing the cord through the straps, behind my heel and tied at the ankle will keep the sandals from getting torn off my feet by fast current when wading rivers. I cross the West Branch Piscataquis River tomorrow and the East Branch on Friday and I doubt I will be lucky enough to find stepping stones. Better to prepare now rather than putter with it at the riverbank.

Drat it, the mosquitoes are back! I think I will resort to using DEET for the first time since Vermont rather than fiddle with my tent again.

136 Miles to Katahdin!

-Mouse

Thursday, September 16, 2004
Destination: Horseshoe Canyon Lean-To
From: Bald Mountain Brook Lean-To
Today's Miles: 13.0
Trip Miles: 2050.6

Another great day to be hiking in Maine!

Moxie Bald is another granite dome like early in Maine only lower and less steep. Most of the ascent is like a gentle ramp. In fact, the granite looks rather like weathered asphalt complete with broken and grown over spots so that it felt rather like parts of the Ramble in New York City's Central Park.

Where the bad-weather bypass split off, the Trail became a bit steeper then veered through giant slabs of granite that had spalled off and piled up. It was like walking under the top of Aslan's Table in Narnia or through the ruins of Stonehenge.

The top seemed not quite above treeline but the wide expanses of bare granite dome still gave it an alpine feel. There were blueberry bushes everywhere but hardly a berry. I took the very short sidetrail to the summit and ruins of an old fire tower. I could see all around but clouds to the east blocked most of the mountains and the valleys all around were still fogbound. A different vista from either a clear day or a foggy one.

Starting down I ran into a patch of big juicy sweet almost alpine blueberries! I picked a handful and ate them one at a time, popping each yummy globe and savoring its goodness. I could have swooned with happiness. There is nothing tastier than blueberries fresh picked from a Maine mountaintop! It really is the true reward for getting up here.

I passed over terrace after terrace of granite, full of berryless bushes. On the east side of each I would go around a corner and find another patch of big sweet berries. They always came as a surprise, after many bare bushes.

Then as I neared the sidetrail to North Peak I found an even bigger surprise! Large bushes packed with whole clusters of a new variety of blueberry. They were even bigger and sweeter, with a taste hinting of cherries, and there were LOADS of them. I ate and ate, picking with both hands at once there were so many. Life just does not get better than that. I was in berry heaven. They were even better than the oh, so refreshing juiciness of the mulberries back in Cumberland Valley PA. A father and son team by the names of Papabear and Badger caught up with me there. They had stayed at the tentsite just before the shelter I had stayed at. We ended up passing and re-passing each other the rest of the day.

Going down was steeper but the path was mostly soft pine needles. I stopped at Moxie Bald Lean-to for lunch and water. It is odd that it is near Bald Mountain Pond while Bald Mountain Brook Lean-to was next to Moxie Pond. Sounds backwards!

Then came a fast two miles to Bald Mountain Stream. It was thirty feet or so wide, with a rough dam of drifted logs forming a pool upstream and rapids downstream. There were inches of fast water pouring over the logs so the only way across was to ford it.

I dropped my poles and pack and sat on a warm sunny slab of rock. Removing my boots and socks I put the socks in the stuff sack I keep at the top of my pack for clothes I need in the day and looped my boots to the back of the pack with the bungee cord. Then I put on my sandals and tied the laces I had made. I put on my pack with the waist belt undone so I could shrug free of it if I fell, took my poles and started across. I went upstream of the logs where it was deeper but calmer and I could see the bottom. The water was a bit cold and came up to just above my knees. Once or twice a pole slipped into a deep hole between the rocks forming the bottom but other than that crossing was easy. On the other side I reversed the process, drying each foot with the top part of a sock before putting socks and boots on, then putting away the wet sandals.

The next four miles were fairly level but varied, with sections of mud and rocks that made me feel like I was back in Vermont or Pennsylvania. Then I ran into ran into Papabear and Badger filtering water and getting ready to ford the West Branch Piscataquis River. I went through the same fording routine as before and went across ahead of them.

Finally were three miles along the canyon of the Piscataquis to the Shelter. There were enough roots and irregularities to make my already tired feet sore and it seemed to take forever. Still, overall it was a really nice day.

I met Papabear and Badger at the spring and a little later someone named Baloo. He came from Pleasant Pond 22 miles back and warned us at least five more hikers were coming. Looks like a full shelter tonight and a stampede to get rooms in Monson tomorrow.

123 Miles to go!

-Mouse

Friday, September 17, 2004
Destination: Monson, ME
From: Horseshoe Canyon Lean-To
Today's Miles: 9.0
Trip Miles: 2059.6

This morning there were stirrings before 5:30 and it became clear there would be a general stampede toward town and its comforts. I was on the Trail by 6, my earliest start in some time.

I scanned the bushes and finally found two raspberries and a blueberry. At the first road a friend of Tennessee Jack's was waiting with Trail Magic for all who passed. A soda and two candy bars later I was flying happily through the woods. Trail Angels are the greatest!

At Highway 15 everyone was at Tennessee Jack's friend's pickup waiting on the last few stragglers when another pickup pulled up and the driver asked if anyone wanted a ride to town. He turned out to be shuttling for Shaws Boarding House, so that is where I decided to stay. I got a nice private room with a comfortable bed with sheets and even a TV set.

By noon I was showered, had picked up my mail drop and had a good cheeseburger at the Monson General Store. Then I sorted everything out, mailed home film and a few odds and ends I would not need the last weeks, and bought food for the Hundred Mile Wilderness. Shaw's has its own store of hiker needs as complete as many outfitters. I was finally able to replace my Spenco Insoles which I had had since Kent Connecticut. They were old and falling apart and had lost nearly all their cushion. I also replaced a bandana I had accidentally left at a shelter two days ago.

I also got a pint of Ben and Jerry's ice cream, a quart of chocolate milk and a half gallon of whole milk as well as some peaches and bananas to devour while I am here.

Then came Shaws' rather legendary AYCE dinner with mountains of ham, potatoes, garden fresh tomatoes, corn and all the trimmings. Yummm!!!!! They were warm hosts, eager to make us feel at home and well cared for.

Wow, I have finally reached Monson. Just the Hundred Mile Wilderness and Katahdin left. The end is really coming up! Now when passersby tell me I am almost finished it really feels true, whereas in the difficult early part of Maine that comment had felt bitterly ironic.

114 Miles to go!

-Mouse

Saturday, September 18, 2004
Destination: Monson, ME (2nd day)
From: Monson, ME
Today's Miles: 0.0
Trip Miles: 2059.6

    I had planned on slack packing 14 miles today. But the rain from a cold front and the remains of Hurricane Ivan came unexpectedly far north so I took off my THIRD hurricane day instead. Mr. Shaw drove me and two others into Guilford to an ATM and then to Dover for groceries and a stop at McDonalds to buy lunch. Then I spent the afternoon napping.

    The rain lasted into the afternoon but it is supposed to clear overnight and stay good for at least a week.

    I will give up the slackpacking idea and hike out tomorrow with five night's food. That will give me 6 days to cover the 73 miles to White House Landing where I sent a food drop.

    -Mouse

Sunday, September 19, 2004
Destination: Long Pond Stream Lean-To
From: Monson, ME (2nd day)
Today's Miles: 15.1
Trip Miles: 2074.7

    A good start into the Wilderness. The weather was cool and overcast but dry with scattered blueberries.

    Breakfast at Shaws starts at 6am and to simplify things it goes by how many of everything you want. "Two by" mean two each of eggs, bacon sausage, ham and pancakes plus potatoes. I had that yesterday and barely got it all down. "One and a Half by" would be ideal but that was not an option so I had a "One by" and filled the remaining empty spaces with donuts.

    After that Mr. Shaw drove me and another hiker who was ready to the Trail at 7am, a record early start from a hostel. Most hostels are just starting breakfast then. He thanked us for staying with them, shook the other hiker's hand and gave me a hug and peck on my cheek. (Blush!)

[Sadly, Mr. Shaw passed away less than three months later, on December 7, 2004. I am glad to have met him. He was an unforgettable character who will be missed by the thruhiking community.]

The trail had ups and downs and I made the 1.5 miles per hour I usually did on rough terrain before New Hampshire. Interestingly the bedrock was slate instead of granite.

Things got interesting when I reached Big Wilson Creek. It looked innocently smooth as I prepared to ford. But the current was swift and before I knew it I was in up to my waist. With even deeper holes between the rocks on the bottom it was hard to find footing. I fell forward into the rushing water and had to let my poles dangle and grab the top of a boulder to keep my face above water. Hanging onto it I inched nervously through a fast sluice of water pouring between it and the next boulder. Finally I got to calmer water and made my way to shore. It may not have been seriously dangerous but it was certainly difficult! If that boulder had not been there and I had pitched face first into waist deep water weighed down by my pack and with the current trying to pump me full of water I might have been in real trouble though! I was relieved to be on dry land again. My pack stayed dry but my shorts and the front of my t-shirt were drenched.

Then came Long Pond Stream. It was not so wide but I surveyed it and found that while I could get most of the way across on rocks in several places, there was always a gap too wide to jump. So I had to ford it as well. It turned out to be only knee deep, much to my relief and I got across without trouble.

Then I finally got to the shelter. I was first there but two others arrived by dark.

99 Miles to go!

-Mouse

Monday, September 20, 2004
Destination: Chairback Gap Lean-To
From: Long Pond Steam Lean-to
Today's Miles: 10.9
Trip Miles: 2085.6

Today was cool with mostly clear skies and continued scattered blueberries. It also marked my sixth month on the Appalachian Trail.

I went over four of the five peaks of the Barren-Chairback Range making for a strenuous day. I started with the 1700 foot climb up Barren Mountain. Then from Fourth Mountain I got my first unquestionable look at Mount Katahdin. No mistaking it peeping up above the horizon in between two nearer mountains.

With all the ups and downs I thought I was on Third Mountain three times before I actually got there. By the time I got to Columbus Mountain I was getting tired and sore-footed. Then to my surprise I burst upon the shelter almost before I realized it.

Finding the privy and water was a bit of an adventure as both were well hidden. By then one of my companions from last night got in. At about 6 a whole herd started arriving from Wilson Creek shelter. Another full house and more tenting.

88 Miles to go!

-Mouse

Tuesday, September 21, 2004
Destination: Carl Newhall Lean-to
From: Chairback Gap Lean-to
Today's Miles: 9.9
Trip Miles: 2095.5

First day of autumn!

When the sun came up a large green caterpillar lay on my air mattress. Its front end moved about searchingly, the way caterpillars do, until it came to a pack of Poptarts nearby. It brought the small puckered opening of its mouth to it and several appendages protruded and delicately tore open the foil pouch. The mouth approached the edge of one Poptart and the caterpillar nibbled away until it was gone. Then it ate the second Poptart as well. After all that activity, the caterpillar rested a while as if worn out by the effort.

Then the skin of the caterpillar split open down one side, starting the mouth. My head and shoulders emerged and I tore open a packet of Jell-O mix, added it to a bottle of water, shook it up, and drank it. Another chilly morning began on the Trail.

The first order of business was scaling Chairback Mountain. Either Katahdin was hiding behind clouds or it just was not in sight. The trail descended down a rockslide alongside the round crested cliff that gave the name Chairback. At first it followed neatly laid stone steps but quickly became just bouldering. I had to guess a bit about which way the Trail went through the chaos of rocks.

Next was a long low ridge topped by stone outcrops, rather like the south end of New York but not as difficult. Making my way along, I ran right into a big patch of those dark cherry-tasting blueberries like the ones I found on Moxie Bald! I stopped to eat them by the handful, picking the hidden or hard to reach ones and leaving plenty in plain sight for other hikers to find.

Then the Trail descended down to the West Branch Pleasant River. I came to where the path dipped down to the water, changed into sandals, and forded across. I got to the far side without trouble but could not see the Trail. I put my boots back on and left my pack to look around. It turned out that I had crossed upstream of the actual ford. What I had thought was the path to the parking lot turned out to have been the Trail continuing downstream. After some searching I found where the Trail went upstream on my side and figured out what had happened. Returning for my pack, I went on my way.

Then the Trail made a fairly gentle climb for five miles alongside Gulf Hagas Brook. Gulf Hagas is supposed to be a spectacular canyon known as "The Grand Canyon of the East" and one sight, Screw Auger Falls, is just .2 miles off the Trail. I was tempted, but when I found the sidetrail started with a wet looking crossing over a swollen stream I decided to skip it and push on.

Ten miles was short for a relatively easy day and there was a campsite about two miles further on. But two southbounders said it already had three thruhikers plus a trail maintenance crew so it was probably packed. What was more, it was on the far side of a mountain and I did not like the way the sky was clouding. So I stopped at the shelter.

Within an hour of my reaching the shelter my decision to stop proved wise as it started sprinkling. NO FAIR, the weather is cheating! It has only been a few days since the last rain. It has not even changed from the cold of a high-pressure zone into the mugginess of impending rain. Well, all right, it DID get comfortably warm this afternoon then dropped into the upper 50s while I was at the shelter. But rain already? Hmmmph!

I cocooned in my sleeping bag against the chill, watched the squirrels and chipmunks cavort in front of the shelter and nibbled Pringles one by one while writing my journal until suppertime.

Just as I was preparing my chili-flavored ramen with bacon bits and peanut butter, Little Bit, Castro and Bluebell arrived. They had tented four miles before Chairback Gap, in between Fourth and Third Mountains.

78 Miles to Katahdin.

-Mouse

Wednesday, September 22, 2004
Destination: Cooper Brook Falls Lean-To
From: Carl Newhall Lean-to
Today's Miles: 18.9
Trip Miles: 2114.4

Today is my 45th birthday! I suppose it is odd spending it in the middle of the Hundred Mile Wilderness with people who know me only as Mouse. On the other hand, this is also Bilbo and Frodo Baggins' birthday and Lord of the Rings starts with a party for their combined age of 144 which if you add the digits together is the same as 45. So it is sort of appropriate that I am in the wilderness carrying a plain gold ring on my way to a great mountain. Don't ask about the ring unless your name is Gollum or Gandolf.

The day started off less than promising, aside from birthday wishes from Little Bit, Castro and Bluebell. It was so cloudy it was long after sunrise before I could see inside the shelter. My hike started with four mountains to climb, each higher than the last with a deep dip between and the final one, White Cap Mountain, is the tallest peak in the Hundred Mile Wilderness at 3700 feet. As soon as I was up the first peak I could see that the other peaks were shrouded by low clouds so a good view was unlikely. Then I discovered that another mouse, perhaps confused about whose birthday was being celebrated, had nibbled one side of a square of chocolate I had left in a pocket of my pack. At least she was nice enough to leave a second square untouched for me.

Then the day started getting better and better! I found a nice patch of blueberries on the third peak. I caught up with TOM and Dave who started two miles ahead of me. They said they were going all the way to Cooper Brook Falls Shelter because a weather report said clear skies on Monday and they wanted to get there in time to summit in the clear spell. The mad idea began to creep into my head to hike to Cooper as well, even though it was 19 miles. Then on White Cap I got to experience again the wild exhilaration of hiking above treeline, complete with wind and even bits of snow drifting about. I got to taste again those special dwarf alpine blueberries. To top it off, the visibility improved enough to see Katahdin looming above low clouds like an enchanted floating mountain. Soon after, blue sky appeared and the day turned nice. A passing southbounder reported the trail ahead was much smoother after White Cap.

I made such progress that I decided to go to Cooper. A Mouse unchained, I raced along like a demented maniac. At the shelter I had planned to stay at I hung a thousand calories of food in a ziplock for Little Bit, who had said she was running low, both to help her and to lighten my pack. Then I wrote the following calm level-headed entry in the register: "Waaaaahoooo!!!! Warp drive engaged, on to Cooper Brook! Yippee!!!!!"

The next river was supposed to be a ford, but I made it across dry shop on rocks and logs, saving even more time. Not even the final thousand foot climb up Little Boardman Mountain slowed me down.

I got to the Lean-to at 5, tired but happy. It was my first 19 mile day since Vermont. I did not think I had it in me anymore!

I had two Little Debbie brownies in lieu of birthday cake. The Trail gave me 19 miles. The mountains gave me berries. The sky gave nice weather. The shelter gave a murder mystery novel to read. Who could ask for a nicer birthday?

60 Miles to Katahdin!

-Mouse

Thursday, September 23, 2004
Destination: White House Landing
From: Cooper Brook Falls Lean-To
Today's Miles: 13.7
Trip Miles: 2128.1

There are espresso shops scattered all through the Maine Woods. Secret hidden espresso shops. I am sure of it. That is the only possible explanation for how hyperactive the squirrels are up here. They skitter about, chase each other and their own tails, chatter furiously at me for intruding.

I check each blueberry bush I passed, looking for the one berry that will keep my berry streak going another day. Finally near Mud Pond I found it. Small but a berry nonetheless. Then I found another. Then my eye fell on not just a berry but a big frosty luscious blueberry. Mmmmmm. Just above it were more and more. Big juicy sweet ones. I waded into the patch and picked several handfuls.

Right after I started hiking again I was brought to a crashing halt by a bush of those dark sweet cherry tasting blueberries. And another. And another. They went on and on for half a mile. I grabbed a handful every few steps. Here it is, almost October and I am inundated with berries! I love Maine!

At Antlers Tentsite I found something even more surprising. Half a dozen bushes of nice big blackberries, many of them not even ripe yet. And more dark blueberries, winding along the shore of Jo-Mary Lake. The path was starting to get bouldery but I was too full of berries to care.

At Pemadumcook Lake a sign said "View of Katahdin." I followed it to the shore and on the opposite side under a clear blue sky and perfectly lit by the midday sun was the entire mountain rising high above the trees. I could finally see it in all its splendor. It was magnificent! For thousands of miles it has been an almost mythical object; now it is real and is tantalizingly close.

About 1:45 I got to the turnoff for White House Landing and followed the sidetrail a mile through the woods to the boat dock. An air horn was hanging there just as the guidebook said, and I gave it a short blast. After a while an outboard came across the lake with a large friendly looking dog sitting in the bow. In a few minutes I was getting situated at White House Landing. My mail shipment was right there waiting for me, with the rest of my warm clothing and food enough to last nearly to the end.

I got a shower and read until suppertime. They serve a ONE POUND cheeseburger that is sensational. I had one, then a pint of Ben and Jerry's and finally an apple to fill in the corners. The amazing thing was I still felt like eating more, but decided enough was enough.

46 Miles to Katahdin!

-Mouse

Friday, September 24, 2004
Destination: Rainbow Stream Lean-To
From: White House Landing
Today's Miles: 15.9
Trip Miles: 2144.0

Breakfast was at 8: orange juice, coffee, scrambled eggs, bacon, scrumptious potatoes, English muffins, and all you can eat blueberry pancakes. Then I got on the first boatload of three back to the Trail. We were dropped off at a spot just .2 miles from the Trail instead of at the boat dock we had been picked up at, saving us a mile of walking.

Still, it was 9:30 and there were 16 miles to Rainbow Lean-to so I had to keep a quick pace to get there at a reasonable hour. Nonetheless I kept my eye on the bushes watching for my first berry. I found one within an hour. Then at Nahmakantu Lake came a somewhat smaller version of the berry feast I had had yesterday at Mud Lake. The berries just keep coming.

I tried asking the squirrels where they hide their espresso but they are not talking. They just scold me vigorously for being so inquisitive.

I came across an amazing rock formation. Two huge boulders support a third roof-shaped boulder forming a neat cottage with a six-foot ceiling inside. It would make a perfect dwelling for a troll!

Nesuntabunt Mountain was a fairly steep thousand foot climb. It has long high flights of well made stone steps that made me think of dwarves. But I knew it was the last time I will make that kind of climb with the load I have, in fact today is the last time I will carry this much at all, as my food could last right to the end.

The "lasts" of my hike are starting to pile up fast. Last resupply. Last heavy load. Last night on the Trail in a real shelter since the rest will be at campgrounds at Abol Bridge and Baxter State Park. I could go on and on. The end of my thru-hike is rushing towards me at unbelievable speed.

Just 30 Miles to the finish!

-Mouse

Saturday, September 25, 2004
Destination: Abol Bridge Campground
From: Rainbow Stream Lean-To
Today's Miles: 15.0
Trip Miles: 2159.0

Wow, I am nearly finished!

The high mileage is beginning to tell on me. My heels are sore, my Achilles tendons protest when I step on rocks, my arches are getting twinges and I took Ibuprofen last night and this morning. But I don't care. This is the last long day and I am going to make the spell of clear weather predicted for Monday.

I started off on the eight mile sweep along the shore of Rainbow Lake. It did not take long to find my first berries. I took my time, knowing I had all day and this would be the last full day of hiking the Maine woods. There were nice views of the lake with the trees reflected in the glassy water. Never quite the perfect photo op, but still nice for memories. Here and there a stretch would look almost just like the woods back in Ohio where I grew up, then around the corner I would know I was in Maine again.

This is bush-pilot country. Again and again I would hear the thrum of a floatplane taking off or flying by and once in a while I would see one through the treetops as it passed overhead.

Rainbow Ledges was the last real hill before Katahdin. Those "Lasts" again! It was a granite dome reminding me of mountains earlier in Maine but much shallower and lower and easier to climb.

On the open space on top is a truly enormous expanse of dark blueberries! For once I gorge myself properly, as there is no lack of either time or berries. I work my way through the bushes as methodically as a bear stuffing herself for winter. Finally even my appetite is sated and I wander on down the Trail again, just stopping now and again for a small handful as a refresher. Mmmmmmmmm!!!! There really is nothing so yummy as Maine mountain blueberries.

On the east rim is a view of Katahdin, its upper reaches shrouded by cloud. Then I descend into the pine forest, the realm of the red squirrels who scold me vigorously as I pass.

Hurd Brook is said to be a dangerous ford in high water, but it has not rained recently and I again get across dry shod over the boulders. At the very last regular shelter there is a maintainer who gives me the latest forecast. It is still expected to be good weather on Monday! Then come more pine woods down to the road. With elation I pass the warning sign that southbounders pass when entering the Hundred Mile Wilderness. I have gotten all the way through! A glow of triumph spreads over me, knowing I am nearly done with the Trail. There is a cooler of sodas and snacks left by a Trail Angel named Don Quixote. I stop for a diet Coke flavored with lime, an odd choice but it sounded too exotic to resist.

At the road it is just a short walk to Abol Bridge. I take a picture of Katahdin with its shroud of clouds. Then to the nearby campsite for the night. I register, get some snacks and a cheeseburger and go to set up my tent and eat and relax.

Tomorrow I make the short 10 mile hike to Baxter State Park. Then if the weather holds, Monday comes the final climb to the summit of Mount Katahdin!

Just 15 Miles left of the entire Trail. This is too amazing!

-Mouse

Sunday, September 26, 2004
Destination: The Birches
From: Abol Bridge Campground
Today's Miles: 9.9
Trip Miles: 2168.9

Abol Bridge Campground has an odd cellular pay phone. You have to pay a dollar per three minute call even to a toll free number. Still I tried it and managed to get my email. I got two welcome surprises.

First, The Walking Stomach is back on the Trail! She fell and hurt her knee back at Mount Mooselauke and had to get off. She is rejoining Little Tree at Monson to hike the Wilderness and Katahdin. I hope her knee holds out and she makes it.

Second, my father is coming to meet me! With the sketchy phone service here and no phones after until Millinocket the best I could do was send him a reply telling him to meet me at the Ranger Station after the climb or contact me at the hostel afterwards.

I managed to send that reply as well as my accumulated journal entries. But when I tried later in the evening to see if there was a reply, it just beeped coyly at me and disconnected.

A thundershower rolled though at dark. I guess my tent needed rained on once more before finishing! When I woke at midnight it was clear with a nearly full moon so I tried getting a moonlit shot of Katahdin from the bridge.

I tried the phone again twice in the morning but no luck. I hope my father gets my message and understands where to meet me.

I got hiking about 8. Late but still first on the Trail. I was the first to get to the entry kiosk and sign up for a spot at the Birches tonight. The Birches is a site for thruhikers with room for 12 in two small lean-tos and in tentsites. TOM (The Old Man) showed up then and signed in right after me.

Just after the kiosk I found three blueberries. That made me glad, as I had worried I might not find any today. I slowly savored them one by one. The last had a marvelous raisin flavor that burst on my senses. Then came a blackberry. Making my way over boulders get to a line of stepping stones leading to a footbridge I slipped and drenched one foot. Along Daicey Pond were still more bushes full of those dark blueberries. I might have eaten quite a few except that I really wanted to get to the Birches. I settled for several handfuls plus a big handful I saved in my water bottle to eat on the summit. Lighter than champagne and in a way more appropriate!

At Elbow Pond I saw TOM standing on the footbridge over the outlet stream looking out over the pond. I looked and there was a moose! It was the first moose I have seen while hiking since my first morning in Vermont. It was too far away to tell if it was male, but later TOM told me he had seen it close up and it was female. Sigh. I have not seen a bull moose the whole hike. They avoid me just like the bears do.

At the Katahdin Stream Campground Ranger Station TOM and I registered, paid the $9 fee and selected daypacks to use on the ascent tomorrow. In the morning we will leave our own packs and heavy gear at the Ranger Station. Then off to the Birches to settle in.

I ate, finished the mystery novel I had gotten from Cooper Brook and relaxed the rest of the day.

I also organized my gear for the climb. I sorted through all my clothing selecting prospective things to bring in one stuff sack, including Gore-Tex top and bottom, wind pants, fleece pullover, balaclava, glove liners and a pair of leather gloves I bought in Monson when someone warned us about sharp rocks. I added a heat pack, spaceblanket and first aid pack and hooked the compass/whistle, knife and flashlight to the stuff sack drawstring. The clothing to leave behind went in the other stuff sack. Map and park permit went into the daypack. Tonight I will use the sack as a pillow, then just add it and a plastic bag with snacks into the daypack in the morning and the daypack will be ready to go.

My main Pack I can load tomorrow for travel home instead of for hiking. Rather unusual after all these months. Everything inside where it won't get lost and I won't have to bother with waterproofing and plastic bags.

5 Miles Left! WOW!

-Mouse

Monday, September 27, 2004
Destination: Mt. Katahdin
From: The Birches
Today's Miles: 5.2
Trip Miles: 2174.1

Woohoo, I finally made it!

I spent a restless night and was ready early. I got to the Ranger Station at 6:40, well before the weather report was due. I set my big pack on the porch and fastened a label to it with my name as I had promised so my father could identify it. In the process I found that the duct tape I had brought would not stick to my pack and I had to use great loops of it to keep the label in place. So much for those little backpacker sized rolls of tape. Next time I use the real stuff and wind it on my poles!

While looking at the previous day's forecast I saw a message for me next to the Trail Register. It said my father would be there at 8am! So I waited to let him see me off. I sat and watched first all the thruhikers and then parties of dayhikers troop past me to the Trailhead. I was a little nervous about the delay, as well as being keyed up and ready to go, so waiting was a bit hard. To make things worse, a sign nearby warned that the ascent would be a frightening experience for anyone having even a mild fear of heights!

How many times have I said that things have a way of working out on the Trail? They do! My father drove in at 7:40 and by 7:45 I had made my greetings and gotten a hug for luck and was starting up the Trail.

As southbounders had said, the first section up to a rock formation called The Cave at the treeline was not too difficult. Then the real work began! After winding up and around a few boulders the Trail came to a wall with a four inch vertical cleft in it. It would be impassible except for a steel T-bar and handrail at the top and several rocks jammed into the cleft. I figured out that you grab the t-bar, put a foot on the first rock, haul yourself by the bar up until you can reach the handrail and get a foot in the next rock, then haul yourself up really far so you can bring one foot as high as it will go and hook it onto the t-bar as a foothold, then pull extra hard on the rail and scramble to the top of the wall. A nice introduction to the sort of climbing that the next mile entails! The Trail goes up the spine of a ridge piled with boulders, going in great loops that start shallow, steepen over a peak then repeat. So you get a view of a great arc of rock to work up, then as you near the top of the loop you see less and less above and more and more below until you pop over the crest, usually in an extra difficult spot due to the steepness, then are confronted with yet another loop arcing upward.

The sheer scale of it was simply enormous! At first I was well below the tops of other mountains to the west. As I made my way up they seemed lower and lower until I was well above them. The Trail went up a fairly wide space on the spine of the ridge, winding back and forth twenty or thirty feet. Not at all like the Knife Edge, has another trail up that followed a VERY narrow ridge with a steep drop to either side. Here I felt secure. To the left I could see a steep drop-off into a valley far far below. Sometimes I had the novel experience of seeing my shadow stretch hundreds of feet below me! But the path never got so narrow and close to the edge of the drop-off as to make me nervous, like when I had vertigo at Lehigh Gap; or climb rocks or ledges steep enough to fall more than a short drop, like the rock walls at Wildcat Ridge. So I felt secure almost the entire climb, just a lot of work! There were just a few "I can't believe it goes THERE!" moments, and most I found a clear route around or they turned out not as bad as they first looked. None of the narrow outward sloping ledges or lack of foot or handholds that made rock climbs in the White Mountains a harrowing experience. What is more, the view of the surrounding countryside got more fabulous by the minute!

But time was passing and as I approached the end of a particularly big loop I fervently hoped the peak I was coming to was the "Gate" up at the top of the ridge and not Hunt Spur only halfway up. The only way to know was to keep going and see what was over the top.

To my joy I came over the crest and saw a big wooden sign at the top of a short less steep section. It HAD to be the top of the ridge. Sure enough, the sign warned to be careful of the delicate alpine vegetation and spreading beyond it was the wide level section called the Tablelands.

THAT was the really exhilarating moment of the climb. Then I KNEW I had made it! Once there, past the ridge, the hard part was over and the rest would be easy. I was ecstatic!

I made my way more than a mile across the Tablelands, past Thoreau's spring in the middle. Contrary to what some local people had predicted, it was bubbling with water. Then came a less steep rise, much of it on those stone dwarf-looking stairs. From the foot the top looked miles away yet was less than half a mile according to a sign I passed. Perspective gets distorted up there and judging heights and distances is confusing. As I got higher I could make out what looked like a group of people on a level spot of a ridge leading to a higher peak to the right. I gradually realized they were at the summit and the "higher" peak was actually the lower end of the Knife Edge. I was nearly there!

A few more minutes and I was at the summit. It was just before noon and the climb had taken 4 hours.

There were a half dozen or so people there and I had someone take pictures of me doing all the summit rituals. The traditional shot of me next to the sawhorse sign marking the north end of the Appalachian Trail. I got out the blueberries I had brought in a ziplock and got a picture of me having a blueberry toast, Daicey Pond Vintage 2004, and shared them with all the other thruhikers. Then I reached in my pack and got out the small rock I had carried all the way from the south end of the Trail at Springer Mountain Georgia. Near the sign was a large cairn of rocks and I got a shot of me adding my rock to it. Then I ate a block of chocolate, made my goodbyes and started down.

Going past Thoreau Spring it seemed only right to scoop up a handful of water and drink it in memory of the trip. Then I enjoyed fresh picked dwarf alpine blueberries one last time and put some in the ziplock for my father.

The climb down took time and one ankle was getting sore but it was not as hard as I had feared. Still I was glad to get below treeline. Just before the falls I picked some dark blueberries for my father and had a last taste of them myself. Right after that I met my father, who had hiked all the way up past the falls to meet me. Not bad for a 75-year old!

We made our way back to the trailhead where I signed off the mountain, then went to the Ranger Station to get my pack and make one last happy entry in the Trail Register. Little Bit had left a thank you note for the food I had left her in the 100 mile Wilderness. She was at the Birches! We drove over so I could say goodbye to her and gave all the next day's summiters sodas.

Finally we drove to Millinocket, where my father had already gotten a motel room for us. We had a triumphant supper at the Appalachian Trail Cafe. My father beamed with pride and told our waitress "This is my daughter, she just finished the entire Appalachian Trail!"

Next morning we started the two day drive to my home in Philadelphia. We found ourselves driving through the heavy rain from the remains of yet another hurricane! I was thankful to be sitting inside the dry interior of the car rather than out hiking. I was ready to go home.

-Mouse